AF435058

REFLECTIONS ON A COMPLEX DEMOCRATIC REPUBLIC

UNVEILING THE SCARS OF THE AMERICAN DREAM

TODD EMERSON

Reflections on a Complex Democratic Republic
Unveiling the Scars of the American Dream

Copyright © 2026 by Todd Emerson.

MILTON & HUGO L.L.C.
1001 3rd Avenue West, Suite 430
Bradenton, FL 34205, USA

Website: *www. miltonandhugo.com*
Hotline: *1- 888-778-0033*
Email: *info@miltonandhugo.com*

Ordering Information:
Quantity sales. Special discounts are granted to corporations, associations, and other organizations. For more information on these discounts, please reach out to the publisher using the contact information provided above.

Library of Congress Control Number: 2026902397
ISBN-13:   979-8-89285-778-9   [Paperback Edition]
                     979-8-89285-779-6   [Digital Edition]

Rev. date: 01/14/2026

NEITHER PARTY HAS CLEAN HANDS: NAVIGATING OUR IDEALS AND SHORTCOMINGS

In "Reflections on a Complex Republic", I embark on a re-exploration of American identity, navigating the intricate tapestry of history, civics, and the numerous nuances that intertwine both America and the broader world. This book serves as an invitation for readers to scrutinize the very fabric of the nation we call home.

I begin this journey by expressing my unwavering love for the United States of America and a steadfast belief in its democratic ideals. Whether defined as a constitutional republic or a democratic republic, the core remains the same: a shared system of governance and legal framework that unites its citizens.

Within these pages, I unveil the fresh and festering wounds, some over 400 years old, and the enduring scars that mark the United States. By holding a mirror to the face of this nation and ourselves, readers are confronted with a sobering reflection, one that reveals the impact inflicted upon the world, the cosmos, and perhaps most poignantly, upon themselves. Amidst these pages lies a message encouraging us all to open our eyes, acknowledge past missteps, make amends, and strive toward a future that embodies the ideals we cherish.

Anchored in rigorous research and a commitment to truth, the book presents a tapestry woven from verified ideas, opinions, events, people, and other subjects.

Readers are invited on a journey of discovery, prompting them to question established narratives and engage with a nuanced understanding of the United States of America's past, present, and potential future.

Reflections on a Complex Republic" is more than a narrative; it is an invitation to dialogue, urging everyone, regardless of whether you agree or disagree, to embark on a path of healing and reconciliation. With openness and dedication, this book dares to imagine a country that learns from its mistakes, transcends its limitations, and ultimately redeems its promises in the eyes of each other and the world.

In an era marked by rapid change and growing polarization, I find myself increasingly drawn to the principles that have long underpinned democratic societies empathy, inclusion, equality, accountability, and acceptance. To me, these are more than just abstract concepts; they are the lifeblood of a democracy. They form the foundation upon which fair and just societies are built, where every individual, regardless of their circumstances, from the homeless to the elite, stands equal under the law.

I invite you to join me on a journey to explore these essential elements of democracy. Together, we'll delve into how they enable societies to thrive amidst diversity and difference. At the same time, I aim to confront our collective shortcomings, those moments and movements where our democracy has
faltered. Where empathy has been overshadowed by indifference, inclusion thwarted by exclusion, and equality denied by systemic injustice.

Through stories and analysis, I hope to uncover how these core values not only sustain democratic governance but also enrich our human experience. We'll journey through history and into the present, examining how democratic ideals have been both championed and challenged across cultures and borders. This includes reflecting on our failures, from the enduring scars of racial inequity to the pervasive influence of wealth that undermines political equality.

This book is not just a reflection on democracy; it is a reason for all of us to get involved. I urge you, to engage actively with the democratic process, to seek out a spectrum of voices, and to recognize the strength in diversity of thought. As we learn to agree to disagree, I invite you to look inward, hold ourselves accountable, and commit to the ongoing work of building a society that honors the dignity and equality of all its members.

By acknowledging where we have fallen short, we create the space to imagine and inspire a democracy that truly lives up to its ideals. Join me as we explore the soul of democracy, a living, breathing entity that requires our compassion, our courage, our compassion, having empathy, and our unwavering commitment.

My Journey in Advocacy

From the outset, I must address a profound misunderstanding about my stance on crucial issues. My advocacy is not confined to a single cause; rather, it encompasses the greater good and seeks justice for all who are disenfranchised. Some assume that because I am white, my concerns are limited to white issues. This perception overlooks the reality that I, too, am part of the disenfranchised in multiple ways, a truth obscured by the prejudices of others.

For over 32 years, I have been an outspoken advocate for a wide array of rights, including those of the LGBTQ+ community, women, immigrants, indigenous peoples, nationalities, and all people of color. My commitment to these causes has been unwavering, even in times when such advocacy was met with significant resistance. My dedication is rooted in a fundamental belief in equality and justice for all, regardless of race, ethnicity, or background.

My concerns about child marriage and the treatment of women across cultures are not confined to one group or demographic. Addressing these sensitive issues requires nuance and a willingness to engage with the complexities inherent in cultural practices. The advocacy against child marriage is not a selective issue; it is a global concern affecting societies worldwide, including those often seen as Western. Any suggestion that my advocacy is selective or biased is simply misguided.

It is important to distinguish between acknowledging cultural practices and condoning them. My discussions around cultural relativism do not advocate for the normalization of practices that violate human rights, such as child marriage. Instead, my goal is to address and combat these issues in a way that respects cultural contexts, without dismissing entire cultures based solely on singular practices. This requires an intersectional understanding of the challenges faced by women and girls globally.

The claim that I ignore atrocities committed by individuals from certain backgrounds while focusing solely on Caucasian perpetrators reflects a misunderstanding of my engagement with these matters. I firmly believe that advocating for one group does not diminish the need to advocate for others. My support extends to all victims of oppression and injustice, irrespective of their ethnicity or cultural background.

I invite you to reassess your understanding of my work and the broader discussions around cultural practices. Engaging in meaningful dialogue requires a willingness to listen and learn, rather than making assumptions or hasty judgments about someone's character or actions.

To gain a deeper understanding of my advocacy and contributions, I encourage you to visit the Mississippi History Archives, where records of my efforts can be found. Additionally, collectible memorabilia related to my work is available on eBay for those interested in learning more about my journey.

I appreciate your passion for these issues and urge you to educate yourself further before passing judgment on my work or that of others. Misunderstandings often stem from a lack of education and information. I hope this chapter clarifies my position and underscores the importance of embracing a comprehensive understanding of human rights advocacy.

Understanding the Disenfranchised Voter's Choice and Why Some Democrats Supported Trump

As Democrats, we continually seek to understand why a significant percentage of disenfranchised voters chose to support Trump.

We touted, "This is the most important election in our lifetime. We are voting to save our democracy!"

Everyone understood what that meant to them individually, but did anyone think to ask a disenfranchised individual what it meant for them?

I didn't ask, but the information was volunteered to me. Once I was told how they felt, I could see how someone might say, "I have tried this my whole life and I wasn't included, but I haven't tried that, so I'm going to try it."

Could it be that the root of this issue lies in our failure to consider the deeper historical context, alongside today's systemic oppression and its impact on their belief in a democratic republic?

We must ask ourselves: What has our conception of freedom truly offered these individuals? We must engage in an honest reflection about the circumstances that led to their disaffection with our party and take proactive steps to address these concerns.

The interplay between the promotion of freedom and the enactment of repression against marginalized communities deserves rigorous exploration, particularly when examining both historical and contemporary political dynamics.

The paradox of a democratic republic is steeped in a historical backdrop of suppression within democratic frameworks. Democracies, especially in the United States, were founded on principles of freedom and equality; however, these ideals have often been applied selectively.

The treatment of Black individuals, Indigenous populations, LGBTQ+ communities, people of color, and undocumented immigrants showcases a long-standing history of systemic oppression that exists alongside the country's professed democratic values.

One glaring example of this foundational hypocrisy is the systematic repression of Black Americans through slavery, segregation, and ongoing systemic racism, which occurred within a democratic structure that claimed liberty for all. This relationship epitomizes the contradiction inherent in a system that promotes freedom while simultaneously undermining it for specific groups.

Another example can be seen in the criminalization of homosexuality through anti-sodomy laws and the marginalization of LGBTQ+ identities, which were implemented in a society that celebrates personal freedoms. The violent backlash against LGBTQ+ communities, especially following the Stonewall Uprising, further illustrates how societal acceptance can be selectively enforced.

Undocumented immigrants frequently face severe repercussions, including deportation and violence, despite the nation's reliance on their labor and its professed democratic ideals. Policies targeting these individuals reveal deeply entrenched xenophobia and racism within our governance.

The current political landscape, particularly initiatives such as Project 2025, illustrates troubling shifts toward authoritarianism. Proposed by conservative groups in the United States, this initiative aims to fundamentally reshape federal governance and policy when Donald Trump, a Republican, regains office in January. Specifically, he appears focused on deporting all immigrants, rolling back progressive reforms, and restoring certain policies that could adversely affect marginalized communities.

The underlying notion of loyalty to a specific political figure, Donald Trump, over constitutional principles represents a disturbing trend; individuals may be categorized not only by party loyalty but also by their identity traits.

As the political landscape becomes increasingly polarized, those who diverge from the prevailing ideology may face repercussions, including public shaming, loss of employment, and even violence. In such an environment, individuals may feel compelled to compartmentalize aspects of their identity, hiding parts of who they are to avoid backlash. As the LGBTQ+ community often says, they are "back in the closet."

This instinct mirrors historical experiences where marginalized communities developed strategies for survival, often living discreetly to evade scrutiny or violence.

As significant political shifts occur, the expression of dissent or nonconformity may become subdued, leading to self-censorship.

People may become increasingly cautious about disclosing their beliefs or identities in public spheres, contributing to an atmosphere of mistrust and anxiety.

In response to escalating repression under initiatives like Project 2025, organized resistance will become necessary.

Liberal and progressive forces must unite to confront authoritarian trends, emphasizing collective advocacy for democratic principles, human rights, and equitable treatment.

Anticipating the consequences of repression is crucial, as the ongoing threat of violence not only impacts immediate victims but also creates a cycle of trauma that affects future generations.

The normalization of fear can stifle societal growth and diminish community spirit and resilience.

The potential regression of rights and freedoms could set a dangerous precedent, unraveling decades of progress and reinforcing systemic inequities.

Vigilance is essential to counteract this trend and reclaim rights for all marginalized groups. The tension between the democratic ideals of freedom and the reality of oppression presents a compelling narrative of systemic injustice.

As political landscapes evolve, particularly under initiatives that may seek to undermine the principles of equality and justice, understanding historical lessons becomes critical.

The call for accountability, advocacy for intersectionality, and recognition of shared fears across identities remains vital.

Mobilizing toward a just and equitable society requires solidarity among those historically faced with repression, as well as those navigating newfound vulnerabilities in an increasingly hostile environment.

In doing so, communities can create a unified front to resist authoritarian tendencies and reaffirm the principles of liberty, justice, and protection for all individuals, regardless of identity.

This requires acknowledging that the fight for freedom and rights is interconnected across marginalized identities. Only through a concerted effort rooted in shared understanding and mutual support can we effectively confront these impending challenges and work toward a society that embodies the values of true democracy for everyone.

Third-Class Citizens

The Outrage of Invisible American Inequality and Representation

The debate over representation and statehood for U.S. territories often remains in the shadow of broader national conversations. Yet, with nearly five million residents unable to fully participate in the nation's democratic processes, the issue demands attention. These residents include those of Washington D.C., Puerto Rico, Guam, the Northern Mariana Islands, American Samoa, and the U.S. Virgin Islands—all of whom contribute to American society yet remain without full political representation.

Unlike the 50 states, U.S. territories do not enjoy full congressional representation. Residents can elect delegates to the House of Representatives, but these delegates cannot vote on the House floor. In presidential elections, only Washington D.C. has electoral college votes, granted by the Twenty-Third Amendment, allowing its over 689,000 residents to have some say in the election of the President. The other territories, despite having U.S. citizenship (or U.S. national status in American Samoa), cannot vote in these pivotal elections.

Residents of these territories contribute to the nation in meaningful ways—most pay certain federal taxes like Social Security and Medicare, actively serve in the U.S. military, and are integral to local economies. However, residents from territories like Puerto Rico generally do not pay federal income tax on income sourced within the island.

Historically, these territories have been marginalized, a situation that mirrors other historical injustices in the U.S., such as those experienced by African Americans after the Civil War or Native Americans throughout history. For over a century, systemic barriers have restricted these territories' access to equal rights and resources, perpetuating cycles of disenfranchisement and socio-economic challenges.

The political stance on statehood has often been divided along party lines, with Democrats generally supporting statehood for territories like Washington D.C., and Puerto Rico. In contrast, Republicans have had reservations, partly due to concerns about shifts in the political balance of power, as these regions tend to lean Democratic.

The strategic importance of these territories cannot be understated. Locations like Guam and the Northern Mariana Islands hold significant military value, serving as key strategic points in the Pacific. Despite these contributions, residents still find themselves without a proper voice in the legislative process that determines their futures.

This ongoing disparity highlights the importance of reform. Statehood or enhanced autonomy would require not only legislative change but also a shift in national consciousness. By integrating these communities through equal representation, the U.S. can uphold its constitutional promises, embodying the values of democracy and inclusivity.

Recognizing and rectifying these internal inequalities is a step toward a more inclusive America. The journey to full citizenship and representation for all residents promises a vision of the United States that truly reflects its foundational ideals. As the nation progresses, it must ensure that all citizens, regardless of geographic location, share in democratic rights and representation. Only then can America fully embody the principles laid out in its Constitution and Declaration of Independence.

Historical Dynamics in U.S. and Philippines Relations: Statehood, Independence, and Racial Attitudes

The relationship between the United States and the Philippines is a complex tapestry of colonial rule, evolving diplomatic ties, and the eventual fulfillment of a promise for independence. Understanding why the Philippines was not on the path to becoming a U.S. state involves examining historical, political, and social contexts spanning several decades.

The United States acquired the Philippines along with Puerto Rico after the Spanish-American War in 1898. During the initial years of American rule, the islands were governed predominantly as a colony, initially under military administration that transitioned to civilian control. The U.S. viewed the Philippines as a strategic territory in the Asia-Pacific region rather than a potential candidate for statehood.

One significant, albeit uncomfortable, factor influencing this trajectory was the prevailing racial attitudes of the time. The early 20th-century United States was marked by a racially stratified society, which often extended to its policies and views on territories. Many in the U.S.

held paternalistic attitudes toward non-European populations, which affected considerations of incorporating such territories fully into the Union. The Philippines, with its predominantly Asian populace, faced substantial racial prejudice that complicated notions of statehood.

Efforts to transition away from colonial rule began with the Jones Act of 1916, which pledged Philippine independence. This legislation established an elected legislature in the Philippines, granting more autonomy and reflecting growing commitments to eventual self-rule, rather than integration as a U.S. state.

The Tydings-McDuffie Act of 1934 further crystallized the path toward independence, creating the Commonwealth of the Philippines and laying out a ten-year timeline to sovereignty. This act formalized plans for the Philippines to become self-governing, backed by significant support within both nations.

Within the Philippines, a robust independence movement thrived, led by influential local leaders such as Manuel Quezon. This movement underscored desires for a distinct national identity and governance, distinct from potential statehood within the United States. The Philippine populace largely favored self-determination and the establishment of an autonomous nation.

The Japanese occupation during World War II caused significant disruptions but did not alter the trajectory toward independence. After liberation, the focus was on reconstruction and fulfilling the long-standing promise of sovereignty. On July 4, 1946, the Philippines was granted full independence, aligning with international decolonization trends and American legislative commitments made beforehand.

The history of U.S.-Philippines relations, from annexation to independence, is marked by strategic considerations, long-standing commitments, and the significant influence of racial attitudes. While geographical and logistical challenges also played roles, these factors combined to steer the Philippines toward independence rather than statehood.

In looking back, these dynamics highlight a crucial period in both nations' histories, rooted in complex interplays of policy, prejudice, and people's aspirations, ultimately paving the way for the Philippines to forge its path as an independent nation.

A Contradiction of Values in America's Foreign Intervention Legacy

Disclaimer: I would like to apologize in advance for my content, and writing style. Someone accused me of being a Russian Bot because I make negative posts. I argue my posts are not negative.

Being negative involves focusing on the flaws or problems with a pessimistic attitude, often leading to discouragement.

In contrast, pointing out wrongdoing means identifying mistakes or unethical behavior to encourage improvement and accountability, typically with a constructive intent.

The key difference lies in the approach and goal: negativity tends to demoralize, while constructive feedback aims to promote growth and positive change.

The United States has long proclaimed itself a champion of liberty, democracy, and human rights.

However, this self-image often collides with the reality of its foreign interventions, revealing a troubling legacy of manipulation, exploitation, and indifference to the well-being of other nations.

We started violating our proclamation long before we became a nation.

At the heart of American identity lies a belief in liberty and justice for all. However, U.S. foreign policy has frequently pursued self-interest over these principles, undermining democratic movements in various regions and raising critical questions about the nation's steadfast commitment to its ideals.

Here are reasons that expose the contradictions inherent in America's interventions abroad. They explore how the rhetoric of freedom often masks a reality shaped by arrogance, economic exploitation, and ethical dilemmas that contradict the very foundations of the American narrative.

United States: Manifest Destiny and Native American Displacement

Manifest Destiny justified the displacement of Native Americans, causing suffering and loss. This contradicted the values of liberty and justice by denying Indigenous rights for territorial expansion.

Mexico: Mexican-American War and Ongoing Influence

The Mexican-American War (1846-1848) was fueled by U.S. territorial greed, undermining Mexico's sovereignty. This contradicted ideals of democracy and self-determination, favoring American interests over respect for Mexico's autonomy.

Central America and the Caribbean

Cuba: Spanish-American War and Interventions

The U.S. engaged in the Spanish-American War to expand its influence in Cuba and establish a foothold in the Caribbean. This contradicted the principle of self-determination, as the U.S. imposed control post-war through political influence and the Bay of Pigs invasion, undermining Cuban sovereignty.

Panama: Independence and Canal Control

The U.S. supported Panama's independence from Colombia to secure control over the Panama Canal. This action conflicted with the principle of sovereignty and self-governance, prioritizing U.S. strategic interests over the rights of the Panamanian people.

Nicaragua: Contra Support and Interventions

U.S. support for Contra rebels against Nicaragua's Sandinista government aimed to counter perceived communist influence. This intervention contradicted democratic values by undermining a legitimate government, demonstrating a preference for influence over local autonomy.

Honduras: Military Interventions and Coup

The U.S. intervened in Honduras multiple times, notably during the 2009 coup, to maintain economic and political influence. These actions undermined democracy and stability, favoring U.S. interests over the will of the Honduran people.

Guatemala: Overthrow of Jacobo Árbenz

The U.S. overthrew President Jacobo Árbenz in 1954 because his agrarian reforms threatened American business interests. This action violated democratic principles by disregarding the elected government and prioritizing U.S. corporate interests over local needs.

Dominican Republic: Military Intervention

The U.S. intervened militarily in the Dominican Republic in 1965 to prevent a leftist government from taking power. This action contradicted the commitment to democracy, as it favored U.S. geopolitical interests over the democratic aspirations of the Dominican people.

South America

Chile: Support for the 1973 Coup

The U.S. supported the coup against President Salvador Allende in 1973 to prevent the spread of socialism in Latin America, fearing it would lead to a Soviet foothold. This action undermined democratic principles by facilitating a military dictatorship under Augusto Pinochet, which inflicted severe human rights abuses and did not represent the will of the Chilean people.

Argentina: Support for Military Regimes

During the "Dirty War," the U.S. provided support to Argentine military regimes to combat perceived communist threats. This support contradicted human rights and democratic values, as these regimes engaged in wide-scale repression, forced disappearances, and violations of civil liberties, prioritizing anti-communism over democratic governance.

Bolivia: Support for Coups and Regime Changes

The U.S. has historically supported coups and regime changes in Bolivia, often linked to anti-drug policies and economic interests. These interventions frequently undermined Bolivia's sovereignty and democratic processes, prioritizing U.S. strategic agendas over the rights and choices of Bolivian citizens.

Europe

Germany: The Marshall Plan

The U.S. initiated the Marshall Plan after World War II to rebuild European economies, prevent the spread of communism, and establish a strong economic presence in Western Europe during the Cold War. While it aimed to foster stability and prosperity, critics argue it propagated U.S. influence and capitalism, sometimes at the expense of local autonomy and economic self-determination.

Italy: Involvement in Italian Elections

Post-World War II, the U.S. intervened in Italian elections to counteract communist influence, fearing Italy might shift towards a socialist government. This violation of democratic principles undermined the electoral process, prioritizing strategic interests over the genuine democratic will of the Italian people.

Greece: Support for King George II

During the Greek Civil War, the U.S. supported King George II's government to prevent a communist takeover. While portrayed as a defense of democracy, this support often aligned with authoritarian governance, contradicting the U.S. stance on promoting democratic values and human rights.

Yugoslavia: Military Interventions

In the 1990s, the U.S. intervened militarily in the Bosnian War and the Kosovo conflict to address humanitarian crises and ethnic cleansing. While the interventions aimed to uphold human rights, they also raised questions about sovereignty and the principle of non-intervention, as they involved significant military action in a sovereign state's affairs. Critics argue that such actions can sometimes be inconsistent with a commitment to international law and peace.

Asia

Korea: Korean War (1950-1953)

The U.S. intervened in the Korean War to stop the communist invasion of South Korea, aiming to contain communism in Asia. This action countered its professed commitment to self-determination and led to a prolonged military presence, contradicting the principle of national sovereignty.

Vietnam: Vietnam War (1955-1975)

The Vietnam War was driven by the U.S. goal to prevent the spread of communism in Southeast Asia. Critics argue that the extensive military involvement violated the rights of the Vietnamese people and demonstrated a willingness to support authoritarian regimes, undermining the U.S. narrative of promoting democracy and freedom.

Laos: Secret Bombing Campaign

During the Vietnam War, the U.S. conducted a secret bombing campaign in Laos and supported anti-communist forces. This operation went against the principle of sovereignty and was conducted without Congressional approval, raising ethical concerns about civilian casualties and the impact on local populations.

Cambodia: U.S. Bombings and Khmer Rouge

U.S. bombings in Cambodia aimed to target Viet Cong sanctuaries but inadvertently contributed to instability and the rise of the Khmer Rouge. This contradicted U.S. rhetoric about protecting human rights and democracy, as the Khmer Rouge regime was responsible for a genocide that resulted in widespread suffering.

Philippines: Military Presence and Conflicts

The U.S. military presence in the Philippines established a strategic foothold but often involved support for repressive regimes and conflict. This compromised the U.S. stance on promoting democracy, leading to accusations of imperialism and violations of Filipino sovereignty.

Middle East

Afghanistan: Military Intervention Post-9/11

The U.S. invaded Afghanistan to dismantle al-Qaeda and remove the Taliban from power. While aimed at combating terrorism, the subsequent long-term occupation raised questions about nation-building and civilian impact, contrasting with U.S. principles of self-determination and non-interference in internal affairs.

Iraq: 2003 Invasion

The U.S. invaded Iraq to overthrow Saddam Hussein based on claims of weapons of mass destruction. This action faced significant criticism for undermining international law and sovereignty, as it was conducted without UN backing, contradicting U.S. claims of promoting global stability and democracy.

Iran: CIA-Backed Coup (1953)

The U.S. orchestrated the 1953 coup to reinstate the Shah and secure Western interests in Iranian oil. While justified as a move against perceived communism, this action contradicted the U.S. stance on democracy and self-determination, leading to decades of repression and anti-American sentiment in Iran.

Syria: Military Operations and Support for Factions

The U.S. engaged in Syria to counter ISIS and influence the outcome of the civil war, supporting various factions. This involvement raised concerns about the lack of a clear objective and the undermining of Syria's sovereignty, conflicting with the U.S. claim of promoting stability and democracy in the region.

Lebanon: Multinational Force Deployment (1983)

The U.S. deployed a multinational force in Lebanon during its civil war, aiming to stabilize the situation. However, this military intervention faced criticism for exacerbating conflict and leading to casualties, raising questions about the efficacy and motives behind U.S. involvement in internal affairs, which at times contradicted its values of sovereignty and non-interference.

Saudi Arabia: Support for the Monarchy

The U.S. has provided military and political support to the Saudi monarchy, prioritizing strategic alliances over human rights. This relationship contradicts the U.S. stance on democracy and human rights, as the Saudi regime is often criticized for its authoritarian governance and repression of dissent.

Other Notable Interventions

Grenada: Military Invasion (1983)

The U.S. invaded Grenada to overthrow a Marxist government and ostensibly protect American citizens. While framed as a defense of democracy, the invasion contradicted principles of national sovereignty and self-determination, raising questions about unilateral military action to impose U.S. ideals.

Bosnia and Herzegovina: NATO Intervention (1990s)

NATO, led by the U.S., intervened to stop ethnic cleansing and humanitarian crises during the Bosnian War. While seen as a moral imperative to protect human rights, the intervention highlighted the tension between sovereignty and the responsibility to protect, questioning when and how outside nations should intervene in internal conflicts.

Kosovo: Airstrikes (1999)

The U.S. conducted airstrikes in Kosovo to protect Kosovar Albanians from Serbian military actions. This intervention was justified as a humanitarian effort. Yet, it raised concerns about bypassing international law and norms regarding state sovereignty, contrasting with U.S. advocacy for self-governance and non-interference in internal matters.

This list highlights the extensive nature of U.S. interventions over the years, a reflection of geopolitical interests frequently veiled in the discourse of promoting democracy, stability, or economic development. Many of these actions have drawn criticism and left long-lasting impacts on the nations involved, leading to complex legacies of conflict, instability, and resentment toward U.S. foreign policy.

Scapegoated and Shortchanged

How Low-Income Families Are Punished by Policy, Business Practices, and Everyday Gatekeeping

Government assistance programs like SNAP, TANF, Medicaid, and housing support aim to help low-income individuals and families, but they are often criticized for perpetuating a system where large corporations can pay wages below a living standard. This dynamic can lead to workers relying on government aid to fill the income gap, effectively allowing corporations to boost profits by keeping labor costs low. As a result, taxpayers, including the middle class, bear the financial burden of subsidizing the cost of living for low-wage workers, which can contribute to ongoing poverty and economic inequality.

In a country where working full-time can still leave a family hungry or homeless, people who rely on assistance for food, clothing, or shelter are routinely cast as the problem rather than the predictable outcome of the problem.

Those earning minimum wage are scapegoated in political speeches, policed at checkout lines, and buried under paperwork at government offices all while many employers and policymakers quietly benefit from the very conditions that force these families to seek help in the first place.

The result is a cycle: low wages push people to public programs, those programs are stigmatized and targeted for cuts, and the same low-wage model persists, subsidized by taxpayers and enforced by policy choices and institutional practices that keep assistance users perpetually looking for aid.

Plenty of people work hard and still can't make rent or buy enough food. They get help just to survive, then get blamed for needing it. Meanwhile, businesses and politicians benefit from the setup that keeps pay low. Taxpayers end up covering basics that paychecks should cover, and the system keeps repeating.

When wages don't meet basic needs, means-tested assistance backfills the gap, and a significant share of the economic benefit is captured by employers and asset owners, not the families forced to navigate stigma and red tape. The public pays twice: once at low retail prices achieved through suppressed labor costs, and again through taxes that fund the safety net. Meanwhile, assistance users are blamed for needing help that the system itself makes unavoidable.

When jobs don't pay enough, the government steps in. That helps keep workers alive but it also lets some companies keep wages low. We all pay for this in taxes, and then we're told to be mad at the people getting help instead of the low wages that made help necessary.

Assistance is not a moral failing; it is a predictable response to pay that lags far behind local costs. When employers offer wages that don't cover rent, food, transportation, childcare, and healthcare, workers turn to SNAP, Medicaid, housing vouchers, and tax credits to survive. That reliance is not rare or fringe. Most benefit recipients are often employed in essential roles in caregiving, retail, hospitality, logistics, and food service, where hours are unstable and schedules unpredictable.

Needing help doesn't mean someone did something wrong. If a job doesn't pay enough to cover basics like rent and food, people turn to programs like food stamps (SNAP), Medicaid, and housing for help. Lots of folks on these programs are working, often in the jobs we all rely on, like caregivers, store workers, and delivery drivers, but their pay and hours are shaky.

Below-minimum pay also happens in practice. Wage theft, off-the-clock labor, misclassification, unpaid overtime, and legal loopholes keep effective wages below statutory floors with little risk to violators.

Even when employers follow the letter of the law, a sub-living wage shifts basic labor costs onto the public: taxpayers buy groceries, fund healthcare, and help pay rent for workers whose paychecks don't stretch.

Some companies break the rules making people work off the clock, not paying overtime, or calling employees "contractors" to dodge benefits. Even when they don't break the law, paying too little means the public has to make up the difference through government programs.

This transfer is sizable. Analyses from the UC Berkeley Labor Center estimate that taxpayers spend well over $100 billion annually on major public programs supporting working families costs that, in a higher-wage equilibrium, would be borne by employers and customers rather than the public. Research on Medicaid and SNAP confirms that a large share of adult enrollees live in working households, especially in low-wage industries.

This isn't small change. Taxpayers spend over a hundred billion dollars a year helping working families because their jobs don't pay enough. Many adults on Medicaid or SNAP are in families where someone works, especially in lower-paying industries.

Public debate often fixates on the person with the EBT card instead of the pay stub that made the card necessary. Shaming benefits users disguises the structural math: if full-time work doesn't cover basic needs, assistance is a rational necessity. It also obscures who truly benefits. Low consumer prices and higher corporate margins are underwritten when taxpayers pick up the tab for workers' essentials. In this sense, safety-net programs function as a quiet subsidy to low-wage business models.

People get shamed for using benefits cards, but the real issue is paychecks that don't cover the basics. When taxpayers cover food and healthcare, it lets companies keep wages low and prices low. That's basically a hidden subsidy, a 100 billion dollar tax break and it's corporate welfare for all business models that refuse to pay a living wage.

Anti-fraud rhetoric further muddies the waters. As long as humankind exists intentional fraud will exist, many so-called "improper payments" arise from complex rules and administrative error not deceit by recipients. Yet the enforcement spotlight falls hardest on poor families, even as wage violations in the private sector go under-enforced.

Yes, fraud happens sometimes, but most "errors" are because the rules are complicated, not because people are cheating. Still, poor families are watched the closest while many companies breaking wage laws don't get caught or punished enough.

The cycle persists because policy is designed to keep it going. Powerful lobbies push for tax cuts skewed toward the wealthiest earners and large corporations; the resulting revenue hole invites austerity that targets discretionary spending, including the very programs that stabilize low-wage households. Program rules often feature sharp "benefit cliffs," where a small raise or extra shift can trigger a disproportionate loss of food, housing, or healthcare support. Families are penalized precisely when they attempt to get ahead.

The rules are set up to keep the system as-is. Big interests push for tax cuts that mostly help the wealthy and big companies. Then, to "save money," we cut programs that help low-income families. On top of that, if someone gets a small raise, they can lose a big chunk of benefits all at once so trying to get ahead can actually set them back.

Meanwhile, enforcement gaps let wage theft and misclassification thrive. Scheduling volatility on-call shifts, last-minute changes, and insufficient hours forces workers to absorb hidden costs for childcare and transportation. The public then subsidizes the fallout through assistance. The system is tight where it burdens the poor and loose where it benefits firms.

Not enough is done to stop companies from underpaying or misclassifying workers. Unstable schedules make life and childcare harder and pricier. Then taxpayers cover the fallout with assistance. The rules are strict when they hurt poor people and loose when they help companies.

Beyond formal rules, ordinary gatekeeping compounds the harm. At grocery stores, benefits users face side-eye and extra scrutiny. In housing, voucher holders encounter denials or subtle steering, sometimes under the guise of neutral criteria. At work, employees who rely on public programs are shamed as "not pulling their weight," even when low pay and erratic hours are the actual culprits.

Every day life piles on. People using benefits get judged in stores. Landlords often turn away renters with vouchers. Workers who get help are shamed, even though low pay and messy schedules are the real problem.

Long waits, repetitive forms, hard-to-meet documentation demands, and frequent recertifications, act as a rationing tool, dissuading eligible families from accessing support. Scholars call this "administrative burden," and it functions as a hidden tax on time and dignity. Notably, wealthy beneficiaries of public largesse from mortgage-interest deductions to corporate tax incentives rarely face equivalent scrutiny or hassle.

Getting help is made exhausting on purpose endless forms, long lines, and constant re-checks so fewer people stick with it. It's like a tax on your time and dignity. Meanwhile, richer people and big companies get tax breaks without this kind of hassle.

Taxpayers shoulder the cost when low wages force families onto public programs. Employers benefit from lower labor costs and turnover; consumers benefit from lower prices; and shareholders benefit from maintained margins. Assistance recipients many of them workers sustaining essential sectors absorb the stigma, instability, and bureaucratic friction.

We all pay for low wages through our taxes. Companies save money on pay and turnover; shoppers get cheaper prices; investors keep profits up. The people who need help are many working essential jobs who face stress, shame, and paperwork.

Some supports are explicitly designed as wage supplements. The Earned Income Tax Credit is effective at reducing poverty, but research shows that in markets where employers have hiring power, part of its value can be captured by firms via lower wage growth than would otherwise occur. In housing, evidence suggests that in tight markets some landlords capture part of voucher value through higher effective rents. These are not arguments against the programs' usefulness; they are reminders that without fair wages and competitive labor and housing markets, public benefits can be partially privatized by those with market power.

Programs like the Earned Income Tax Credit help a lot, but in places where bosses have more power, some of that benefit can end up helping companies instead of workers because wages don't rise as much as they should. With housing vouchers, in crowded rental markets, landlords can sometimes raise rents to capture some of the benefit. The programs still help but fairer wages and fairer markets would keep more of the benefits with families.

If the low-wage model is subsidized by the safety net, why do some upper-income interests push to cut it? Because weak, stigmatized assistance can still serve as a labor stabilizer while keeping workers insecure. The playbook is consistent: suppress wages and bargaining power, stigmatize the safety net to divide workers, keep support stingy and conditional, and reap the profits from a compliant, low-cost labor force. In this dynamic, the safety net is tolerated as a pressure valve, just enough to maintain labor supply, not enough to confer real bargaining power or security.

Why do some powerful people attack the very programs that help their business model? Because small, complicated, and stigmatized work helps keep workers desperate enough to accept low pay. The safety net is allowed to exist just enough to keep people working and not enough to give them real leverage or stability.

Raise the wage floor to a local living wage and index it to inflation. This shifts the cost of labor back to firms and reduces dependence on means-tested programs.
Enforce existing labor laws. Crack down on wage theft, misclassification, and abusive scheduling that push effective pay below legal floors.

Gradual phase-outs, income averaging, and continuous eligibility prevent small raises from triggering large losses.

Support small businesses in transition. Temporary, targeted credits, technical assistance, and access to low-cost capital can ease adjustment while preserving jobs.

Strengthen worker voice and standards. Sectoral wage boards, transparent scheduling rules, and fair contracting reduce monopsony power and prevent subsidy capture.

Modernize administration with dignity. Simplify eligibility, reduce paperwork churn, and invest in outreach so that it supports function as bridges, not barriers.

In plain language: We can fix this. Pay a true living wage and keep it updated with inflation. Enforce the laws we already have. Change benefits so people don't lose everything when they get a small raise. Help small businesses adjust during the change. Give workers a real voice and fair schedules. Make getting help simpler and more respectful.

Evidence from numerous minimum wage increases shows modest price effects, reduced turnover, improved morale, and productivity gains that offset part of the higher wage bill, with small to neutral employment effects at commonly enacted levels. Fewer families would need assistance; more low-wage workers would become net taxpayers; and public dollars could be targeted toward mobility-building investments like childcare, housing, and education.

Studies of minimum wage increases show prices don't jump much, workers stick around longer, morale and productivity go up, and jobs usually don't disappear. With better pay, fewer families need benefits, more people pay taxes, and we can invest public money where it builds a better future.

Assistance users are not the problem; they are the result of the problem. When an economy is built on sub-living wages, the public is asked to backfill the basics and then asked to resent the people who need that help. That cycle does not serve the public interest. It props up low-wage business models, socializes their costs, and punishes the families who keep essential sectors running.

People who need help show us that wages are too low not that they're doing something wrong. The current setup makes the public pay for basics and then blames the poor. That protects low-wage business models and hurts the families we all rely on.

A living wage, stronger enforcement, and safety-net rules that avoid punishing progress would reduce reliance on assistance and restore a fairer alignment between who pays and who profits. Most importantly, these changes would shift the conversation from blaming those at the bottom to fixing the systems at the top that make help necessary.

If we pay a living wage, enforce fair pay, and fix benefits so a small raise doesn't wreck a family's budget, fewer people will need assistance. We'll match costs with profits more fairly and we'll focus on fixing the system, not blaming people who are doing their best.

These sources back up the points above. They show how much taxpayers spend to support working families, how many benefit recipients are working, how wage supplements can get partly captured by employers or landlords, how paperwork creates barriers, and how raising wages tends to help workers without big job losses.

UC Berkeley Labor Center. The High Public Cost of Low Wages: Taxpayer Costs of Public Assistance to Working Families. https://laborcenter.berkeley.edu

USDA. Characteristics of Supplemental Nutrition Assistance Program Households. https://www.fns.usda.gov/snap/characteristics

KFF. Medicaid coverage and employment analyses. https://www.kff.org

Rothstein, J. (2010). Is the EITC as Good as an NIT? NBER Working Paper 14966. https://www.nber.org/papers/w14966

Eriksen, M., & Ross, A. (2015). Housing Vouchers and the Price of Rental Housing. The Review of Economics and Statistics.

Herd, P., & Moynihan, D. (2018). Administrative Burden: Policymaking by Other Means.

Dube, A.; Cengiz, D.; et al. Research on minimum wages, turnover, and employment effects.

Let's End Subsidized Rental Housing: A Radical Reimagining of Supportive Solutions

I Bet MAGA is Excited and Confused That a Democrat, Left, Liberal is Calling for an End to Subsidized Housing.

Subsidized rental housing has long been a pillar of support for low-income individuals and families across the United States. While well-intentioned, the current model has inherent flaws that perpetuate dependency and long-term government expenditure. To create a sustainable housing solution, we must consider a groundbreaking alternative: transitioning from subsidized rentals to a system that focuses on subsidized sales of no-frills homes. This new paradigm can provide better economic stability for individuals and reduce costs for taxpayers over time.

In the subsidized rental housing system, tenants pay a portion of their rent, with the government covering the remainder. For example, if an individual pays $400 of a $1,500 rent, the government effectively subsidizes the remaining $1,100 each month. This dynamic results in a continuous financial commitment from the government for as long as the individual requires housing assistance.

If we project this over a typical timeframe of 40 years, the financial impact becomes staggering. The government would spend approximately $528,000 ($1,100 x 12 months x 40 years) on a single individual's rental subsidy. Such expenditures can accumulate significantly when multiplied across the millions of Americans relying on subsidized housing.

Instead of perpetuating this cycle of ongoing subsidy, I propose a new model: the government should contract construction firms to build basic, low-cost homes tailored for low-income families. These homes would be designed with minimal frills effectively stripped of non-essential features allowing them to be built and sold at a significantly lower price point.

Non-Profit Sales: The government would ensure these homes are sold at cost, foregoing any profit margins. This approach would keep housing affordable while relieving the taxpayer burden.

Closed-End Contracts: Under this model, individuals would enter into closed-end contracts to buy these homes. A fixed payment plan could be established, allowing them to pay a set amount, similar to how rent works, until the home is paid off. This creates an expiration date on their financial obligation, transforming a perpetual rent into a clear path to ownership.

Long-Term Financial Planning: Once the home is paid off, the individual not only gains equity but also moves away from government dependency. They become responsible homeowners rather than lifelong tenants of subsidized housing.

While the Department of Housing and Urban Development (HUD) operates various programs aimed at providing rental assistance, including the Housing Choice Voucher Program (Section 8) and public housing initiatives, these programs fundamentally maintain the status quo of providing ongoing subsidies for rental properties. Here's how the proposed model differs:

Transition to Ownership vs. Rental Assistance: HUD's programs primarily focus on subsidizing rental costs, ensuring that low-income individuals can afford to rent private market housing or live in public housing. In contrast, this proposal emphasizes a transition from rental assistance to homeownership, which empowers individuals by allowing them to build equity over time and gain financial stability.

End of Dependency: Current HUD programs can inadvertently create a state of dependency on government support. Participants may remain in subsidized settings without a clear path toward financial independence. This plan introduces a closed-end contract for home purchases, providing a clear endpoint to government assistance and encouraging self-sufficiency.

Economic Mobility: HUD schemes, while beneficial in the short term, may not effectively promote long-term economic mobility. Homeownership opens avenues for wealth accumulation and financial growth that rental assistance cannot offer. By providing low-cost homes that can be purchased with manageable payments, we facilitate a gateway to economic advancement and empowerment.

The proposed system carries a myriad of benefits that extend far beyond mere cost savings. Decreased Long-Term Costs: By transitioning from an open-ended rental subsidy to a close-ended home subsidy, the government can eliminate the lifetime commitment to rental assistance, ultimately achieving a zero-cost model for taxpayers.

Empowerment and Stability: Homeownership fundamentally changes the game for low-income families. It fosters a sense of community, stability, and personal investment in one's living situation. Beyond financial savings, homeownership can lead to improved social outcomes, such as better education for children and lower crime rates.

Encouragement of Economic Mobility: Owning a home can serve as a springboard for economic advancement. Families with equity in their homes may find it easier to access loans for higher education or business ventures, contributing to upward mobility and breaking the cycle of poverty.

Community Development: Investing in neighborhoods through building homes, rather than merely providing subsidies for existing rentals, fosters community development and engagement. Homeownership often leads to greater civic involvement, enhancing the health of local communities.

The time has come for policymakers to rethink their approach to housing assistance. The burdensome cycle of subsidized rental housing is unsustainable, both for individuals who rely on it and for the taxpayers who fund it. By transitioning to a model of subsidized home sales that empowers individuals through ownership, we can create a system that fosters community, supports economic mobility, and ultimately leads to a decrease in future government spending on housing assistance.

Ending subsidized rentals and embracing a vision of affordable homeownership can pave the way for a more equitable and economically viable future for all. It's a necessary step toward not just housing security, but a broader commitment to investing in individuals and communities.

Join the conversation on how we can reimagine housing policy to support sustainable, long-term solutions that empower individuals and families. Together, we can create a brighter future through homeownership.

Understanding Social Security Without All Of The Rhetoric

Social Security is designed to be self-sustaining, primarily funded through payroll taxes that generate a surplus. This surplus is then invested in Treasury bonds, creating a significant asset pool. Critics argue that some politicians, particularly from the Republican Party, have used these Social Security funds as collateral for various spending projects, essentially masking them under the guise of Social Security revenues.

Such actions contribute to the federal deficit by diverting funds from their intended use for Social Security, allowing for increased discretionary spending without adequate transparency.

This practice raises ethical concerns and has sparked discussions about the long-term viability of the program and fiscal responsibility.

The debate surrounding Social Security often gets mired in political rhetoric, particularly from conservative factions. Analyzing this issue requires a clear understanding of what Social Security represents, how it functions, and the implications of proposed changes to the program.

Social Security is a social insurance program established in 1935 to provide economic security for the elderly, disabled, and survivors of deceased workers.

It is primarily funded through payroll taxes collected under the Federal Insurance Contributions Act (FICA). Employees and employers each contribute 6.2% of wages to the Social Security Trust Fund, totaling 12.4% for employees' wages. Self-employed individuals pay a combined rate of 12.4% (which includes both the employee and employer share).

As of recent data, the Social Security Trust Fund has a reserve of approximately $2.9 trillion. It's important to note that while Treasury bonds are held in trust as assets for future obligations, the characterization of "collateral" in connection with spending projects is misleading. These funds are intended to be preserved for Social Security benefits, and the use of surplus funds for other expenditures indeed raises concerns about the program's long-term

This trust fund is crucial, as it ensures the program can continue paying benefits even during periods when expenditures exceed revenues from payroll taxes. Social Security is structured to be self-sufficient and is not designed to contribute to the federal budget deficit.

Many conservative politicians and commentators have perpetuated the narrative that Social Security contributes to the national deficit, suggesting that it requires significant reforms or even cuts. This portrayal is fundamentally misleading. Social Security operates distinctly from the general budget; it is not part of the discretionary spending that contributes to the federal deficit, and its funding mechanism is separate from general tax revenues.

While Social Security itself is stable for the foreseeable future, debates often conflate it with discussions about Medicare and Medicaid, which face funding challenges due to rising healthcare costs.

The conflation of these separate programs can lead to misconceptions, reinforcing a narrative that paints Social Security in a troubled light when that is not the case.

Social Security serves as a critical lifeline for millions of Americans. Approximately 65 million beneficiaries depend on these payments, including retirees, disabled individuals, and survivors of deceased workers. For many, Social Security represents a significant portion of their retirement income, helping to alleviate poverty among older adults. In fact, without Social Security benefits, it is estimated that the poverty rate for seniors would increase substantially.

Social Security is vital for maintaining the economic stability of the middle class. It allows individuals to retire without fearing destitution and contributes to overall economic health by providing a steady stream of income to consumers, who in turn spend it on goods and services.

Proposals from conservative lawmakers, often under the guise of reform, have included suggestions to privatize Social Security or reduce benefits. Such measures pose significant risks, including exposing retirees to the volatility of the stock market and undermining the guaranteed income that Social Security provides.

The push for cuts or privatization disproportionately affects younger generations, Generation Alpha, Generation Z, Millennials, and Generation X, who supply the majority of the Social Security revenue and are relying on Social Security to provide a safety net in their retirement.

While there are legitimate concerns about the long-term financial viability of the program, the focus should be on reforming the funding structure through means such as raising the payroll tax cap, which currently applies only to earnings up to a certain threshold. Increasing this cap could enhance the program's solvency without diminishing benefits.

The MAGA movement, which has gained a foothold in the Republican Party, often emphasizes populist themes that resonate with working-class voters. While this movement includes criticism of the "establishment," it can also perpetuate confusion regarding Social Security, framing it as a burden rather than a benefit.

One of the more concerning aspects of the MAGA movement is its tendency to foster distrust in government institutions, including social safety nets like Social Security. This skepticism can lead to support for politically motivated changes that threaten the program's core function as a guaranteed source of income for millions.

The discussion surrounding Social Security should focus on its merits, foundational structure, and the importance of preserving its integrity as a self-sustaining program.

Mischaracterizations that link Social Security to the national deficit are not only factually inaccurate but also undermine the program's vital role in American society.

The focus should be on enhancing the program, ensuring it remains funded and viable for future generations, rather than diluting or dismantling it under misleading pretenses. Constructive dialogue is essential to combat misinformation and advocate for policies that protect and strengthen Social Security while reflecting a commitment to economic stability and security for all Americans.

Medicare-for-All: Transforming American Healthcare for a Healthier Future

Misconception: Medicare is free

Truth: There are four parts of Medicare: Part A (hospital), Part B (medical), Part C (Medicare Advantage), and Part D (prescription drug coverage).

The prices vary by part and individual circumstances, but in 2025, the standard premium for Part B is $185 per month, while Part A is free for most people who have paid Medicare taxes for at least 10 years. The average Part C premium is about $17 per month, and the average Part D premium is around $38 per month.

The ongoing debate over Medicare-for-All (MFA) has emerged as a pivotal topic in reshaping the American healthcare landscape, driven by the urgent need for affordable and accessible healthcare solutions.

Advocates argue that implementing a single-payer system could not only secure universal healthcare for all citizens but also yield substantial financial benefits for families.

However, despite growing public support, the proposal has yet to pass, largely due to powerful opposition from entrenched interests, including insurance companies, lobbyists, and the political establishment.

A transition to MFA would significantly reduce profits for private insurers, curtail lobbyist influence, and diminish campaign contributions that many politicians rely on to fund their electoral efforts.

These stakeholders have mounted robust campaigns against MFA, fearing that its implementation could disrupt the lucrative healthcare market that currently prioritizes profit over patient care.

This comprehensive analysis delves into the multifaceted implications of a Medicare-for-All model, leveraging extensive research and data available.

From anticipated savings in insurance premiums and out-of-pocket expenses to the promise of universal coverage, this exploration aims to present a detailed assessment of how MFA could revolutionize healthcare in the United States while navigating the complex landscape of political resistance and vested interests.

One of the most critical aspects of the Medicare-for-All proposal is the anticipated reduction in insurance premiums for American households.

Analysis from institutions such as the Political Economy Research Institute suggests that average households could save approximately $2,400 annually in premiums due to the elimination of private insurance.

The shift from multiple private insurance plans to a single-payer system removes the middle layer of private healthcare, which tends to incur high administrative costs.

Medicare's operations are much more streamlined, with lower overhead, allowing savings to be redirected toward patient care rather than administrative bureaucracy.

Lower Out-of-Pocket Expenses
Currently, many Americans face significant out-of-pocket expenses, such as high deductibles and co-pays that can make healthcare access financially burdensome.

In a Medicare-for-All system, the elimination of these costs is a focus, leading to projected savings ranging from $1,000 to $5,000 annually.

The complete removal of deductibles and co-pays means individuals would not face unexpected financial burdens when seeking necessary care, resulting in greater access to preventive services and reduced barriers to treatment.

Universal Coverage
With over 29 million people currently uninsured and even more underinsured in the U.S., a universal coverage model like Medicare-for-All promises to eliminate out-of-pocket costs for all necessary medical services.

For those who currently lack adequate healthcare access, estimates suggest that they could save between $1,500 and $3,000 annually, which factors in enhanced access to medical care that can lead to improved health outcomes.

The implementation of such a system would also reduce uncompensated care, which is costly for taxpayers who frequently subsidize emergency services for uninsured individuals.

Healthcare Access Improvement
The principle of improved access to healthcare is inherently tied to any universal healthcare plan.

By enabling broader access to routine check-ups and preventive screenings, emergency room utilization would likely decline.

Analyses indicate that reducing emergency room admissions alongside increased preventive care can result in meaningful savings for the healthcare system.

Although the figure of $24 billion in potential savings may feel generalized, various studies support the argument that a proactive approach to healthcare could significantly lessen overall healthcare spending.

Economic Impact
Advocates of Medicare-for-All assert that transitioning to this system could reduce national healthcare spending by an estimated $600 billion to $1 trillion annually.

These projections stem from analyses conducted by reliable organizations like the Urban Institute and the Center for American Progress.

By eliminating insurance company profits, unnecessary administrative costs, and systemic inefficiencies prevalent under the current model, a single-payer system has the potential to foster a more efficient distribution of healthcare resources ultimately contributing to substantial savings.

Furthermore, these significant savings could theoretically bolster economic activity, as the funds that would have otherwise gone into healthcare costs are reallocated to consumption, savings, or investment.

This reallocation has the potential to improve overall disposable income, subsequently leading to increased wages and job creation in other sectors of the economy, thereby enhancing the overall economic landscape.

Comprehensive Coverage
A key feature of the Medicare-for-All initiative is its promise of comprehensive coverage that meets the health needs of all individuals.

Under this system, all essential services including preventive, hospital, vision, dental, and mental health care would be fully covered.

This positions Medicare-for-All as a marked improvement over the current landscape, where coverage may vary widely, leaving patients vulnerable to significant medical bills for services deemed non-essential by private insurers.

Tax Adjustments and Redistribution
While the savings for individuals are a significant part of the conversation, it's also essential to examine the tax implications of a Medicare-for-All framework.

To support the funding necessary for such a comprehensive system, the government would need to adjust revenue collection through progressive taxation measures.

Interestingly, while higher-income buyers may face increased taxes, many low- to middle-income families are expected to see a net reduction in overall healthcare spending.

By profoundly simplifying the structure of healthcare financing, individuals could be relieved of premiums and out-of-pocket costs that currently consume a significant portion of household budgets.

Economic Impact and Job Creation
The transition to a Medicare-for-All model may also impact jobs in the economy positively, especially within the healthcare sector.

While there may be a decrease in administrative jobs tied to private insurance companies, the overall demand for healthcare services is likely to grow, necessitating new hires in hospitals, clinics, and supportive roles.

A healthier population, empowered by better access to care, could foster increased productivity across various sectors, further contributing to economic growth.

Policy Considerations and Challenges
Bear in mind that while these savings sound beneficial, the transition to such a system involves substantial policy considerations, potential tax adjustments, and political debates that affect how these savings are realized.

The exact outcomes may differ based on the specific structure of the Medicare-for-All program implemented, as well as regional healthcare dynamics and cost-of-living variations across the U.S.

The complexity of these considerations underscores that while the theory behind Medicare-for-All is promising, its practical implementation will require nuanced policy development to ensure equity and efficiency.

The Medicare-for-All proposal offers a transformative opportunity to revamp the American healthcare system notably, presenting substantial potential savings for voters through lowered premiums, reduced out-of-pocket expenses, and comprehensive coverage.

By emphasizing universality and financial accessibility, advocates argue that such a system could enhance healthcare access while ensuring a healthier population overall.

As a deeper understanding of these issues is developed through ongoing research and analysis, both public opinion and legislative objectives may evolve regarding the potential implementation of a Medicare-for-All structure.

In summary, achieving projected savings of approximately $1.9 trillion annually entails a cumulative effect of cost reductions across multiple facets of the healthcare system, including premium reductions, lower out-of-pocket costs, and increased administrative efficiency, ultimately making healthcare a fundamental right accessible to all Americans.

To cover the cost of Medicare For All the following would need to happen:

To cover the cost of Medicare-for-All, a multifaceted funding strategy would need to be employed. Increasing the Federal Insurance Contributions Act (FICA) tax rate from 6.2% to 9% would significantly enhance the revenue pool dedicated to healthcare funding.

This adjustment could substantially increase the funds available to support a universal healthcare system. However, alone, this increase in FICA would not be sufficient to fully cover the projected costs of such a program, which has been estimated by various analyses to exceed $30 trillion over ten years.

To effectively bridge this gap, additional funding sources would need to be identified:

Including increased income taxes on the top 10%. Raising income tax rates on the highest earners could yield substantial revenue. For instance, implementing higher marginal tax rates for individuals making over $400,000 could ensure that the wealthiest individuals contribute a fairer share towards the public healthcare system.

Corporate tax increases could serve as another source of funding. Corporations often benefit from a healthy workforce; hence, their contribution to Medicare-for-All could be justified as a reciprocal benefit to ensure their employees are healthier and more productive.

Additionally, higher taxes on wealth and capital gains can provide more revenue.

Adjusting tax structures to increase rates on capital gains and implementing wealth taxes can ensure that those who have accumulated wealth contribute equitably.

Other tax revenue options could include increasing taxes on tobacco and sugary beverages and potentially introducing financial transaction taxes.

Each of these could generate revenue while also promoting public health initiatives.

While raising the FICA tax to 9% would bolster the healthcare funding pool, the cumulative effect of these measures would be essential to adequately finance a Medicare-for-All program.

Such a comprehensive system would result in a healthier population, ultimately benefiting the economy and businesses alike, thus justifying the expectation that the top 10% of earners should contribute their fair share.

Overall, a socially equitable funding approach is critical not just for meeting budgetary needs, but also for ensuring public support and enhancing the impact of a universal healthcare system.

Fact-checking notes indicate that various analyses, including studies by the Political Economy Research Institute (PERI), estimate the cost of a Medicare-for-All program to exceed $30 trillion over ten years, though estimates vary widely based on assumptions and methodologies used. The current employee portion of the FICA tax is 6.2% for Social Security and 1.45% for Medicare, totaling 7.65%. The proposal to increase the FICA tax by 2.8% to 9% refers specifically to the income earner's part and aligns with efforts to improve the funding base for Medicare.

Corporate taxation is an essential consideration in comprehensive funding strategies, as businesses benefit from a productive workforce. Currently, the capital gains tax rate is typically lower than standard income tax rates, leading to proposals for tax reform aimed at equity. This information encapsulates both the mechanics of funding a Medicare-for-All program and some pivotal points of broader tax policy discussions in the U.S.

Corporate Greed Will Undermine And Destroy Any Democracy: Time To Hold The Elite Accountable

In a landscape marked by pervasive inequality and systemic issues, it has become increasingly clear that the burgeoning wealth of the elite demands scrutiny and concerted action.

As billionaires accumulate unprecedented wealth with over two trillion dollars enriched since 2019 largely through tax cuts benefiting the wealthy during the first Trump administration the question arises:

Why should we allow a select few to hoard wealth while the majority of the population struggles to make ends meet?

It's time to challenge our socioeconomic frameworks that enable this disparity and advocate for policies that compel the wealthy to contribute to the common good, addressing crises largely perpetuated by corporate greed, all within a framework of democracy and equitable opportunity.

When individuals accumulate wealth that exceeds the limits of what they and their descendants can utilize, a moral obligation arises.

Billionaires to do business in the United States should be required to embody a sense of responsibility to society, particularly towards their employees and consumers, many of whom are often denied a living wage.

Instead of rewarding their workforce and contributing meaningfully to the community, too many wealthy individuals resort to union-busting tactics and corporate strategies designed to maximize profits at the expense of their staff. Price hikes and profit doubling can become the norm, resulting in a detrimental cycle that exacerbates socio-economic divides.

In discussions of wealth inequality, it's important to consider the significant financial disparities that define the landscape of the American economy.

While the term "monopoly" traditionally applies to market structures where a single entity dominates supply and pricing, the concentration of wealth among the elite can resemble monopolistic power in its effects on society.

Recent data highlights that the wealthiest segment of the population holds an overwhelming share of national assets.

The top 50% of earners in the United States control approximately $156 trillion, a figure that exceeds 88% of the country's total wealth.

This leaves the bottom 50%, which owns only about $4 trillion, in a markedly precarious position. Among these wealth holders, the top 1% or approximately 1.3 million households individually command nearly $49 trillion, representing about one-third of the entire national wealth.

This staggering wealth concentration underscores the difficulties faced by lower-income households in achieving upward mobility and financial stability.

While the elite do not fit the traditional governmental definition of a monopoly, their extensive financial resources yield considerable influence over economic policies and outcomes, potentially affecting market competition and living standards for the broader population.

Such disparities raise vital questions about the fairness and functionality of our economic system. They compel us to examine the mechanisms that facilitate this wealth accumulation and the implications it has for democracy and social equity.

True success in a democracy should not be defined solely by financial accumulation but by the positive impact, one can have on society.

A Responsible capitalist would achieve their financial goals and then redirect their efforts toward philanthropy and improvements in the lives of others.

However, many choose the path of political involvement with ulterior motives, pushing agendas that undermine the public interest. The emergence of billionaires, such as Donald Trump and Elon Musk, in politics demands vigilance; how can we trust individuals who have garnered immense wealth while promising to serve the public for a fraction of their earnings?

Unchecked corporate greed coupled with the overwhelming influence of the top 1% is not merely an economic concern it poses an existential threat to our democracy.

When wealth becomes concentrated in the hands of a few individuals or corporations, the fundamental tenets of democracy, equality, representation, and accountability are undermined. Elites wield disproportionate power over the political landscape, enabling them to manipulate democratic processes to their advantage.

As we witness figures like President Trump and Musk who blatantly defy court orders and constantly violate our constitutional rights since becoming prominent voices, their vast resources allow them to sway public opinion, influence legislation, and perpetuate a narrative that serves corporate interests.

This concentration of power erodes the diversity of voices essential for a functioning democracy. Political decisions increasingly reflect the whims of billionaires, sidelining the needs and concerns of everyday citizens.

Furthermore, the lack of accountability for such individuals fosters a cash-and-grab society. When wealth and influence go unchecked, the ethical boundaries that typically govern business operations blur.

Decisions made in boardrooms and with politicians prioritize short-term financial gain over the long-term health of communities and the environment.

This greed-driven mentality not only exacerbates economic inequalities but also cultivates a culture of cynicism and disengagement among the populace.

When citizens perceive that their voices and votes do not matter against the backdrop of unchecked corporate influence, trust in democratic institutions erodes, leading to increased polarization and instability.

This moment calls for a reevaluation of our economic priorities. For instance, consider that with $162.5 million, we could significantly address the nation's homeless crisis through innovative housing solutions. Moreover, ending hunger in the United States would only require approximately $25 billion, according to estimates from Joel Berg, CEO of Hunger Free America. This figure accounts for ensuring adequate nutrition for all Americans while also addressing related factors like poverty and unemployment.

Ending hunger would yield broader positive effects, such as reduced healthcare costs, improved educational outcomes, and increased economic productivity. A 2020 Hunger Report illustrates that the U.S. spends $160 billion annually on healthcare costs driven by food insecurities. This statistic underscores the urgent need for comprehensive solutions:

Investing in the well-being of citizens can lead to substantial savings for the healthcare system and strengthen the economy.

Critics often express concerns about assisting those in need, arguing that it is unfair to those who pay for their homes or basic needs. However, the reality is that stable housing and adequate nutrition help foster economic participation and consumerism. When individuals have a place to live and food to eat, they are more likely to invest in their communities, boosting local economies and creating a thriving middle class. In contrast, those without stable housing or access to nutritious food cannot contribute as they should leading to diminished purchasing power and a stagnating economy.

An essential aspect of addressing corporate greed and ensuring fair treatment for employees is the mandatory establishment of independent, outside unions that advocate for workers' rights.

These unions would play a crucial role in representing employees across all sectors, negotiating fair wages, and advocating for improved working conditions and benefits.

By being organized collectively, employees can exert pressure on corporations to recognize their rights and prioritize their well-being.

Outside unions can serve as powerful advocates for employees, enabling them to voice their grievances, negotiate for better standards of living, and hold their employers accountable.

This representation not only empowers workers but also helps to balance the power dynamics within companies, ensuring that employee interests are considered in decision-making processes.

When employees are collectively represented, businesses are compelled to acknowledge their needs, leading to a healthier workplace culture, increased productivity, and ultimately enhancing the overall economy as well.

Capitalists would not lose any money or profits by paying their employees a comfortable living wage. Paying a living wage would actually increase their profits.

The more expendable income workers have, the more buying power they gain, ultimately leading to a higher accumulation of wants and needs.

Increased purchasing power aligns with corporate interests, as satisfied consumers drive demand and boost profits. Yet the prevailing attitude among the wealthy often revolves around power and control rather than genuine consideration for the well-being of their employees.

Currently, only 56% of full-time workers in the U.S. are earning a living wage, while 44% struggle to cover their families' basic needs, according to the inaugural Dayforce Living Wage Index. This alarming statistic emphasizes the disconnect between corporate profits and employee welfare and highlights the urgent need for change in our compensation structures.

As active participants in a democracy, we hold significant power. One of the most effective ways to challenge the dominance of billionaires and abusive corporate practices is through strategic boycotts. Companies whose leaders are worth billions must be held accountable for their practices. By redirecting our purchasing power, we signal to these corporations that the public demands responsibility, equity, and ethical behavior. We must raise our voices against those who exploit the system for their gain while disregarding the struggles of everyday people. A concerted effort to boycott can serve as a robust statement against greed and push for systemic changes, urging lawmakers to create regulations that require the wealthy to give back.

By opting to support businesses that prioritize fair wages, ethical labor practices, and community investment, we can foster a marketplace that values integrity over sheer profit.

The simple act of choosing where to spend our money is a potent tool in shifting corporate behaviors. Collective action can create ripple effects, encouraging companies to adopt more socially responsible practices, lest they find themselves on the receiving end of consumer backlash.

The dangers of unchecked corporate greed and the influence of the top 1% cannot be overstated. As we grapple with crises stemming from economic inequality, environmental degradation, and erosion of democratic principles, we must advocate for policies compelling the wealthy to contribute to solutions, all within the framework of democracy.

By supporting independent unions that advocate for employee well-being and holding billionaires accountable through boycotts, we can pave the way for a fairer, more just society. Our collective action can dismantle the barriers erected by corporate greed and generate a new economic landscape where the wealth generated by society is shared more equitably.

The call for billionaires to give back isn't just a plea for fairness; it is a necessity for a sustainable future. Let us embrace a system that champions democratic values while ensuring that those at the top also do their part. A truly responsible capitalist should not merely seek profit but strive to elevate the very fabric of society. Together, we can demand a world where the wealthy use their resources to uplift others, truly embodying the principles of social responsibility and equity that are essential for building a better future for all.

Ending corporate greed and implementing laws that require corporations to reinvest a portion of their profits into society is essential, especially in light of the prevailing greed demonstrated by the top 1% of the population and its social consequences.

Government mandates aimed at curtailing corporate behavior would not only mitigate negative impacts, such as environmental degradation and wage stagnation, but would also promote consumer spending, ultimately benefiting the economy as a whole.

Regulating corporations and fostering a culture of social responsibility will help build public trust. When companies are held accountable and forced to visibly contribute to societal well-being, it enhances their reputation and encourages customer loyalty both of which are vital for long-term success and sustainability.

Investing in sustainable practices and community development can also spur innovation. Such investments not only address pressing societal challenges but can also lead to economic growth in emerging sectors, creating new job opportunities and fostering a healthier ecosystem.

Corporate greed is a leading contributor to income and wealth inequality. Enforcing regulations that mandate corporate investment in social programs can help level the playing field, reducing disparities and contributing to a more equitable society.

Requiring corporations to reinvest some of their profits into society through regulatory frameworks, as well as addressing tax obligations, is not merely a moral imperative; it is a necessary strategy for fostering a sustainable and equitable economy. It will also ensure we have a healthy operating and functional Democracy.

Holding businesses accountable for their actions and the roles they play in environmental degradation, income inequality, and public health issues will also restore faith in our elected officials by ensuring they serve their constituents rather than succumbing to financial influence.

We must ensure that the benefits of economic activity are shared broadly, leading to a healthier society, a secure Democracy, and a more resilient economy.

The condition of our Democracy today is that we are on the verge of a total collapse. Why? Just so that the greed and entitlement of 1.3 million people get their way, which is hoarding wealth, power, and control.

America's Facade Of Democracy and Equality Exposed

Pulling Back the Curtain and Exposing the Dark Underbelly of the United States Practice in Regards to Diplomacy

America's Complex Role it Plays on the Global Stage: Can a Nation Exhibit Narcissism?

The United States publicly praises democracy, civil rights, human rights, and the principle that all men are created equal; however, privately, we often overlook these ideals. Not only are we complicit in global injustices, but we also frequently initiate the discord. In reality, much of the hostility and hatred toward America and its citizens stems from our government's initial interactions with various countries, including their demographics and the resources at stake.

It is important to note that from the time the first Anglo colony was established in North America, a troubling trend began that the United States continues to find acceptable. Whether out of habit or an inability to change, we are not only complacent but also actively participate in atrocities, both foreign and domestic: the exploitation, annexation, and annihilation of people of color, along with entire nations and continents.

This trend was initiated with the systematic plundering, pillaging, and stealing of land from the Indigenous American people, acting as though we were the first to occupy this continent and treating them as if they were not human. We set out to systematically annihilate and we nearly caused the extinction of the Indigenous peoples of the Americas, who had occupied this land for thousands of years.

As if that weren't far enough, the U.S. continued to exploit, plunder, and pillage the very peoples of the African continent, considering this human demographic a commodity for the USA to own. Our arrogance and failure to recognize them as human only compounded these injustices.

Despite proclaiming itself a promoter and advocate of democracy, the U.S. does not have clean hands and is the root cause of the hostility and animosity the world has toward the United States through its treatment, actions, and interactions with nations of color, continents of color, and people of color throughout its history.

The treatment of nations of color beyond our borders and the people of color within America's own borders speaks to a legacy of systemic aggression that has persisted since the inception of its first colony.

To perpetuate these hostilities toward the USA, the United States has never held itself accountable and continues to refuse to admit its wrongdoing. Instead, it often doubles down and portrays itself as a victim, claiming that attacks are unprovoked and necessitate retaliation whenever nations or continents of color rise against the injustices they endure. This mentality of the U.S., claiming it is defending its interests under the guise of democracy, perpetuates a cycle of unrest and resentment.

The United States frequently approaches international relations with a paternalistic attitude, attempting to impose its values on other nations. This mindset reflects a failure to learn from history and to emulate the democratic practices of older civilizations that have thrived for millennia. The U.S. has exploited nations of color since its inception, a practice that continues to shape its foreign policy and international relations. As a result, America's democracy now teeters on the brink of collapse.

Numerous countries harbor resentment toward America and its citizens due to a long history of exploitation, in which we have taken their people as commodities, along with their land, resources, and governance, for our gain. Notably, around 90% of these nations are countries of color.

Remarkably, the United States has never formally acknowledged these transgressions or made any meaningful reparations, including to the indigenous peoples or to the descendants of captives possessed by our citizens. Most within the American public have largely remained silent on the need to address these injustices.

This persistent arrogance and reliance on intimidation can only lead us so far. Since the beginning of humankind, when oppressed people reach their breaking point, they will inevitably react, regardless of the consequences they may face.

At the heart of this issue lies a deeply ingrained attitude of American exceptionalism, which holds that the U.S. not only has the right but also the obligation to intervene in the affairs of other nations.

This mindset often disregards the historical contexts and complexities of foreign societies, leading to poorly conceived policies that exacerbate existing tensions.

Due to America's arrogance and its feelings of entitlement to anything the globe has to offer, many countries, including Iran, perceive American cultural and political imposition as a form of imperialism, fostering resentment and resistance.

The fact that the U.S. is willing to impose its values at the expense of others' dignity only deepens international divides and hostilities, hindering progress toward mutual understanding and cooperation with countries and continents of color.

Most countries of color have voiced sentiments similar to those of Iran.

While Iran is a focal point due to its current prominence in global events, many countries and territories of color share similar feelings of resentment and hostility toward the United States.

We exploit even our own territories and our allies that are countries of color, often without regard for the consequences of our actions.

The relationship between the United States and Iran, in particular, is a complex tapestry woven from historical events, political decisions, and cultural misunderstandings, all of which significantly influence today's relations.

A central truth of this narrative is that American actions over several decades have not only shaped Iran's trajectory but also sown the seeds of resentment, anger, and hostility toward the U.S. The imperialistic and geopolitical maneuvers of the U.S. government have left lasting scars on Iranian society, making it crucial for Americans to acknowledge and confront the responsibility we bear in shaping this fraught relationship.

Acknowledging these histories and examining the ongoing implications of U.S. actions in all countries of color is crucial for fostering a more comprehensive understanding of international relations and repairing relationships adversely affected by American policies.

The origins of this complex relationship with Iran can often be traced back to critical events since the end of World War I, when the Middle East was divided into countries with borders.

The 1953 coup of Iran, when the CIA orchestrated the overthrow of Iran's democratically elected Prime Minister, Mohammad Mossadegh. This intervention aimed to secure Western control over Iranian oil resources and counter the perceived threat of communism during the Cold War. As a direct result, the Iranian people witnessed the crushing of their democratic aspirations and the undermining of their sovereignty. This coup set the stage for a monarch who ruled for decades as an authoritarian Shah Mohammad Reza Pahlavi.

Backed by the United States, the Shah ruled as a shadow puppet of the USA, with an iron fist, employing a brutal security apparatus known as SAVAK to suppress dissent.

During this period, the Iranian populace endured oppression, censorship, disappearances, and the ruthless enforcement of a regime that prioritized Western interests over the well-being of its citizens.

This painful chapter in Iranian history is what fostered deep-seated animosity toward the United States, a sentiment that continues to resonate in the Iranian consciousness today.

The 1953 coup, known as Operation Ajax, was a watershed moment in U.S.-Iran relations. The U.S. intelligence community viewed Mossadegh's nationalist policies, particularly the nationalization of the Anglo-Iranian Oil Company (now BP), as a direct threat to American and British oil interests.

Following the coup, the Shah instituted a regime characterized by widespread human rights abuses, which created long-lasting grievances among the Iranian people toward the United States of America.

The Shah's secret police, SAVAK, was notorious for its torture, killings, suppression, and the disappearance of Iran's citizens of political dissent.

Supported and trained by the CIA and Israeli intelligence, SAVAK played a crucial role in maintaining the Shah's regime, yet contributed significantly to public discontent toward Israel and the United States.

The Shah's alignment with the U.S. often alienated ordinary Iranians who felt their culture was being undermined in favor of Western values. Socioeconomic disparities increased, with much of Iran's wealth concentrated among a small elite, exacerbating widespread unrest.

The culmination of this resentment led to the 1979 Iranian Revolution, which resulted in the overthrow of the Shah and the establishment of the Islamic Republic under Ayatollah Khomeini. This marked a significant turning point in U.S.-Iran relations, as the new government adopted a vehemently anti-American stance, rightly blaming the U.S. for the country's previous hardships.

The animosity stemming from the coup and the subsequent years of U.S. support for the Shah has had enduring consequences. Events such as the U.S. Embassy hostage crisis in 1979 and ongoing tensions over Iran's nuclear program have continued to exacerbate the adversarial relationship.

Acknowledging this history is crucial for understanding current dynamics in U.S.-Iran relations and the broader Middle East. A more nuanced perspective can help facilitate constructive dialogue and potentially mend the fractures of the past.

Furthermore, the lack of authentic democratic practices under the Shah's government exposed the contradictions in American foreign policy. The U.S. supported the Shah even as evidence of his systematic human rights and civil rights violations became increasingly apparent.

This collaboration meant that Iranian dissenters faced repression not only from local authorities but also from foreign influence. Such actions starkly contrast with the democratic values the U.S. professes to champion. This duplicity did not go unnoticed; it sparked revolutionary sentiments among Iranians who viewed the U.S. not as a promoter of democracy but as a key enabler of tyranny.

The complicity of the U.S. in these human rights violations and its indifference to the suffering of the Iranian people intensified feelings of betrayal, resentment, and hostility toward Americans, shaping the tumultuous relationship that persists to this day.

Under the Shah, various reports and accounts documented widespread human rights abuses, including torture, imprisonment of political dissidents, and censorship of the press. Organizations such as Amnesty International and Human Rights Watch have chronicled these abuses, noting that the U.S. turned a blind eye due to strategic and economic interests.

Cold War dynamics partly drove the U.S. support for the Shah, as American policymakers viewed Iran as a bulwark against Soviet expansion. This geopolitical strategy often overshadowed concerns about democracy and human rights, leading to a foreign policy prioritizing stability over ethical considerations.

The fact that the U.S. was complicit in the Shah's oppressive regime galvanized various factions in Iranian society, including leftists, Islamists, and nationalists, contributing to a coalition that ultimately led to the 1979 Iranian Revolution.

Anti-American sentiment was a unifying theme during this period, as many Iranians saw the U.S. as an imperialist power imposing its will on Iran.

The aftermath of the Iranian Revolution saw the establishment of a theocratic regime that has maintained a hostile stance toward the United States. The U.S. Embassy hostage crisis in 1979 epitomized this animosity, leading to decades of adversarial relations characterized by sanctions, military standoffs, and mutual antagonism.

This history demonstrates the U.S.'s refusal to acknowledge any wrongdoing.

The events in Iran raise important questions about the ethical implications of U.S. foreign policy and the genuine promotion of democracy abroad. The tension between political realities and democratic ideals remains a sensitive topic in discussions about American intervention and foreign relations in the Middle East.

Understanding these complexities is vital for comprehending the current state of U.S.-Iran relations and the underlying tensions that continue to shape them.

By acknowledging the U.S. in the historical context and the repercussions of past actions, there is an opportunity for the U.S. to right its wrongs and foster a narrative through which both nations might find pathways to more constructive engagement in the future.

The consequences of American policy did not end with the fall of the Shah in 1979; instead, the U.S. decided to double down, and its actions evolved and magnified. The Iranian Revolution dramatically altered the political landscape, and the subsequent hostage crisis further strained an already tense relationship.

In response to the hostage situation, the U.S. imposed a series of severe economic sanctions aimed at isolating Iran. These sanctions were unilateral and drastic, effectively punishing the Iranian populace for the actions of their government.

As a result, ordinary Iranians faced dire hardships, starving to death and struggling with shortages of essential goods, medicines, and basic services. The elite in Iran felt none of these hardships, effectively punishing the right hand for what the left hand was doing.

The economic distress inflicted by these sanctions became a catalyst and served as fertile ground for the growing resentment and anti-American sentiment, as it reinforced the belief that the U.S. would sacrifice the welfare of the poor and disenfranchised Iranian people to meet its geopolitical objectives, which were only concerned with the Iranian elite.

The U.S. Embassy hostage crisis in 1979, in which 52 American diplomats and citizens were held hostage for 444 days, not only soured U.S.-Iran relations but also emboldened hardline elements within Iran, leading to an even more authoritarian political climate.

The sanctions imposed by the U.S. after the hostage crisis were comprehensive and targeted various sectors of the Iranian economy, including critical oil exports. Over the years, these sanctions have expanded to include measures that target financial transactions, trade, and access to key technologies.

While economic sanctions often aim to leverage change in government behavior, they invariably lead to unintentional humanitarian crises. Reports indicate that sanctions have adversely affected access to medical supplies and healthcare for ordinary Iranians, fostering further anti-American sentiments.

The long-term impacts of these sanctions have perpetuated economic instability in Iran. Inflation and unemployment rates have soared, with many Iranians facing poverty, starvation, and deprivation, which deepens their resentment toward the U.S. as they perceive it to be responsible for their suffering.

The sanctions policy has proven controversial, with various international bodies and humanitarian organizations arguing that such measures only hurt civilians more than they pressure the elite or the government. This dynamic has led to a complex relationship where calls for reform among Iranians are overshadowed by nationalistic sentiments opposing foreign interference, particularly from the U.S.

The ongoing sanctions and the U.S. withdrawal from the Joint Comprehensive Plan of Action (JCPOA) in 2018 have further complicated relations. Donald Trump's decision to reinstate sanctions has driven Iran to assertively pursue its nuclear program, fueling further tensions between the two nations.

These sanctions have laid an additional foundation for a humanitarian crisis, solidifying the perception of the U.S. as a harmful influence within Iranian society.

The sanctions severely damaged not only Iran's economy but also the lives of millions of non-political Iranian citizens, exemplifying how American foreign policy decisions can lead to devastating consequences for populations. When the U.S. employs economic sanctions as a diplomatic tool, it often overlooks their human impact, resulting in extensive suffering among innocent people.

Once again, the U.S. is willing to throw aside what it claims publicly and make decisions that reveal a broader pattern whereby human rights considerations are sacrificed for strategic ends, further entrenching mistrust and animosity in regions affected by American policies.

Moreover, U.S. support for military interventions in the Middle East during the late 20th and early 21st centuries has further complicated the situation with Iran.

For example, the U.S. backing of Saddam Hussein during the Iran-Iraq War (1980-1988) directly contradicted its stated goals of promoting stability and democracy in the region.

The U.S. freely provided Iraq with crucial military intelligence and financial support, even as Saddam's regime committed heinous atrocities against its people and neighboring nations.

By prioritizing a short-term alliance based on immediate strategic interests rather than investing in long-term peace-building initiatives, the U.S. caused lasting regional instability and conflict.

This pattern of duplicity fostered an environment of fear and mutual suspicion, leading Iran to feel compelled to seek its own security solutions, including the development of nuclear capabilities—a significant point of contention between Iran and the U.S. in recent decades.

Initially, the U.S. viewed Saddam Hussein as a counterbalance to the Islamic Revolution in Iran, supporting Iraq financially and logistically throughout the Iran-Iraq War. This support included providing intelligence and selling weapons, despite awareness of the humanitarian crises created by Saddam's regime.

During the Iran-Iraq War, Saddam Hussein's regime was responsible for numerous human rights violations, including the use of chemical weapons against Iranian troops and Kurdish civilians, resulting in the deaths of millions.

The U.S. government's knowledge of these actions did not deter its support, highlighting a complex and often contradictory foreign policy approach.

The lasting effects of U.S. interventions in Iraq extended beyond the Iran-Iraq War, leading to further instability in the region. The 2003 invasion of Iraq, following 9/11, exacerbated sectarian tensions, and the U.S. is responsible for the rise of various extremist groups in the Middle East, such as ISIS, al-Qaeda, and the Taliban, complicating the security landscape.

The perceived need for security has driven Iran to develop its nuclear program, which Tehran views as a deterrent against potential military threats. The U.S. response, including sanctions and military posturing, has created a cycle of provocation and distrust, significantly impacting diplomatic efforts.

The history of U.S. military interventions in the Middle East underscores the complexities of foreign policy driven by strategic imperatives. The contradictions in supporting authoritarian regimes while advocating for democracy and stability have contributed to enduring instability and conflict. This reality has not only shaped regional dynamics but has also spurred nations like Iran to pursue alternative security measures, complicating U.S.-Iran relations and raising questions about the efficacy of American involvement in the region.

The fallout from Trump's decision to withdraw the U.S. from the Joint Comprehensive Plan of Action (JCPOA) in 2018 further illustrates the pattern of American diplomacy that often overlooks broader implications. By unilaterally rescinding this agreement, which was designed to effectively curtail Iran's nuclear program in exchange for sanctions relief, the U.S. not only undermined diplomatic goodwill but also sent a clear signal to Iran and the international community that it could easily abandon its commitments.

This action triggered a renewed cycle of conflict and distrust, prompting Iran to reassert its sovereignty while beginning to explore its nuclear options.

Consequently, this decision further isolated Iran from the international community. It highlighted a retreat by the U.S. from constructive diplomacy, marking a shift from engagement to confrontation that entrenches divisions and alienates potential regional allies and beyond.

The consequences of such actions are profound, underscoring the complexities and possible pitfalls of American foreign policy rooted in short-term strategic calculations rather than long-term diplomatic vision.

The JCPOA, signed in 2015 between Iran and the P5+1 (the five permanent members of the UN Security Council plus Germany), aimed to limit Iran's nuclear capabilities in exchange for lifting economic sanctions. The agreement was seen as a landmark achievement in diplomacy.

Following the U.S. withdrawal, Iran began to gradually breach the limits set by the JCPOA, including expanding uranium enrichment levels and stockpiling enriched materials—actions that raised concerns among the international community regarding the potential for weapons development.

The withdrawal strained U.S. relations with European allies, who remained committed to the agreement and sought to salvage it. It illustrated a divergence in strategic priorities among traditional partners.

Trump and the U.S. are responsible for all of the actions that have taken place since the withdrawal, leading to increased military tensions in the region, including confrontations between U.S. and Iranian forces, as well as a series of attacks on shipping in the Gulf that were attributed to Iranian proxies. This environment has led to a renewed call for increased hostilities and fears of a wider conflict.

Subsequent attempts by the Biden administration to revive negotiations on a revised nuclear agreement have met with mixed responses from Iran, complicating efforts to restore the diplomatic framework established by the JCPOA.

The U.S. withdrawal from the JCPOA reflects a broader trend in American foreign policy that prioritizes immediate strategic gains over sustained diplomatic engagement.

The resultant instability raises questions about the viability of future diplomatic efforts and serves as a cautionary tale about the long-term consequences of unilateral actions on international relations initiated by the U.S.

Recognizing and addressing the historical grievances caused by U.S. actions is vital for improving U.S.-Iran relations and establishing a more stable and cooperative Middle Eastern landscape overall. Understanding the long-term consequences of interventionist policies and engaging in genuine dialogue rooted in mutual respect is essential for breaking the cycle of animosity and mistrust that has characterized U.S.-Iranian relations for decades.

To move forward, Americans must critically engage with their country's historical and ongoing actions in Iran and other nations of color by acknowledging how American actions have shaped the current state of relations.

The impacts of U.S. interventions, economic sanctions, and diplomatic failures have left an enduring imprint on Iranian society and continue to stoke animosity. Recognizing this responsibility demands a transformative shift in perspective that prioritizes diplomacy, respects national sovereignty, and honors the humanity of all individuals involved.

Historical U.S. interventions in Iran, particularly the 1953 coup, have fostered a narrative of external control that still resonates in Iranian society today.

Ongoing economic sanctions imposed by the U.S. have significantly affected the Iranian economy and civilian population, often leading to widespread hardship. Critics argue that these sanctions exacerbate anti-American sentiment and hinder diplomatic resolution.

The inability to constructively engage with Iran, especially following the Iran nuclear deal (the Joint Comprehensive Plan of Action) in 2015 and the subsequent U.S. withdrawal in 2018, has contributed to deteriorating relations. A lack of trust hampers progress toward mutual interests.

Engaging with nations of color requires cultural sensitivity and an understanding of historical contexts. This approach is vital for fostering relationships based on respect and equality rather than power dynamics.

Successful diplomacy must consider the lives and perspectives of ordinary citizens. Fostering people-to-people connections and understanding local political contexts can help mend relations at a grassroots level.

Acknowledging and addressing historical grievances is crucial for improving U.S.-Iran relations and ensuring a more collaborative Middle East. A commitment to understanding and respecting the complexities of these relationships will pave the way for more productive dialogue and cooperation in the future.

Only through this lens of accountability and understanding can the U.S. redefine its role on the global stage, fostering relationships grounded in respect, mutual understanding, and a genuine commitment to shared values rather than dominance or coercion.

Through such critical reflection, we can address the root causes of animosity and strive toward a more peaceful and cooperative future.

Acknowledging past mistakes and adopting a policy framework centered on empathy and constructive engagement can foster a more stable and prosperous relationship between the U.S. and Iran, ultimately benefiting both nations and the wider international community.

Historical U.S. foreign policy often leaned toward dominance, particularly during the Cold War. Shifting to a partnership model instead of a dominant and possessive stance would emphasize collaboration and respect for national sovereignty, which is essential for long-term stability.

Policies that prioritize empathy and understanding can help mitigate conflicts. By recognizing the unique historical, cultural, and political contexts that shape Iranian society, the U.S. can build trust and open lines of communication.

Identifying shared values, such as economic cooperation, regional stability, and the fight against extremism, can serve as a foundation for dialogue and collaboration between the U.S. and Iran.

Fostering constructive engagement requires consistent and open dialogues, highlighting the need for back-channel communications, cultural exchanges, and diplomatic initiatives.

A peaceful and cooperative U.S.-Iran relationship has implications beyond bilateral ties. Stability in Iran can contribute to broader regional stability, impacting global issues such as energy security, migration, and counterterrorism.

The U.S. must acknowledge historical grievances, make reparations, and shift towards an approach based on empathy and respect.

The U.S. can foster positive nation-to-nation relationships globally. Such a transformation would not only enhance ties with Iran but also contribute positively to the international community, paving the way for a more collaborative and peaceful world.

Eight other countries of color we have exploited, are: Puerto Rico, Venezuela, Cuba, Panama, Honduras, Mexico, Syria, and North Korea (Korea as a whole).

Resentment over U.S. interventions, economic sanctions, and support for opposition groups has significantly contributed to the longstanding tensions between the U.S. and these nations.

The following eight nations exemplify the complex and often damaging relationship the U.S. has fostered through its various forms of exploitation or intervention:

Puerto Rico: The relationship between Puerto Rico and the United States is fraught with historical, political, and economic tensions that contribute to resentment among many Puerto Ricans. Since becoming a U.S. territory in 1898, Puerto Rico has lost its sovereignty and operates under U.S. governance without full rights.

Puerto Ricans are U.S. citizens but cannot vote in presidential elections and have no voting representation in Congress, leading to feelings of political marginalization.

Furthermore, U.S. policies, such as the Jones Act, have adversely affected the island's economy, exacerbating issues like the recent debt crisis and contributing to a pervasive sense of economic exploitation and neglect.

Culturally, many Puerto Ricans feel a loss of identity due to the imposition of American norms and values, alongside facing discrimination in mainland America. This complex dynamic fuels calls for either statehood or independence, a multifaceted grievance that illustrates the disconnect between Puerto Rico and the U.S. mainland.

Venezuela: The complex relationship between the United States and Venezuela is marked by long-standing resentment fueled by a series of interventions, economic sanctions, and perceived political meddling. Historically, the U.S. has intervened in Latin America under the pretext of promoting democracy and stability, but many Venezuelans view these actions as imperialistic. This includes U.S. support for various opposition groups during tumultuous times, notably during Hugo Chávez's presidency when the U.S. was perceived as backing a coup attempt in 2002. Such interventions fostered a narrative of the U.S. as a neocolonial power attempting to control Venezuela's political landscape, galvanizing nationalism and anti-American sentiment among both the populace and the government. Furthermore, economic sanctions targeting Venezuela's oil sector the backbone of its economy have exacerbated the nation's economic woes and contributed to a humanitarian crisis. Many Venezuelans blame these sanctions for widespread shortages of basic goods, food, and medicine, viewing them as punitive measures that deepen the suffering of ordinary citizens rather than encourage reform. This perception of U.S. interference has entrenched resentment and unified a national identity against what is seen as an external oppressor, deepening the rift between the two nations.

Cuba: Long-standing animosity between the U.S. and Cuba is rooted in the U.S. embargo and interventions in Cuban affairs. After Fidel Castro came to power in 1959, Cuba sought assistance from the U.S., but the USA's refusal to aid the island unless it aligned with American interests significantly contributed to Cuba's shift toward communism. The U.S. response included the embargo that economically isolated Cuba, escalating hostilities, and prompting Castro to turn to the Soviet Union for support. This realignment not only solidified Cuba's communist regime but also deepened anti-American sentiments within the country. The U.S. interventionist policies and economic sanctions pushed Cuba into the arms of a superpower willing to provide the aid and support that the U.S. denied, illustrating how U.S. actions can directly shape the political landscape of other nations. This historical context highlights the complexities of U.S. foreign policy and its unintended consequences on international relations.

Panama: Panama's animosity toward the United States has historical roots deeply embedded in its complex relationship with U.S. involvement in its sovereignty, particularly concerning the Panama Canal. The U.S. played a pivotal role in Panama's separation from Colombia in 1903, subsequently gaining control over the Canal Zone. This control was formalized through the Hay-Bunau-Varilla Treaty, which many Panamanians perceived as inequitable and forced upon them. For most of the 20th century, the U.S. exercised significant political and military influence in Panama, leading to resentment toward American interventionism. The Canal, a symbol of U.S. dominance, was critical to Panamanians, who felt that their land and resources were being exploited without fair compensation or respect for their sovereignty. This legacy fostered humiliation and anger exacerbated by U.S. military actions and political machinations, including support for the oppressive regime of Manuel Noriega. Noriega's eventual fall from grace led to the U.S. invasion of Panama in 1989, resulting in extensive casualties and damage, deepening distrust of American motives. Many Panamanians continue to harbor bitterness toward American policies, viewing them as exploitative and damaging to their national identity.

Honduras: Resentment and hostility toward the United States in Honduras can be traced back to a tumultuous history of U.S. involvement in political affairs, particularly the backing of military coups that subverted democratic processes. One glaring example is the 2009 coup that ousted President Manuel Zelaya, who had initiated progressive reforms aimed at addressing social inequality and poverty. The U.S. response to the coup was perceived as tacit approval, as it did not take immediate action to restore Zelaya's leadership. This complicity entrenched distrust toward the U.S. among many Hondurans, who see American influence as undermining their sovereignty and democratic institutions. Additionally, economic exploitation linked to U.S. corporate interests has contributed to resentment, as American companies in agriculture and textiles have often employed exploitative labor practices with inadequate wages. This perception of the U.S. as a nation that exploits local resources fosters feelings of injustice, contributing to a cycle of resentment that affects diplomatic relations.

Mexico: Mexico's animosity toward the United States is rooted in colonial history, territorial disputes, and economic disparities. The Mexican-American War (1846-1848) dramatically reduced Mexico's territory, fostering a deep-seated resentment toward the U.S. Policies that maintain cycles of dependency and underdevelopment contribute to poverty and violence in Mexico, which are often oversimplified in American discourse focused on cartel violence. Many Mexicans view U.S. actions as imperialistic, undermining their sovereignty and exacerbating domestic challenges.

Syria: The United States' actions in Syria have significantly contributed to deep-seated distrust and hostility toward America among many Syrians. Historically, the U.S. has supported Israel in its conflicts with Syria, fostering animosity due to perceived imperialistic tendencies. During the Syrian Civil War, the U.S. intervened by backing various rebel groups, including those affiliated with extremist factions, which many saw as direct interference in Syria's sovereignty and governance. This military involvement was perceived as exacerbating the conflict rather than promoting stability, particularly as U.S. airstrikes targeted both ISIS and government forces, leading to civilian casualties and destruction of infrastructure. The consequences of U.S. sanctions and military actions have resulted in widespread suffering among the Syrian populace. The Caesar Act, aimed at crippling the Syrian regime, has further complicated the humanitarian crisis, inflicting economic pain on ordinary citizens rather than solely the governing elite. The lack of a comprehensive approach that represents the diverse voices of the Syrian population in peace negotiations has also bred resentment, solidifying a narrative that the U.S. prioritizes its strategic interests over the welfare of the Syrian people. As a result, many Syrians view the U.S. not as a promoter of democracy but as an imperialist entity that fuels suffering and instability.

Korea: America's need to dominate and control the political landscape after World War II significantly contributed to the animosity toward the United States in Korea. Following the end of the Japanese occupation, rather than supporting Korea's bid for independence, the U.S. and the Soviet Union chose to divide the nation along the 38th parallel. This move was not driven by an understanding of Korean aspirations for self-determination but rather by the superpowers' desire to establish military strongholds in the region. The division artificially imposed by foreign powers created deep divides within Korea and led to the establishment of two antagonistic regimes: a communist dictatorship in the North guided by the USSR and an authoritarian government in the South propped up by the U.S. Ultimately, this failure to honor the Korean people's desire for unity and autonomy sowed seeds of discontent and hostility toward the U.S. as a colonial participant in their ongoing struggle. In the years that followed, America's actions in Korea were largely dictated by the context of the Cold War, where containing communism became a critical objective. The U.S. chose to back Syngman Rhee, an anti-communist leader whose regime was marred by authoritarianism and corruption, further alienating the population. The U.S. arrogance and disregard for the Korean perspective resulted in increased instability, which contributed to the outbreak of the Korean War. Throughout this conflict, U.S. military intervention was less about supporting Korean independence and more focused on asserting control in the region, fueling the animosity that had already begun festering post-WWII. The desire to dictate the narrative of democracy, coupled with a lack of genuine engagement with the Korean populace, not only jeopardized the possibility of a cohesive Korean state but also led to profound, lasting repercussions that have shaped U.S.-Korean relations to this day.

At the heart of these issues lies a deeply ingrained attitude of American exceptionalism, which conveys the belief that the U.S. has both the right and obligation to intervene in the affairs of other nations. This mindset often disregards the historical contexts and complexities of foreign societies, leading to poorly conceived policies that exacerbate existing tensions. Nations like Iran and Cuba perceive American cultural and political imposition as a form of imperialism, fostering resentment and resistance.

Manifest Destiny and Territorial Acquisition

The ideology of Manifest Destiny was a powerful driving force behind U.S. policy in the 19th century. This belief that the U.S. was destined to expand across the continent was rooted in a sense of American cultural and racial superiority. It provided a moral justification for the annexation of lands and the displacement and eradication of indigenous peoples.

The people from the south of today's United States populated almost all of the Southwest of what we now know as the US. The Mexican-American War (1846-1848) was a direct manifestation of this ideology. The war culminated in the loss of 38,000 lives and the Treaty of Guadalupe Hidalgo, which forced Mexico to cede approximately 55% of its pre-war territory to the U.S., including present-day California, Nevada, Utah, Arizona, and parts of Colorado, Wyoming, New Mexico, and Texas. The financial compensation of $15 million was minimal compared to the vast resources and strategic advantages the U.S. gained. This annexation had profound implications for the indigenous and Mexican populations living in these regions, who suddenly found themselves under U.S. jurisdiction, facing new laws, cultural pressures, and often discriminatory practices.

The U.S. also attempted to purchase additional Mexican territory after the war, such as in the Gadsden Purchase (1853), emphasizing its relentless pursuit of territorial expansion. The combination of military action and economic inducements highlights the aggressive nature of U.S. expansionism during this era.

Throughout U.S. history, immigration policies have favored certain groups over others, reflecting broader societal attitudes and prejudices. In the late 19th and early 20th centuries, policies were designed to encourage immigration from northern and western Europe, regions seen as culturally compatible with the U.S.

However, immigrants from non-European regions, particularly Latin America, Asia, and Africa, faced restrictive measures. For instance, the Chinese Exclusion Act of 1882 was one of the first major laws restricting immigration based on ethnicity, setting a precedent for future policies that discriminated against non-European immigrants.

In the 20th and 21st centuries, immigration debates have increasingly centered around the U.S.-Mexico border. Policies such as the Bracero Program during World War II indicated a willingness to allow Mexican laborers into the country when economically beneficial, yet subsequent periods saw heightened restrictions and border enforcement. This reflects a dynamic where economic considerations occasionally overrode racial biases, yet these were not sustained beyond periods of immediate economic need.

Before European contact, indigenous peoples in North America had diverse societies, ranging from nomadic tribes to advanced civilizations with agricultural networks, cities, and trade systems. European colonization severely disrupted these societies, leading to massive population declines caused by disease, warfare, and displacement.

In contrast, the Spanish colonization of Mexico, while also brutal, involved more integration between Europeans and indigenous peoples. Intermarriage and cultural blending led to a mestizo identity that is a fundamental part of modern Mexican culture. This contrasts sharply with the United States' approach, which frequently involved the marginalization and forced relocation of Native American peoples onto reservations, often in undesirable or remote areas.

Today, the U.S.-Mexico border is a focal point of immigration policy and debate, complicated by historical context and ongoing racial dynamics. Many immigrants crossing the border seek to escape violence, economic hardship, or political instability, driven by factors often linked, directly or indirectly, to U.S. policies in Latin America.

The treatment of immigrants at the border has been widely criticized, with reports highlighting overcrowded detention centers, family separations, and inadequate access to basic services. These issues are often exacerbated by underlying racial biases, where immigrants from Latin America are treated differently from those from European countries. For example, in moments of crisis, U.S. immigration policies have sometimes shown preferential treatment to refugees from European nations, reflecting deeply ingrained racial and cultural prejudices.

To address these complex issues, it is critical to acknowledge the interconnected histories of the U.S., Mexico, and indigenous peoples, understanding the legacies of displacement and cultural erasure.

Promoting equitable immigration policies requires dismantling racially biased frameworks and ensuring that all individuals, irrespective of their heritage or skin color, are treated with dignity and respect.

Moreover, meaningful reform must address both immediate humanitarian concerns at the border and broader systemic issues that drive migration. This includes support for economic development, political stability, and human rights in Latin American countries. Engaging in international cooperation, alongside domestic policy changes, is essential for fostering a more just and equitable approach to immigration that honors shared histories and upholds human dignity.

By reflecting on these profound historical narratives and inequalities, we can work towards policies that not only address immediate concerns but also promote long-term justice and reconciliation.

A Case for Open Borders Across the Americas: Embracing Our Shared Heritage

In the modern-day pursuit of freedom and opportunity, the concept of open borders within the Americas is emerging as not only a practical solution to economic and societal challenges but also as a profound acknowledgment of our shared historical and cultural heritage. Imagine an America where people from all over the continent, North, Central, and South, move and interact freely, fostering richer communities and a deeper sense of unity. This vision, rooted deeply in historical continuity, economic pragmatism, and ethical considerations, calls for a reevaluation of contemporary borders.

Long before European colonization defined the geopolitical landscape of the Americas, the indigenous peoples of the continent were interconnected through complex networks of trade, kinship, and cultural exchange. This pre-colonial mobility allowed for fluid movement across vast territories, a tradition abruptly altered by colonial borders but never fully extinguished. These historical networks remind us of a world where the peoples of the Americas were one, long before the territorial claims of distant empires drew lines upon maps.

The colonial era saw the mingling of indigenous, European, and African cultures, creating a shared legacy that continues to resonate today. This mixing of heritages laid the foundation for regions in the United States that were once part of New Spain and later Mexico, California, Texas, New Mexico, and Arizona, to become cultural beacons of this continental blend. These states' names themselves are a testament to their deep cultural ties with Latin America, suggesting that the notion of separate, impermeable borders stands in contrast to centuries of interconnected histories.

From an economic perspective, the benefits of open borders within the Americas are profound. Greater freedom of movement can unlock tremendous economic potential through inter-American trade and collaboration. Allowing people to move freely would enable a more dynamic allocation of labor and skills, spurring innovation and economic growth across the continent. Such mobility is not merely an ideal; it is a practical step toward economic synergy.

The U.S. economy, in particular, has long benefited from the labor of immigrants, especially from neighboring countries. Migrant workers play critical roles in various industries, from agriculture to technology, often addressing labor shortages and helping maintain economic stability. Furthermore, remittances sent by immigrants to their home countries in Latin America and the Caribbean are vital economic lifelines that reduce poverty and promote development. Open borders could strengthen these economic ties, creating a more stable and prosperous region, where the pressures driving migration are significantly alleviated.

At the heart of the call for open borders lies a profound ethical obligation to recognize and uphold the rights and dignity of all individuals. The current immigration system subjects many to dangerous journeys, detention, and separation from loved ones conditions that starkly oppose the ideals of human rights. Embracing open borders for people of the

Americas is a step towards respecting and affirming their inherent dignity, treating the movement of people as a natural and legitimate act.

Addressing historical inequalities also forms a crucial part of this ethical discourse. Socio-economic challenges driving migration often stem from past policies and interventions that have destabilized regions, leading to cycles of poverty and displacement. The U.S., acknowledging its role in this shared history, bears a responsibility to pursue equitable solutions that foster opportunity for all peoples of the Americas.

Moreover, an open-border policy invites cultural reciprocity, enriching societies through the exchange of ideas, customs, and traditions. It echoes the multicultural fabric of the Americas, celebrating the diversity that defines our continent.

Reimagining U.S. borders to be open to individuals from anywhere across the Americas is not merely a dream. It is a practical and ethical imperative that acknowledges our intertwined destinies. Such a policy would honor the longstanding tradition of interconnectedness, address economic needs, and rectify historical injustices, laying the groundwork for a more equitable and harmonious future.

By embracing this vision, we can create a society rooted in the principles of freedom, opportunity, and justice an America that acknowledges its shared heritage and looks towards a united future. In doing so, we transform borders from barriers into bridges, strengthening our communities and honoring the impeccable continuity of the Americas, a land meant to be open to all its people.

Ignorance Has Run Out of Excuses

We live in the most information-rich era in human history. With a smartphone, a library card, or a modest internet connection, anyone can access world-class lectures, textbooks, simulations, and expert communities at little to no cost. Public libraries provide free computers, WiFi, and research databases, and universities offer complete courses through open initiatives. If you can read, write, and persist, the raw materials for an education are at your fingertips.

Learning still demands time, focus, and discipline, but the idea that ignorance is excusable because resources are scarce no longer holds. You can audit university courses for free, build foundations with high-quality open textbooks, and prepare for credit-bearing exams using open courseware. Entire degree pathways can be pieced together using open courses and low-cost assessments from reputable providers, many of which carry credit recommendations recognized by thousands of colleges. For those seeking tuition-free university options, there are accredited programs that charge only modest assessment or proctoring fees, and state systems that aggregate open educational resources from public institutions.

How to Earn Most of a College Education for Little or No Cost

Access to learning has never been broader. With free online courses, public libraries, credit by exam, prior learning assessments, and low-cost competency-based universities, many people can complete most of a degree at minimal cost. Real barriers do exist, including caregiving duties, disabilities, broadband gaps, unsafe housing, work schedules, and opaque college policies. The goal is to show practical paths while acknowledging these challenges and offering ways around them.

The key idea is simple. You can learn nearly any subject for free online. You can also earn accredited college credit cheaply through exams, portfolio assessment, industry certifications, and transfer-friendly universities. A paid, traditional pathway typically bundles campus services, registration, advising, and a diploma. A low-cost pathway unbundles those pieces so you learn for free or at low cost, then convert learning into credit and a degree.

Free and low-cost ways to learn are plentiful. Open courseware and textbooks allow you to access high-quality content without tuition. Many platforms provide free auditing with optional paid certificates, while others offer fully free courses paired with low-cost, proctored credit exams. Tuition-free universities can reduce costs further by charging only assessment fees. State systems publish complete materials through open educational resources. Local public libraries add free internet, study spaces, databases, and often test prep tools.

Turning learning into credit can save thousands of dollars. College credit by examination lets you demonstrate mastery in subjects equivalent to lower division courses at a fraction of the price of tuition. Many colleges accept these credits, and some programs provide free prep and even cover exam fees. Additional exams cover business, social sciences, and technology, with cost waivers for many active duty military learners. High school credentials such as Advanced Placement and International Baccalaureate can award credit before you start college; policies vary, so verify each institution's chart.

Alternative credit providers evaluated by national credit recommendation services offer more low-cost options. Subscription platforms and self-paced courses can fulfill general education and introductory major requirements for a fraction of university tuition. Transfer policies differ, so always confirm alignment with your target college before enrolling.

Prior Learning Assessment and portfolios can convert work and training into academic credit. Many institutions award credit for military training and for industry certifications in IT, project management, HR, and cloud technologies. Adult-friendly institutions specialize in portfolio assessment aligned to recognized standards and publish transparent transfer rules for exam and alternative credit.

Competency-based and transfer-friendly universities make finishing economical. Flat tuition per term allows you to accelerate as you master competencies, sometimes earning a term's worth of credit in weeks. Degree completion schools for adults accept large amounts of transfer, exam, and alternative credit, then focus your remaining effort on upper-division and major requirements. Other flexible institutions publish clear transfer pathways and accept alternative credits in select programs.

A proven route is to begin at a low-cost community college with last-dollar scholarships, then transfer to a public university.

A straightforward strategy minimizes cost dramatically. Define your target degree and school early, pull the official degree plan, and mark which requirements allow exams or alternative credits. Learn for free using open resources to prepare for standardized exams, then take credit by exam first to knock out general education. Add alternative provider credits that map cleanly to your target school's transfer guide. Leverage prior learning and certifications by documenting work experience and securing industry credentials that your program values. When you have accumulated enough lower-division credits, transfer into a degree-completion school known for generous acceptance of alternative credits and transparent degree audits. Finish your upper division or major coursework in residence as required, which is still far cheaper overall after testing out of many lower division courses. Throughout, use every aid and support for which you qualify, including federal and state grants, employer tuition assistance, and scholarships.

Understanding what free college usually means avoids disappointment. Learning is often free, but converting that learning into accredited credit typically carries assessment, transcription, or proctoring fees. Some programs charge modest per-course assessment fees despite no tuition and also offer scholarships. With credit by exam providers and prep platforms, preparation and even the exam can be free if you receive vouchers, although some test centers charge small proctoring fees unless covered. Public libraries provide free internet, study spaces, and sometimes proctoring and test prep databases that reduce out-of-pocket costs further.

Time, motivation, and structural realities all matter. Willpower and time management are necessary, but so are accessible materials, stable connectivity, and supportive policies. Broadband and device access can be limited in rural areas. Disabilities require accessible content and accommodations that not all providers deliver equally. Caregiving, shift work, and health conditions squeeze study time, while hidden costs such as childcare, proctoring, transportation, and textbooks add up. College transfer rules differ widely, and not every institution accepts the same alternative credits. Plan with these realities in mind by choosing asynchronous, mobile-friendly resources where possible, working with disability services early to secure accommodations, batching exams and assignments around work and family schedules, and prioritizing institutions with clear, published transfer and prior learning assessment policies.

Illustrative pathways show how this comes together. For a business or IT bachelor's, you might build fundamentals with open textbooks and courseware, pass standardized exams in math, literature, microeconomics, and macroeconomics, complete subscription based general education and business core courses, earn industry certifications for recommended credit, then transfer sixty to ninety credits into a transfer friendly university to finish remaining major courses at a fraction of the usual cost. For health sciences or allied health, you could use open resources to prepare for anatomy and physiology, microbiology, and chemistry, fulfill non-lab requirements through alternative credit providers approved by your target program, complete lab sciences at a community college for smooth transfer, and apply for hospital tuition benefits or paid clinical pathways.

Avoid common mistakes by confirming transfer policies before taking exams or courses, tracking any time limits your school imposes on older credits, respecting lab and upper division residency requirements, seeking free open educational resources before buying materials, and never skipping the federal aid application since even part-time adult learners often qualify for grant aid.

Ignorance thrives on isolation, shame, and the belief that learning is reserved for someone else. Today you can start with a free textbook, watch a lecture, join a study forum, practice with adaptive exercises, and schedule a credit exam within weeks. You can assemble a largely free education and convert much of it into accredited credit at low cost. The smartest route is to map your target degree early, learn with free resources, earn credit by exam and alternative providers, document prior learning, and finish with a transfer-friendly, accredited university. It is not effortless and not everyone's circumstances are equal, but with a clear plan and the right links at hand, you can drastically reduce both time and money while earning the same accredited degree. In an age of abundant learning, ignorance is a choice we no longer have to make.

MIT OpenCourseWare — https://ocw.mit.edu
OpenStax — https://openstax.org
Coursera — https://www.coursera.org
edX — https://www.edx.org
Khan Academy — https://www.khanacademy.org
Saylor Academy — https://www.saylor.org
Sophia Learning — https://www.sophia.org
StraighterLine — https://www.straighterline.com
ACE National Guide — https://www.acenet.edu/National-Guide
University of the People — https://www.uopeople.edu
USG Free Campus — https://freecampus.usg.edu
Modern States — https://modernstates.org
CLEP — https://clep.collegeboard.org
DSST — https://www.getcollegecredit.com
CompTIA — https://www.comptia.org
Google Career Certificates — https://grow.google/certificates
Thomas Edison State University — https://www.tesu.edu
Charter Oak State College — https://www.charteroak.edu
Excelsior University — https://www.excelsior.edu
Western Governors University — https://www.wgu.edu
UMPI YourPace — https://umpi.edu/yourpace
Southern New Hampshire University — https://www.snhu.edu
ASU Universal Learner Courses — https://ea.asu.edu
Purdue Global — https://www.purdueglobal.edu
University of Maryland Global Campus — https://www.umgc.edu
FAFSA and Federal Student Aid — https://studentaid.gov

A Chronological Overview of Social Justice Movements in American History, from our inception to today. Sometimes, a small ripple can cause a huge wave.

During the colonial period (1600s-1700s), many marginalized groups, including Indigenous peoples and enslaved Africans, faced significant oppression. Early resistance to these injustices laid the groundwork for future social justice movements.

Enslaved Africans resisted their conditions through rebellions, such as the Stono Rebellion (1739) in South Carolina, demonstrating early acts of defiance against the injustices they faced.

Figures like Phyllis Wheatley emerged as prominent voices against slavery, advocating for freedom and equality through her poetry.

The abolitionist movement (Early 1800s-1865) sought to end slavery and racial discrimination, gaining momentum in the early 19th century.

The publication of "The Liberator" by William Lloyd Garrison (1831) and conventions like the "Seneca Falls Convention" (1848) brought together activists advocating for both abolition and women's rights.

Frederick Douglass, Harriet Tubman, and Sojourner Truth played crucial roles. Douglass famously criticized the hypocrisy of American democracy and called for immediate emancipation.

Abolitionists faced violent backlash and were often labeled as radicals or traitors to the nation. For instance, Garrison was threatened and even attacked for his beliefs.

The fight for women's rights and suffrage (mid-1800s to 1920) grew alongside abolitionist movements, with women advocating for voting rights and equal treatment in society.

The Seneca Falls Convention (1848) marked the formal beginning of the women's suffrage movement. Key milestones included the publication of the "Declaration of Sentiments" and the establishment of various suffrage organizations.

Susan B. Anthony and Elizabeth Cady Stanton emerged as leading advocates for women's enfranchisement, challenging societal norms.

Suffragists were often ridiculed and opposed by segments of society, who framed their activism as unfeminine and radical. Assertions about women's roles in society were used to delegitimize their movement.

The Civil Rights Movement (1950s-1960s) sought to end racial segregation and discrimination against African Americans, addressing systemic injustices across the United States.

Major events included the Montgomery Bus Boycott (1955), the March on Washington (1963), and the passage of landmark legislation such as the Civil Rights Act (1964) and the Voting Rights Act (1965).

Leaders like Martin Luther King Jr., Rosa Parks, and Malcolm X became symbolic figures of the movement, advocating for different approaches to achieving equality.

Activists faced violent opposition, including the bombing of churches, intimidation, and arrests. They were often framed negatively as troublemakers or threats to social order.

The LGBTQ+ rights movement (1960s-Present) has evolved significantly since its inception, with pivotal moments shaping the landscape for current advocacy.

The modern LGBTQ+ rights movement gained traction as activism emerged around the Stonewall riots in 1969, marking a turning point in the fight against discrimination and for equal rights.

The first pride parades were held in the aftermath of Stonewall, and over the years, the movement has led to important legal and cultural milestones, including the decriminalization of homosexuality, the repeal of "Don't Ask, Don't Tell," and the legalization of same-sex marriage in 2015.

Activists like Marsha P. Johnson, Sylvia Rivera, and later figures such as Evan Wolfson have been central to the movement's progress, advocating for visibility, rights, and societal acceptance.

From colonial times through modern movements, each social justice initiative in American history reflects a complex interplay of resistance, advocacy, and societal change. The work of individuals causes crucial developments within the larger context of civil rights and social justice, illustrating the enduring struggle for equality and dignity across various marginalized communities. This commitment to activism continues to inspire new generations in their fight for justice and equality.

***

Blame, Deny, Repeat: America's Role in the Cross-Border Drug Trade

America's illegal drug market is driven primarily by American demand. Blaming Canada or Mexico for fentanyl and other illicit drugs oversimplifies a crisis rooted in U.S. policies, culture, and health systems. The central problem is not foreign supply; it is untreated addiction, pervasive stigma, and decades of prioritizing punishment over care. Whatever legislative steps Canada or any other country takes are their sovereign decisions. The United States should stop chasing headlines and start shrinking demand through treatment, harm reduction, and economic opportunity.

The United States' appetite for drugs fuels cartel profits, crossborder smuggling, and violence that destabilize neighboring countries. When possession is criminalized but treatment and prevention are neglected, cartels step in to meet demand, especially where poverty and limited opportunity make illicit markets attractive. Reduce demand at home, and the incentive to smuggle declines. Assigning blame to neighbors is like faulting a manufacturer for televisions appearing in U.S. stores; without demand, supply withers.

A healthfirst approach is overdue. The war on drugs filled jails, not treatment centers, and disproportionately harmed Black and Brown communities despite similar rates of use across racial groups. Declaring and acting on a public health emergency would align policy with reality. Millions meet criteria for a substance use disorder, yet only a fraction receive evidencebased care. Provisional federal data show more than 100,000 overdose deaths in 2023—the worst on record—driven by synthetic opioids like fentanyl. Persisting with punitive responses guarantees more loss, while a healthdriven model has repeatedly shown measurable reductions in deaths, infections, and crime.

The burden of addiction and overdose appears across mortality, treatment access, and economic cost. Overdose deaths surpassed 100,000 annually in 2021 and have stayed at or above that level through 2023, with synthetic opioids implicated in most fatalities. Regions from Appalachia to the Pacific Northwest have faced fentanyl waves and, increasingly, xylazine contamination, which complicates overdose response and increases severe wounds. Treatment remains fragmented: many counties lack opioid treatment programs, prior authorization delays medication starts, and people leaving jail or prison often lose access to care at the moment of greatest risk. The economic toll of the opioid crisis alone is estimated at well over one trillion dollars annually when considering healthcare, criminal justice, lost productivity, and the value of lives lost.

Culture, economics, and policy interlock to sustain the crisis. The United States both stigmatizes addiction and normalizes certain drug use through aggressive pharmaceutical marketing and media glamorization. That contradiction feeds shame and deters people from seeking help. Surveys consistently find that most people with a substance use disorder receive no treatment in a given year, often due to stigma, cost, or lack of accessible services.

Economic distress intensifies risk. Communities facing poverty, unstable housing, and limited access to education and mental healthcare experience higher rates of use, trafficking, and overdose. Deindustrialization, rural hospital closures, and underfunded behavioral health systems have created care deserts. In these conditions, drugs can appear to offer relief or income, often ending in dependency and criminalization. Meanwhile, firearm availability in the U.S. elevates the lethality of drugmarket disputes compared with many peer countries, magnifying crossborder violence that critics wrongly attribute solely to foreign actors.

The criminal justice system's emphasis on punishment over treatment has not reduced use or deaths. It has entrenched cycles of incarceration and relapse, created lifelong barriers to work and housing, and diverted resources away from services that reduce harm. Drug arrests surged after the 1980s even as addiction persisted, with profound racial disparities in who is policed and imprisoned. Stigma continues after sentencing, increasing homelessness, family separation, and return to use. A growing consensus—including medical associations and many lawenforcement leaders—recognizes addiction as a treatable medical condition rather than a moral failing.

Prevention must be honest, skillbased, and developmentally appropriate. The DARE program, widely deployed in the 1980s and 1990s, often failed to reduce drug use and sometimes heightened curiosity. Its scarebased approach did not equip students with practical decisionmaking skills, and its reliance on law enforcement as instructors could foster fear rather than understanding. Multiple evaluations over decades questioned its effectiveness, leading many districts to abandon or substantially revise it.

Modern prevention emphasizes skills, relationships, and realism. Groupbased programs that teach coping strategies, peer support, and socialemotional learning help adolescents navigate realworld risks. Programs such as Life Skills Training and Too Good for Drugs focus on resilience, selfefficacy, refusal skills, and goalsetting rather than fear. Schools and community centers that host open, nonjudgmental discussions—sometimes facilitated by trained peers or counselors—create early opportunities for helpseeking. Moderated online platforms extend this safe space, allowing youth to ask questions, understand the risks of today's drug supply, and access resources without stigma. The goal is not to pretend drugs do not exist but to equip young people with the skills and supports to say no, seek help, or intervene for a friend.

Treatment and harm reduction work when they are accessible, immediate, and evidencebased. Medications for opioid use disorder, including buprenorphine and methadone, cut mortality roughly in half compared with no medication and improve retention in care when paired with counseling and practical supports such as housing and transportation. Initiating buprenorphine in emergency departments after an overdose increases treatment engagement compared with referral alone. Correctional systems that offer all three FDAapproved medications have reported substantial drops in postrelease overdose deaths, a period of extremely elevated risk due to reduced tolerance.

Harm reduction is indispensable. Broad naloxone distribution reverses overdoses and lowers death rates when available at pharmacies and through community organizations. Syringe services programs reduce HIV and hepatitis C transmission and connect people to treatment, vaccinations, and wound care. Drugchecking tools—including fentanyl and xylazine test strips and, where available, spectrometry—help people avoid the most dangerous exposures. Supervised consumption sites, longstanding abroad and piloted in limited U.S. settings, have reversed thousands of overdoses onsite, reduced public syringe litter, and increased referrals to care. These strategies do not condone drug use; they keep people alive and stabilize communities.

To scale what works, policy barriers must fall. Prior authorization delays for buprenorphine, methadone's tightly restricted clinic model, and inadequate reimbursement for counseling and peer services suppress capacity. Telehealth flexibilities introduced during the COVID19 public health emergency improved access in underserved regions without compromising safety. Preserving these flexibilities and investing in the addiction workforce—clinicians, nurses, counselors, and peers—can turn sporadic access into a reliable care continuum.

International experience reinforces a healthfirst model. Portugal's 2001 reform decriminalized personal possession while investing in treatment, outreach, and harm reduction. The country recorded lower overdose deaths and dramatic declines in new HIV infections among people who inject drugs, alongside improved treatment uptake. Switzerland's heroinassisted treatment, combined with supervised consumption and robust social services, reduced streetlevel crime, lowered overdose deaths, and stabilized employment and housing among participants. Germany's harm reduction and opioid substitution treatment similarly reduced mortality and infectious disease spread. These models do not legalize trafficking; they redirect people who use drugs away from courts and toward care while maintaining focused enforcement against criminal networks.

Domestic examples show the same pattern. Jurisdictions that saturate communities with naloxone, expand medications for opioid use disorder, and fund syringe services experience slower growth or declines in fatal overdoses and fewer infectiousdisease outbreaks than places that restrict harm reduction. Emergency department–initiated buprenorphine increases engagement and reduces repeat overdoses. Rhode Island's statewide MOUD program in correctional facilities cut postrelease overdose deaths by more than half, demonstrating the payoff of treatment continuity.

Many substances once sold openly became criminalized as public attitudes hardened, particularly in the late twentieth century. Moralpanic politics drove harsher laws and longer sentences, fracturing families, increasing foster care placements, and deepening poverty. Criminalization has also increased mortality by pushing use underground and deterring people from calling for help during overdoses. Good Samaritan laws can mitigate this problem, but uneven awareness and trust limit their impact. The cumulative effect of punitive policy is visible: high arrest numbers, persistent use, and tragic mortality—an expensive detour from what works.

Family and community support are central to recovery. Outcomes improve when loved ones are engaged and stigma is replaced with empathy. Peer recovery coaches, groups such as Narcotics Anonymous and Families Anonymous, and community networks providing housing, employment assistance, child care, and mental health services create conditions where change can take hold and last. Stable housing is a powerful predictor of treatment retention and reduced overdose, underscoring the need to align addiction policy with housing and labor policy rather than treating them as separate silos.

Owning our role is the first step. The United States cannot demand that neighbors solve a crisis sustained by American demand and American policy choices. Reducing demand through treatment, harm reduction, prevention, and economic investment is both humane and strategically effective. Law enforcement should concentrate on trafficking, money laundering, and precursor chemicals, not possession for personal use. Health systems should guarantee sameday access to medications, integrate care into emergency and primary settings, and eliminate administrative hurdles that delay lifesaving treatment. Education systems should deliver modern prevention that teaches skills and fosters connection, not fear.

Data systems should enable rapid response. Realtime overdose surveillance, wastewater monitoring for drug trends, and public alerts about dangerous batches allow communities to act quickly. Publishing transparent dashboards on treatment access, wait times, and outcomes helps target resources to where they are needed most and builds public trust. When people know treatment is available today, naloxone is free and ubiquitous, and help comes without judgment, the illicit market begins to lose its customers.

Overdose mortality has exceeded 100,000 deaths per year since 2021, with synthetic opioids involved in most fatalities. Communities that blanket pharmacies, libraries, and first responders with naloxone and train residents in overdose reversal consistently report lower fatality rates than similar areas without widespread access.

Emergency department–initiated buprenorphine, offered immediately after an overdose or withdrawal presentation, produces markedly higher 30day treatment engagement compared with a paper referral. Postrelease medication access in jails and prisons reduces overdose deaths dramatically in the first weeks after release, when tolerance is low and risk is high.

Syringe services programs reduce HIV and hepatitis C infections and increase entry to treatment without increasing drug use. Where supervised consumption sites have operated, staff reverse overdoses onsite, reduce public syringe litter, and connect participants to housing and medical care. Life Skills Training and Too Good for Drugs demonstrate that socialemotional learning and copingskills curricula can delay initiation and lower use, unlike fearbased approaches typified by classic DARE.

The economic case is clear. The opioid crisis costs exceed a trillion dollars annually; by comparison, investments in medications for opioid use disorder, harm reduction, housing, and workforce supports are relatively modest and yield savings via reduced hospitalizations, lower incarceration, and increased employment. Housing stability, in particular, is associated with better treatment retention and fewer emergency department visits, reinforcing the need to embed addiction strategy within broader social policy.

When the United States stops blaming and starts healing, the illegal market loses its fuel. A comprehensive, compassionate response— prevention that teaches skills, treatment that is immediate and evidencebased, harm reduction that keeps people alive, and communities that provide housing and opportunity can cut overdose deaths, undermine smuggling, and help people rebuild their lives. Decriminalizing personal possession while maintaining pressure on trafficking aligns incentives correctly: people who use drugs get health care, and criminal networks lose customers. This is not leniency; it is effectiveness.

Focusing on demand through care, not punishment, is the surest way to save lives at home and reduce the violence and instability that spill across borders. It honors the realities families face, respects the evidence from here and abroad, and finally aims our resources at what works.

White Male Bigot's Pushback Against DEI

The perception among some white males, particularly those with bigoted views, that they are being oppressed or discriminated against due to diversity, equity, and inclusion (DEI) initiatives can be explained through various social, psychological, and historical contexts.

Historically, white males have held dominant positions in politics, business, and society in many Western countries, particularly in the United States. This overrepresentation has sparked debates about systemic inequality and privilege.

When laws or policies are introduced to address these disparities, some may perceive them as a loss of power or status. The legacy of power held by white males creates an environment where initiatives aimed at correcting imbalances are viewed as challenges to long-held societal norms. As this shift occurs, some white males may experience feelings of alienation or resentment, perceiving their traditional roles as being undermined.

Psychological factors further complicate this perception. Many individuals derive a significant part of their self-worth from their identity and social status. For some white males, the spotlight on systemic racism and sexism can feel like a threat to their identity, leading them to see themselves as oppressed.

This phenomenon is often characterized by zero-sum thinking, where one group's gain is perceived as another's loss. Clinging to group identity in the face of perceived cultural or demographic shifts can foster a sense of victimhood, even when significant privileges remain intact.

Misinterpretation of DEI initiatives significantly contributes to this mindset. DEI initiatives aim to level the playing field and address historical injustices. However, some may interpret these policies as preferential treatment for underrepresented groups, viewing them as discriminatory against white males. Media that perpetuates narratives of white victimization can shape beliefs and amplify feelings of oppression, particularly in social media echo chambers where these sentiments are reinforced.

The sociopolitical climate also influences perceptions. Recently, Donald Trump has proposed significant changes to education in the United States, including fining schools for implementing DEI programs and using those seized funds as restitution for "victims," specifically targeting white individuals affected by these policies. Ironically, the fact that Trump is suggesting a willingness to pay restitution to white individuals, raises questions about whether Black people will also receive restitution for the 300-plus years of slavery in the U.S.

Such political moves tap into existing fears and frame discussions around DEI as threats to the rights of certain groups, exacerbating feelings of victimization among those who already feel marginalized.

It is crucial to highlight the disparity between perception and reality regarding statistics. Although white males make up around 30% of the overall U.S. population, they occupy a major majority of powerful positions, 62% of elected offices, and 89% of private companies' management and above.

This statistical dominance might clash with the perception of being marginalized, revealing a disconnect in understanding societal structures and advantages.

This disconnect can lead to cognitive dissonance, whereby individuals hold conflicting beliefs about their societal status and the changes occurring around them. To resolve this discomfort, they might adopt narratives that affirm their perceived oppression.

Lastly, these oppression narratives can have significant social consequences. Believing oneself to be oppressed can create division rather than fostering dialogue and understanding across different social identities. Such narratives can hinder progress toward genuine equity and understanding.

The feelings of oppression articulated by some bigoted white males in response to DEI initiatives are complex and multifaceted. These feelings reflect a combination of historical privilege, psychological identity defenses, cultural narratives, and political mobilization, as exemplified by recent political proposals.

Understanding these factors is essential for addressing these sentiments in ways that encourage constructive dialogue and collaboration toward a more equitable society.

The American Enigma: Unpacking the Contradictions of Freedom, Aggression, and Hypocrisy

I often find amusement when discussing my travels with others, particularly regarding their perceptions of the United States.

The typical response I receive is a claim that these countries are merely jealous of America's greatness.

However, the reality is far more complex and revealing: many do not harbor jealousy but perceive a fundamental mistrust.

America's portrayal on the global stage often seems steeped in contradictions, and hypocrisy emerges as a glaring hallmark of its international identity.

The United States was founded upon transformative ideals articulated in the Declaration of Independence principles such as "life, liberty, and the pursuit of happiness."

These values have shaped the nation's self-image and its claims to be a beacon of freedom and opportunity.

As a democratic republic, America positions itself as a model government that other nations should aspire to emulate.

Yet, a careful examination reveals an ongoing struggle between these proclaimed principles and the actions often taken on the world stage.

Issues of aggression in foreign policy, domestic inequality, and social injustices highlight the chasm between America's ideals and realities.

The juxtaposition of America's advancement as a symbol of freedom and its frequent acts of aggression, whether military interventions or economic sanctions, presents a paradox.

This dissonance invites scrutiny: how can a nation that champions liberty simultaneously engage in behaviors that undermine the essence of the freedom it purports to promote?

This self-portrayal becomes increasingly complicated due to inherent contradictions, particularly evident in the aggressive stance taken toward other nations and the unequal treatment of marginalized groups within its borders.

These realities starkly contradict the very principles the nation claims to uphold.

At the heart of America's identity is its promise of unparalleled freedoms, an ideal meant to be inclusive rather than exclusive.

The belief that every individual can express themselves freely and pursue their aspirations is a powerful narrative that has led many to regard America as the freest country in the world.

Americans take great pride in their democratic values, perceiving their nation as a global leader advocating for civil rights and individual liberties.

Yet, despite these lofty ideals, the United States's actions on the international stage frequently undermine its foundational principles.

The U.S. has a long and complex history of military interventions and foreign policy decisions driven by aggressive actions, often justified under the pretext of spreading democracy or ensuring national security.

In pursuit of geopolitical and economic objectives, the United States has at times overlooked the authoritarian regimes and dictatorial leaders who grossly violate fundamental human rights, as long as these alliances are perceived to further American interests.

When it comes to American foreign policy, we are willing to engage with oppressive regimes if such collaboration provides the U.S. with access to valuable resources, strategic locations, or other economic benefits.

This inconsistency raises critical questions about the true nature of our commitment to the values it espouses and its role on the world stage.

America's support for regimes such as those in Saudi Arabia and Egypt exemplifies a compromise of its core values, as it endorses authoritarian leaders in the name of stability and resource acquisition.

This approach profoundly contradicts the ideals of promoting democracy and freedom for all.

While conservatives, particularly those aligned with the MAGA movement, often endorse stringent immigration policies that undermine the nation's foundational ideals, liberals and Democrats are advocating for an expansion of civil rights aimed at rectifying injustices and promoting inclusivity.

This fundamental disconnect highlights a domestic struggle over what America truly stands for, whether it embodies equality and opportunity or fosters division and exclusion.

America's immigration policies have become emblematic of this contradiction.

Policies that separate families, detain asylum seekers, and foster a climate of fear and distrust run counter to the ethos of welcoming the "tired, poor, and huddled masses yearning to breathe free," as famously articulated in Emma Lazarus's poem inscribed on the Statue of Liberty.

Such harsh measures contradict the principles of liberty and justice for all, reinforcing a narrative that positions immigrants as threats rather than as potential contributors to society.

In contrast to the conservative approach, liberals and Democrats strive to advocate for the expansion of civil rights, seeking to address systemic inequality and ensure that marginalized communities—including racial minorities, the LGBTQ+ community, and immigrants, have access to the same freedoms that many Americans take for granted.

Movements for racial justice, gender equality, and immigrant rights exemplify a commitment to overcoming the profound disparities within American society.

America's contradictions create a complex and often conflicting image on the international stage.

While some perceive the United States as a land of opportunity, others view it as a hypocritical nation that professes freedom while denying it to specific groups domestically and abroad.

The aggressive nature of U.S. foreign policy and strategic alliances with authoritarian regimes further complicates this image.

This creates skepticism regarding the country's steadfast commitment to democracy, mainly when its actions prioritize geopolitical interests over humanitarian concerns.

To reconcile these discrepancies, America must deeply self-reflect and implement corrective actions that more closely align with its founding principles of liberty, equality, and justice for all.

Acknowledging our hypocrisy in its treatment of marginalized groups and our aggression toward other nations is vital for fostering a robust democracy.

It is essential to reduce the influence of toxic nationalism and military arrogance propagated by conservative factions, recalibrating foreign relationships based on ethical considerations rather than mere utility to create a more just society.

A commitment to genuine American values requires humility, open dialogue, and a willingness to learn from diverse experiences.

Recognizing past failures, particularly in foreign interventions and domestic civil rights issues, is critical for progressing toward a more equitable society.

They are making restitution for past discrepancies towards other nations, their population, and our citizens.

Emphasizing collective well-being over individual superiority can help bridge the gap between America's lofty ideals and the harsh realities many face.

By addressing its contradictions, especially its alignment with dictators and support of authoritarian regimes in exchange for economic benefits, America can strive to be a true leader in the global pursuit of freedom and opportunity.

This transformative change begins with recognizing that true greatness is not found in mere declarations of superiority but in an unwavering commitment to equality, respect, and the dignity of all individuals.

Ensuring that the ideals of life, liberty, and the pursuit of happiness are genuinely realized for everyone is the challenge that will define America's future and its role in a global society.

The Political and Cultural Battle Over Critical Thinking, Critical Race Theory, and Accurate American History

Critical Race Theory (CRT) is not taught in K-12 schools. However, public school teachers in the more progressive states have started integrating critical thinking into their subject-specific standards and curricula. In blue states, educators, including K-12 teachers, university professors, and organizations like the Zinn Education Project and Learning for Justice, are committed to presenting a comprehensive and unbiased history. This includes diverse perspectives and the challenge of dominant narratives. Conversely, Republican state lawmakers have introduced measures aimed at preventing teachers from discussing the history of racial oppression in the United States.

The discussion surrounding the suppression of critical race theory (CRT), critical thinking, and a nuanced view of American history by factions such as the "Make America Great Again" (MAGA) movement involves several intertwined issues. CRT originated from legal studies in the late 20th century, focusing on how societal structures, laws, and practices perpetuate racial inequalities. Politically, Trump and MAGA Republicans depict CRT as a divisive ideology that frames all white individuals as oppressors, MAGA Republicans claim erroneously that teaching this perspective can hurt white students by instilling feelings of guilt or shame regarding their race.

Critical thinking is essential in educational institutions, and CRT encourages questioning established norms and exploring multiple perspectives. For example, critical thinking might involve analyzing different interpretations of historical events, such as the impact of the Civil War beyond merely a fight to preserve the Union; it involves understanding its roots in slavery and the ongoing implications of that conflict. This questioning threatens those in power, as it challenges the status quo. By promoting a simplified version of history, particularly concerning colonization, systemic racism, and injustices, limiting what we teach about our history helps political factions to control public perceptions and discourse. The MAGA movement advocates a version of U.S. history centered on American exceptionalism, often glossing over or outright denying the narratives of racism, slavery, and imperialism

Those who refuse to learn about the past the way it happened are doomed to repeat it.

Many states, particularly those aligned with the MAGA ideology, have introduced legislation banning the teaching of "divisive concepts," including CRT. Such initiatives aim to standardize educational content while claiming to preserve educational integrity. However, critics argue this stifles the necessary discourse on history and systemic inequalities.

Red states are particularly active in this movement, implementing policies to suppress teachings that challenge traditional narratives upheld by conservative white MAGA members' ideologies, effectively curtailing educators' ability to present comprehensive historical perspectives.

The cultural resistance and differing value systems play a significant role in this tension. Adherents of MAGA ideology often value rugged individualism, personal responsibility, and a meritocratic view of society that suggests anyone can succeed through hard work. CRT, however, challenges these beliefs by emphasizing systemic issues that create barriers for marginalized communities, which may be seen as undermining the American ethos of personal agency and self-determination.

The reasons behind the opposition from Trump, MAGA Republicans, and many white Americans to CRT and comprehensive historical education are complex and multifaceted. Many white Americans feel their identity and societal position as superior to everyone else are being threatened by discussions of systemic racism and inequality.

CRT challenges the notions of a racially neutral and fair society, which may provoke defensive reactions among those who see themselves as part of the dominant culture. This defensive stance reinforces a desire to maintain a familiar worldview that prioritizes their experiences and perspectives.

Acknowledging systemic inequalities can evoke feelings of guilt, anger, embarrassment, denial, and shame among individuals who identify as white, particularly if they believe that the teachings may imply personal complicity in historical injustices.

It is important for individuals to recognize that they are not accountable for events that occurred before their birth; those historical circumstances and injustices are not a reflection of their personal character or values.

However, it is also crucial to acknowledge that many white individuals today benefit from advantages inherited from past injustices. For instance, white people often find it easier to secure jobs, receive shorter sentences or probation when they encounter the legal system, and are generally perceived, erroneously, as more trustworthy and credible compared to people of color.

This systemic bias is a result of historical inequities that continue to shape societal norms and narratives. This emotional response can lead to a defensive posture against CRT, as many prefer narratives that allow them to view themselves and their communities in a more positive light, without the burden of confronting uncomfortable truths.

Instead of feeling guilt or responsibility for these historical advantages, what truly matters is how we engage with and address issues of equality and inclusivity through our present-day actions.

White individuals, in particular, have a significant opportunity and responsibility to leverage their societal status to advocate for others who face systemic discrimination and marginalization. This can include standing up publicly for those who are disadvantaged, using their voice to amplify marginalized perspectives, and actively participating in conversations about race and equity.

By committing to fostering a more equitable and inclusive society today, we can work toward rectifying past injustices and creating a better future for everyone. It is essential to recognize our privileges while using them as a platform to support equality and justice, ultimately transforming society's narrative into one that encompasses all voices.

The teachings associated with CRT are often viewed as a direct challenge to traditional American

Values, including patriotism, meritocracy, and individualism. For those aligned with the MAGA movement, any perceived attack on these values is seen as an attack on the very foundations of the country. Consequently, there is a perception that CRT seeks to undermine the principles that have historically defined American society.

Trump and MAGA Republicans have effectively used opposition to CRT as a political mobilization tool. By framing the issue as a defense of conservative values against progressive ideologies, they have galvanized their base. This political strategy creates a dichotomy between "us" (those who defend traditional values) and "them" (those who support perceived divisive concepts), capitalizing on existing societal divisions.

On the other hand, Democrats often view the opposition to CRT as a misguided attempt to suppress critical thinking and honest discussions about race and history. They argue that teaching CRT is essential for understanding systemic racism and its impact on American society. Democrats believe that acknowledging and discussing uncomfortable aspects of history is necessary for progress and healing. They fear that banning CRT undermines educational integrity and prevents students from grappling with complex social issues, ultimately hindering their ability to think critically.

Democrats also assert that opposition to CRT stems from misinformation and a misrepresentation of its core tenets. This rhetoric is often seen as a strategy to motivate a conservative base by generating fear around the idea of teaching systemic racism in schools. Many Democrats argue that such fears distract from addressing real issues of inequality and create further division in society.

The emphasis on American exceptionalism fosters a narrative that downplays or ignores disparate racial and historical experiences. Many people in MAGA circles embrace a simplified timeline in which America is portrayed only as a land of opportunity and freedom, which contradicts the realities of racial injustice and inequality highlighted by CRT. For example, an accurate understanding of U.S. history involves discussing the Tulsa Race Massacre, which illustrates the violent suppression of Black success, as a key event that alternative narratives often overlook. The acceptance of this simplified history allows for a sense of community and shared identity that feels threatened by more complex, inclusive narratives.

Racial and economic anxieties can intertwine, creating a complex landscape where fears of social change are compounded by concerns over job security and economic stability. Economic uncertainties can drive individuals to cling to familiar narratives that protect their societal status. The idea that systemic inequality might require systemic change can be frightening for many white Americans, leading to resistance against discussions that bring these issues to the forefront.

The role of media in shaping the discussions around CRT cannot be underestimated. Sensationalized portrayals can misrepresent the tenets of CRT, turning it into a boogeyman for conservatives. Media narratives often frame educational debates as battles over freedom of speech, leading to polarization and a lack of nuanced understanding of the concepts that CRT promotes. This can further entrench opposition among those who feel they are under attack for simply wanting to preserve traditional educational values.

The dynamics of suppressing critical thinking, CRT, and a more inclusive history are closely connected to political power, cultural identity, and social psychology.

For Trump and the MAGA movement, these issues represent existential battles over who defines the American narrative, what values are upheld, and how history is interpreted. The resistance to these changes among many white Americans stems from a complex mix of identity defense, fear of change, and a deeply entrenched belief in a specific vision of American history.

On the other side, Democrats advocate for a deeper understanding of systemic inequalities and emphasize the importance of critical discussions in education. Understanding these factors is crucial for fostering meaningful discourse on race, history, and education in America, paving the way for a more inclusive society that acknowledges its complexities.

The Historical and Contemporary Landscape of Political Representation in the United States

In a nation as diverse as the United States, the journey toward equitable political representation has been a complex and ongoing battle. By reflecting on our past, understanding our present, and envisioning a more inclusive future, we can actively work to enhance our chances of winning more seats in office for underrepresented communities.

In the early years of American democracy, political power was largely concentrated among elite white males. Voting rights were limited to white male property owners, rooted in the belief that only those with a vested interest in society, who owned land, should have a say in governance. This exclusion laid the foundations for a political landscape that favored a select demographic, sidelining women, people of color, and economically disadvantaged individuals.

The issue of slavery significantly impacted the political landscape of the United States. Enslaved individuals were considered property and thus lacked any civil rights, including the right to vote. The Three-Fifths Compromise (1787) allocated congressional representation based on three-fifths of the enslaved population, granting disproportionate power to slaveholding states while further entrenching the political disenfranchisement of enslaved people.

As the nation expanded westward, Native American tribes were systematically stripped of their rights and sovereignty. The federal government regarded Native Americans as wards of the state, with limited say in political processes. It wasn't until the Indian Citizenship Act of 1924 that Native Americans were granted U.S. citizenship and the right to vote, though many states employed barriers to continue their disenfranchisement.

Women began organizing for the right to vote during the 19th century, with pivotal moments such as the Seneca Falls Convention in 1848. After decades of struggle, the 19th Amendment in 1920 granted women the right to vote; however, this right was systematically undermined for women of color, particularly in the Jim Crow South, where discriminatory practices like literacy tests and poll taxes disenfranchised many.

Fast forward to the 1960s, when the Civil Rights Movement sought to dismantle barriers to representation for African Americans. The Voting Rights Act of 1965 was a pivotal moment, affirming the right to vote and paving the way for increased political engagement among marginalized populations. This law aimed to eliminate racial discrimination in voting, a landmark achievement in the ongoing fight for equality.

As decades passed, various movements emerged, including feminism, LGBTQ+ rights, and immigrant advocacy, each striving to challenge traditional power structures in American politics. While representation for these groups grew, systemic barriers continued to impede progress, often exacerbated by divisive political tactics. Today, non-Hispanic white straight males comprise about 27-29% of the total U.S. population, yet they represent a striking 62% of officeholders, dominating both chambers of Congress and 42 state legislatures. This staggering disparity highlights a critical imbalance, underscoring that our political representation must evolve to reflect the diverse voices of the nation instead of remaining disproportionately controlled by a small minority.

The current political climate is rife with challenges. Populism and polarization can create divisions that hinder cooperation across communities. Voter turnout remains a concern, particularly among marginalized groups facing systemic obstacles like gerrymandering and voter ID laws. The lingering influence of such barriers can lead to apathy and disengagement, further entrenching the status quo.

On a brighter note, activism has taken on new dimensions thanks to social media, allowing for rapid mobilization and awareness. Movements like Black Lives Matter and the Women's March have ignited grassroots efforts, emphasizing the necessity of inclusive representation. These movements not only raise awareness about systemic inequality but also advocate for policy changes that address the root causes of disenfranchisement.

Looking ahead, we must recognize the demographic shifts continuing to reshape our nation. By 2045, the U.S. is projected to become a majority-minority country, presenting an unprecedented opportunity for greater representation—if we seize it. As diverse populations grow and evolve, their voices will increasingly demand representation that aligns with their experiences and needs.

To improve our odds of winning more seats for underrepresented groups, we can implement several key strategies. Engaging the community is crucial. Building relationships and trust within communities through town halls, workshops, and information sessions can foster a sense of ownership and connection to the political process. Active participation from local leaders and influencers can also help mobilize support and encourage civic engagement. Creating narratives that resonate with diverse demographics is essential. Highlighting the multifaceted identities within communities can foster empathy and expand the electorate. This includes addressing the unique challenges faced by different groups and framing political issues in a manner that connects with their lived experiences.

Launching targeted voter registration drives and events designed to educate and motivate can enhance voter mobilization efforts. Collaborating with local organizations will further strengthen outreach efforts and ensure that information reaches those who need it most. Establishing mentorship programs for aspiring leaders from underrepresented backgrounds can provide valuable training in campaign strategy, fundraising, and public speaking. These programs can empower the next generation of leaders, ensuring that they have the skills and support necessary to navigate the political landscape. Advocating for legislative measures that expand voting access, eliminate voter suppression tactics, and ensure fair redistricting processes is vital for creating an equitable political landscape. Engaging in coalition-building with other advocacy groups can amplify the call for reforms that facilitate greater participation.

Encouraging alliances among different movements can create a united front that amplifies voices and demonstrates the power of diversity. Utilizing data to analyze community demographics will also help tailor outreach effectively, prioritizing issues that matter most to constituents. The path to achieving diverse political representation requires commitment and collaboration.

By understanding our historical context, capitalizing on present opportunities, and working together for a more inclusive future, we can transform the political landscape. Empowering underrepresented communities to gain seats in office not only enriches democracy but also ensures that our governance reflects the diverse voices of all Americans.

Let us take action today for a more inclusive tomorrow, where every citizen's voice resonates in the halls of power. Together, we can pave the way for a political system that truly represents the rich tapestry of our nation a democracy that is vibrant, equitable, and just.

Understanding America's Political Landscape: Examining How a Party with the Fewest Registered Voters Secured Most National Elections

The political landscape in the United States is characterized by three main factions MAGA Republicans, mainstream Republicans (often referred to as Establishment Republicans), and Democrats each embodying distinct beliefs, platforms, leaders, and approaches to governance. Collectively, these factions significantly influence the lived experiences of Americans, particularly regarding critical social issues such as racism, misogyny, LGBTQ+ rights, and women's issues. To interpret the electoral landscape and the strategies that have led to notable successes for MAGA Republicans despite their comparatively smaller base, it is essential to understand the dynamics within and among these groups.

Populist and Nationalist Sentiments
MAGA Republicans, inspired by the slogan "America First," advocate for a populist agenda characterized by nationalism, immigration control, economic protectionism, anti-women's health choices, and traditional family values, one man and one woman connected by lifelong, monogamous marriage, together with the children of this couple. Their appeal resonates largely with working-class voters who feel alienated by globalization and traditional political structures. By positioning themselves as outsiders fighting against the political elite, they effectively attract those who believe their socioeconomic struggles have been overlooked, particularly in rural and economically disadvantaged regions. However, this nationalist lens often exacerbates tax cuts for the wealthy and inflation for the working class, by focusing on divisions related to race and gender while sidelining LGBTQ+ rights.

Resistance to LGBTQ+ Rights

Regarding LGBTQ+ issues, MAGA Republicans generally promote a conservative stance aligned with traditional family structures, resisting advancements in LGBTQ+ rights, including same-sex marriage and non-discrimination protections. This creates a hostile environment for LGBTQ+ individuals, marginalizing them and leaving them vulnerable to social exclusion. The rhetoric and policies of this faction frequently frame LGBTQ+ advocacy as contrary to "family values," reinforcing societal divisions and limiting the progress toward inclusivity.

Despite comprising only about 30% of the registered Republican vote, MAGA Republicans have achieved significant electoral victories, including the presidency in 2016 and 2024. This success can be attributed to several interconnected strategies:

MAGA Republicans effectively connected with working-class voters, even though MAGA is publicly against unions and a living wage, disillusioned by traditional politics, presenting themselves as champions of the "forgotten" Americans. They tap into feelings of anger and frustration, transforming these emotions into political action by verbally advocating for policies that prioritize American workers, often underpinned by anti-immigration sentiments and with no actionable follow-through.

In an increasingly polarized political environment, MAGA Republicans engage their base by addressing fears surrounding immigration, economic instability, and cultural changes. They capitalize on anxieties regarding demographic shifts, framing their platform to protect traditional values against perceived threats. This strategy has proven particularly adept at mobilizing support for White Nationalists and those feeling threatened by changes in societal norms around race, gender, and sexuality.

The rise of conservative media outlets has enabled MAGA Republicans to craft compelling narratives that resonate deeply within their base. These outlets often depict MAGA supporters as champions of "real Americans," reinforcing a collective identity that motivates voter engagement. This media ecosystem occasionally overshadows moderate perspectives within the Republican Party, leading to further entrenchment of extreme views.

The MAGA movement has fostered a dedicated and enthusiastic voter base that is exceptionally motivated to participate in elections. MAGA spent the last four years changing voter laws, voter districts, and purging voter rosters. Also, grassroots mobilization efforts encompass extensive outreach, large rallies, and leveraging social media platforms to galvanize support. This engaged base not only votes but also actively encourages others to do the same, further consolidating the MAGA Republicans' political influence.

The fear of losing cultural hegemony is prevalent among MAGA Republicans, feeding into a broader narrative that portrays changing demographics as threats. Scapegoating immigrants, minorities, and LGBTQ+ individuals creates a divisive ingroup-outgroup dynamic, reinforcing a false sense of unity. By framing societal changes as assaults on core values, this faction successfully mobilizes support by tapping into anxiety-driven political engagement.

The divisive language and policies promoted by MAGA Republicans contribute not only to a culture of animosity but also to normalizing hate-filled rhetoric in the broader political discourse. The reluctance of mainstream Republicans to distance themselves from this extreme rhetoric can lead to an environment where hateful views gain traction and acceptance, further marginalizing targeted communities.

Establishment Republicans advocate for conservative principles centered on fiscal responsibility, limited government, and traditional values. Their approach to addressing racism often emphasizes recognition of individual rights but lacks comprehensive engagement with systemic inequalities. While mainstream Republicans may publicly denounce overt racism and advocate for equality under the law, they have historically been criticized for their failure to confront the structural aspects of racial injustice.

When it comes to women's issues and misogyny, mainstream Republicans typically favor an economic perspective, focusing on workplace equality. However, critiques arise regarding the party's overall commitment to advancing gender equality more broadly. Some establishment Republicans have spoken out against misogyny and promoted women's leadership, but these efforts are often overshadowed by broader party dynamics or lack the intensity needed to drive systemic change.

In recent years, mainstream Republicans have shown a degree of evolution regarding reproductive rights, and LGBTQ+ rights, with a number supporting non-discrimination protections and marriage equality. However, this shift faces pushback from more traditional, conservative party members who resist such changes. Consequently, the Republican Party finds itself divided, with some advocating for inclusive policies while others cling to outdated views that marginalize LGBTQ+ individuals and won't let reproductive rights pass.

The Democratic Party generally aligns with a more progressive agenda that emphasizes social justice, equity, and inclusivity. This party actively prioritizes addressing racism, sexism, and LGBTQ+ rights as core components of its platform. Demands for racial justice are deeply embedded in their policies, with Democrats advocating for reforms aimed at dismantling systemic racism and uplifting marginalized communities.

Democrats are vocal proponents of policies designed to address systemic racism, including police reform, expanded access to healthcare, and educational equity. They advocate for initiatives that aim to dismantle barriers faced by racial minorities while promoting opportunities for economic and social mobility. The party's commitment to these issues is frequently framed as essential for the health of democracy and society.

In terms of misogyny and women's issues, Democrats promote gender equality vigorously, pushing for policies that protect reproductive rights, combat domestic violence, and enhance workplace equality. Democratic leaders often highlight issues like the gender pay gap and advocate for women's representation in political and corporate leadership to create a more equitable society. Their platform usually includes comprehensive measures to support women in leadership roles and address systemic barriers faced by women in various sectors.

The Democratic Party is strongly supportive of LGBTQ+ rights, evolving to champion measures that protect and uplift the LGBTQ+ community. This includes supporting same-sex marriage, anti-discrimination laws, and policies that promote inclusivity and acceptance within society. Prominent Democratic figures advocate for comprehensive protections against discrimination based on sexual orientation and gender identity, framing LGBTQ+ rights as fundamental human rights. This alignment with LGBTQ+ issues reinforces the party's broader commitment to civil rights and social justice.

In evaluating these political factions, it is clear that their approaches to critical social issues such as racism, misogyny, LGBTQ+ rights, and women's issues significantly shape their proposed standards of living for the American public. MAGA Republicans often adopt a nationalist lens that can exacerbate divisions related to race and gender while sidelining LGBTQ+ rights. Mainstream Republicans generally recognize individual rights but may lack depth in engaging with systemic inequalities regarding race and gender. In contrast, Democrats vigorously advocate for inclusive policies that address systemic injustices and promote equity across all social dimensions.

To challenge the prejudices among segments of the electorate and promote a vision of inclusivity, several strategies can be considered:

Engaging in conversations that share personal stories can be powerful. By fostering empathy and understanding, voters may be more open to reconsidering their views on social issues. In-person dialogues and community gatherings can create spaces for genuine connection.

Emphasizing common values—such as family, personal dignity, and community—can bridge divides. By framing inclusivity as a way to enhance the well-being of all citizens, campaign messaging can resonate with a broader audience.

Educational initiatives that address misunderstandings or stereotypes can help shift perceptions. Providing resources and information about the struggles of marginalized communities may foster compassion and support for inclusive policies.

Electing leaders who embody inclusivity and demonstrate its benefits can inspire a shift in public opinion. When constituents see effective policies that elevate marginalized voices leading to tangible societal benefits, they may become more receptive to broadening their views.

Advocacy for inclusivity should extend beyond electoral cycles. Engaging communities through dialogue and mutual support around shared goals can help build trust and reduce prejudicial attitudes over time.

As the political landscape continues to evolve, understanding these nuanced positions on social issues and their implications for the lives of diverse communities remains crucial for voters seeking to make informed decisions in upcoming elections. The ongoing discourse surrounding racism, misogyny, LGBTQ+ rights, and women's issues will play a pivotal role in shaping the future direction of American politics and society. Addressing the underlying prejudices that fuel divisive politics is essential for creating a more inclusive and equitable future, enabling progress toward a society where all individuals, regardless of their identity, can thrive.

Navigating the Tightrope of Gun Ownership: Balancing Rights and Responsibilities

Gun control has become one of the most contentious issues in contemporary society, especially in the United States, where the culture of gun ownership is deeply rooted and constitutionally protected by the Second Amendment. The ongoing debate surrounding gun control encompasses various perspectives on the regulations governing firearm possession, use, and distribution. At the core of this dialogue lies a profound tension between the individual right to bear arms and the collective responsibility to ensure the safety of all citizens. Let us delve into the complexities of this issue, raising important ethical questions about personal freedoms, societal duties, and the intricate balance required to navigate these conflicting ideals.

We want you to keep your guns and all the weapons you plan to buy, but not at the expense of any loss of life due to your choices. If you can't figure it out, it is society's responsibility to handle it for you.

The right to bear arms is not merely a legalistic point; it is a reflection of historical contexts that emphasize self-defense and personal liberty. Advocates for gun ownership often cite the Second Amendment as an essential safeguard against tyranny and a means to protect oneself and one's family.

MAGA Republicans often view gun ownership as an essential component of American identity and frame it as a fundamental right under siege by government overreach. This group argues that increased regulation endangers individual liberties and personal safety.

MAGA and fanatical gun owners tend to see calls for tougher gun laws as part of a broader narrative of liberal governance that seeks to control citizens when it is actually to protect citizens and save lives. However, the assertion that "we want you to keep your guns" also comes with an important caveat: "not at the expense of any life loss." This nuanced position compels us to consider crucial questions about what responsible gun ownership truly means in a society grappling with high rates of gun violence.

The Second Amendment of the United States Constitution, which protects the right to bear arms, remains one of the most contentious issues in American society. As the debate over gun control intensifies, advocates assert that individual rights and public safety must take precedence. While there are no constitutional amendments that explicitly supersede the Second Amendment, a closer examination of existing rights and the potential for new amendments reveals avenues for prioritizing societal well-being alongside individual liberties.

One constitutional provision often referenced in the context of gun control is the First Amendment, which guarantees freedoms including speech and assembly. Proponents of gun control argue that these rights are inherently tied to the safety and security of individuals in society. Living in a safe environment is crucial for the free exercise of these rights. Thus, enhancing regulations surrounding firearms can be framed as essential for allowing individuals to engage in public discourse and assembly without fear of violence or intimidation, thereby reinforcing the tenets of the First Amendment.

The Fourteenth Amendment's Equal Protection Clause provides a foundation for addressing disparities exacerbated by gun violence. Communities disproportionately affected by gun-related incidents may claim that they are denied equal protection under the law, leading to calls for legislation that safeguards their rights. This perspective invites a reevaluation of the Second Amendment's application, suggesting that individual rights should be balanced with the necessity of protecting vulnerable populations from gun violence. Enhancing public safety through effective legislation can ensure that the rights of all citizens are upheld equally.

The discussion surrounding gun control could benefit from the introduction of a balanced rights amendment. Such a proposal might assert that while the right to bear arms is recognized, it should not infringe upon the rights of individuals to live in safety and security. This hypothetical amendment could serve as a legal framework for laws prioritizing public safety while respecting the Second Amendment. As society grapples with these complex issues, the ongoing dialogue will shape the future of individual rights and community safety in America, emphasizing the need for thoughtful consideration and innovative approaches to gun legislation.

Gun control refers to the legal framework designed to regulate firearms, encompassing a range of measures, such as background checks for prospective gun buyers, mandatory waiting periods between purchase and delivery of firearms, permit requirements for carrying firearms, restrictions or bans on specific types of firearms, like automatic weapons, regulations on gun dealers, and licensing requirements that expire and must be renewed. These measures aim to enhance public safety while still allowing for lawful gun ownership.

This comprehensive approach underscores the complexity of the gun control debate. While critics of gun control argue that these regulations infringe upon individual rights, proponents maintain that such measures are necessary to protect the individual rights of the general public and communities from gun violence. Thus, the question arises: how do we implement these regulations without infringing on the personal freedoms that many Americans cherish?

Opposition to gun control often stems from a cultural identity that intertwines gun ownership with personal freedom, self-reliance, and a deep-seated mistrust of government authority. Many Americans see gun ownership as a symbol of independence and individual rights enshrined in the Constitution. The National Rifle Association (NRA) plays a crucial role in this opposition. Founded in 1871, the NRA advocates for gun rights and opposes most forms of gun control. It engages in lobbying efforts to influence legislation and politics to protect the rights of gun owners.

The NRA has a significant financial footprint in lobbying against gun control measures. Reports indicate that the organization spends millions annually on political contributions and lobbying efforts. For instance, in 2023, the National Rifle Association donated $27,413,008 to individuals in the legislature or used in efforts to elect these individuals. Additionally, the NRA's Political Victory Fund, a PAC, received $613,600 in contributions to federal candidates, with 100% of these funds allocated to Republicans and 0% to Democrats.

Several politicians have received substantial financial contributions from the NRA. Notable recipients include Ted Cruz, Mitt Romney, Lindsey Graham, and Mitch McConnell. According to OpenSecrets, for example, Ted Cruz has received over $1.2 million, while Mitt Romney has received over $1.1 million. Other notable recipients include the Republican National Committee, the National Republican Senatorial Committee, and various Republican congressmen. While the bulk of NRA contributions flow to Republicans, it's worth noting that eight Democratic congressmen have also accepted funding from the NRA, illustrating a more complex political landscape regarding gun rights.

The narrative that "no one wants to ban weapons or take your guns" resonates strongly with these groups, emphasizing a desire to uphold lawful gun ownership while resisting perceived government overreach.

The phrase "if you can't figure it out, it is society's responsibility to do it for you" urges us to confront a significant ethical dilemma: How do we reconcile individual liberties with the imperative of collective safety?

This call for societal accountability raises profound questions about the implications of our choices regarding firearms. Should individuals bear the full weight of responsibility for their actions, or does society have an obligation to intervene when personal decisions endanger the lives of others?

This tension invites a reflection on the ethical dimensions of freedom—how do we define the limits of individual autonomy in situations where personal actions may have severe repercussions for community safety?

The contemporary landscape presents a paradox: While societies champion liberty, they must also prioritize the well-being of their members. This dilemma is not merely philosophical; it has practical ramifications. How do we strike a balance that allows for personal freedom while ensuring communal safety?

Consider various models of governance worldwide. Some nations have enacted stringent gun control measures that permit ownership yet prioritize gun safety education, mental health evaluations, and comprehensive training. These approaches suggest that it is possible to foster responsible gun ownership while instituting safeguards that mitigate risks. Such discussions prompt us to ask: What systems and regulations should be developed to create a framework that harmonizes personal rights with public safety?

Governments play a critical role in shaping the frameworks within which individual choices unfold. If society is responsible for addressing the complexities surrounding gun ownership, the question arises: What regulations and educational initiatives can be implemented to ensure safety without infringing on personal rights?

This approach requires careful consideration of various factors, including the provision of gun safety courses, the establishment of background checks, and the encouragement of mental health support. It also beckons a more profound examination of how we engage with the topic of gun ownership, suggesting a shift from polarized debates toward collaborative efforts aimed at minimizing risks associated with firearms.

At the heart of this issue lies the human element. Each gun owner brings a unique set of experiences, motivations, and contexts influencing their relationship with firearms. This diversity demands introspection: How well do we understand the consequences of our choices, and are we equipped to wield our rights responsibly?

As a society, we must ask ourselves whether individuals possess the necessary information and training to make informed decisions about gun ownership. This includes understanding the ethical responsibilities that accompany the right to bear arms, a responsibility that extends beyond personal safety to encompass community welfare.

To fully grasp the implications of gun ownership and the necessity of balanced regulations, we must confront the statistics surrounding gun violence in America.

Homicide refers to the intentional acts of violence resulting in death, which includes both murder and manslaughter. In 2023, there were a total of 19,252 reported homicide cases in the U.S. When examining murder victims by gender and ethnicity, the vast majority were male, and just over half of the victims were identified as Black.

Mass shootings are defined as high-profile incidents in which multiple individuals are shot in a single attack. According to the Gun Violence Archive, there have been over 488 reported mass shootings across the U.S. in 2024 so far. A mass shooting is classified as an incident in which four or more people are injured or killed. The figures from the Archive include shootings that take place in both public spaces and private residences.

Suicides, particularly those involving self-inflicted gunshot wounds, account for more than half of all gun-related deaths in the U.S. In 2023, there were 27,300 firearm suicides, marking the highest recorded number to date. Approximately 90% of suicide attempts that involve a firearm result in death, while around 3,000 additional attempts are unsuccessful. In contrast, only about 4% of suicide attempts that do not involve a gun result in death.

Accidental shootings, and unintentional discharges of firearms that lead to injury or death, also add to the tragic statistics. In recent years, these incidents have resulted in several hundred deaths annually, with approximately 500 fatalities resulting from accidental shootings.

Law enforcement-related shootings refer to incidents where police use firearms, which can be justified in some cases and controversial in others, leading to fatalities. In 2024, a record-breaking 1,365 people were reported killed by U.S. law enforcement, making it the deadliest year since tracking began in 2013, according to Campaign Zero.

Gun-related injuries are not always categorized as homicides or suicides. More people suffer nonfatal firearm-related injuries than die from them. More than 70% of medically treated firearm injuries are the result of firearm-related assaults, while nearly 20% stem from unintentional firearm injuries. Intentional self-inflicted firearm-related injuries are less frequently observed in hospital emergency departments, but the majority of those who attempt suicide with a firearm do not survive.

Critics contend that while millions are spent on research aimed at enhancing the lethality of firearms, creating weapons capable of inflicting mass casualties in a matter of seconds, almost no resources are directed toward initiatives that could reduce accidental shootings or gun-related deaths. This imbalance raises questions about societal priorities regarding gun violence compared to other forms of injury and death prevention or public safety.

Research indicates a complex relationship between gun ownership and violence. Studies show that gun ownership increases the risk of firearm-related incidents. The American Journal of Public Health has reported that households with firearms face higher risks of homicide and suicide compared to those without guns. Internationally, countries with stricter gun control, like Australia and the UK, have seen declines in gun-related deaths following mass shootings. Advocates of gun rights reference defensive uses of firearms, but research indicates these scenarios are rare compared to instances of gun homicides and suicides.

The debate is complicated by emotional factors, including fears of confiscation among gun owners. This concern is particularly pronounced among MAGA Republicans, who often mobilize around the belief that their rights are threatened by progressive policies. Misinformation surrounding gun laws also fuels tensions and creates confusion. Despite the high rates of gun-related injuries and deaths, significant funding is often allocated to safety measures in other areas, such as homes, appliances, automobiles, toys, and clothing. These industries invest heavily in research and development to improve safety standards and reduce accidents. However, gun safety has not received a similar commitment to prevention; there is little to no investment aimed at making firearms safer, despite their responsibility for thousands of fatalities each year. These overwhelming figures prompt a critical need for dialogue and action aimed at addressing not only the rights of gun owners but also the safety of all citizens.

The discussion surrounding gun ownership is not merely a legal or political issue; it is an ethical imperative that challenges us to reflect on our values as individuals and as a society. As we grapple with the significance of maintaining the freedoms we cherish, we must simultaneously commit to ensuring that these freedoms do not encroach upon the rights and safety of others.

Moving forward, the dialogue should not dwell solely on the retention of rights but on fostering a future where personal freedoms and societal responsibilities coexist in harmony. The question extends beyond legislation; it asks us to envision pathways that empower all individuals to exercise their rights responsibly, ensuring that the tragic loss of life does not define our choices. How we choose to navigate this intricate landscape will significantly shape our communities and the legacy we leave for future generations.

The Correlation Between Historical Lynchings, Modern Police Killings, and Capital Punishment in America

The concept of "blind justice," embodied by Lady Justice in her blindfold, is meant to signify a legal system that treats all individuals without bias. In practice, it is a white superiority justice system with an abundance of evidence revealing that systemic racism and societal bias have significantly shaped judicial outcomes across various facets, including arrest rates, sentencing, and access to legal resources.

The historical backdrop of lynching in the United States resonates in today's police killings, prompting critical conversations about race, justice, and societal values. Similarly, the application of capital punishment sheds light on ongoing racial disparities and systemic inequality within the justice system.

While lynchings, police violence, and capital punishment stem from different historical contexts, they collectively underscore persistent issues related to racial dynamics and reflect the lasting impact of white supremacy in America. Investigating these connections unearths historical continuities and exposes systemic flaws within the U.S. justice framework.

Between the late 19th century and the mid-20th century, the United States witnessed a harrowing wave of lynchings targeting Black individuals. The Equal Justice Initiative notes that more than 4,400 Black men, women, and children were lynched from 1877 to 1950, serving as instruments of white terror and social enforcement, particularly in the South.

In states like Mississippi, which recorded at least 579 lynchings from 1882 to 1968, these public spectacles not only incited severe violence but also illustrated community complicity in perpetuating racial terror.

Witness accounts reveal that many lynchings were performative, attracting large crowds, including members of law enforcement, who often treated these horrific acts as entertainment

Legal consequences for lynchers were virtually nonexistent, with a study by the NAACP indicating that between 1882 and 1968, fewer than 1 percent of these cases resulted in prosecution. However, a troubling statistic, it is higher than today when compared with modern police killing prosecution rates.

In the present day, modern police killings have garnered national scrutiny, with high-profile cases like those of George Floyd, Breonna Taylor, and Michael Brown igniting nationwide calls for reform. Current data reveal that Black individuals are significantly more likely to be killed by police than their white counterparts; for instance, the Mapping Police Violence database indicates that Black Americans are three times more likely to be victims of fatal encounters with law enforcement.

In 2021, over 1,058 people were killed by police, with approximately 25 percent of these individuals being Black, even though Black Americans make up only about 13 percent of the U.S. population. In 2022, this number increased to around 1,192, while for 2023, it indicates there have been 1,329 police killings. The year 2024 saw 1365 police killings. The rate of prosecution for police killings remains starkly low. A 2021 analysis by the Washington Post revealed that, since 2005, only about 2 percent of police officers involved in fatal shootings have been charged with a crime. Specifically, in 2021, out of over 1,058 police killings, only seven officers were arrested and convicted. In 2022, only five officers were convicted in connection with approximately 1,192 killings. As of 2023, 2 officers faced convictions concerning the over 1,300 killings, showcasing a conviction rate of roughly 0.17 percent for the current year.

The death penalty in the U.S. further complicates the narrative of racial bias and inequality. Since its reinstatement in 1976, there have been 1,632 executions, predominantly in a handful of states. Shockingly, around 47 percent of those exonerated after being wrongfully sentenced to death are Black, highlighting a glaring disparity in how justice is administered. Ignominiously, there have been documented cases of individuals executed who were later proven innocent, a sobering reminder of the irrevocable nature of capital punishment.

Examining the timing of executions reveals an unsettling pattern: Black individuals in certain jurisdictions face swifter executions than their white counterparts. Additionally, studies indicate that the race of the victim dramatically influences whether a defendant receives the death penalty, with crimes against white victims resulting in harsher sentences. The disproportionate number of people of color among those executed—over 70 percent since 1976—further amplifies the urgency for reform.

Specific states have been identified as executing Black individuals at a faster rate.

Texas accounts for approximately 37% of all executions since 1976, with Black individuals representing about 35% of those executed in the state.

In Florida, about 40% of those executed are Black, despite African Americans making up roughly 13% of the state's population.

Georgia has seen about 57% of those executed since 1976 being Black, showcasing a significant racial disparity.

In Virginia, approximately 48% of those executed have been Black, reflecting substantial racial imbalances.

Alabama presents a particularly stark picture, with nearly 60% of those executed being Black.

In Mississippi, about 80% of those executed since 1976 have been Black individuals, demonstrating extreme racial disparity in its application of the death penalty.

The assertion that white individuals often receive more lenient sentences than people of color for similar crimes is supported by various studies and statistics regarding racial disparities in the U.S. criminal justice system. Research has shown that white individuals typically receive lighter sentences compared to their Black or Hispanic counterparts for similar offenses.

A study by the U.S. Sentencing Commission found that, on average, Black male offenders received sentences that were 19.1% longer than those of white male offenders for similar crimes.

Numerous studies indicate that racial bias can influence judicial outcomes, including charging decisions, sentencing lengths, and the likelihood of receiving plea deals.

Black defendants are often more likely to face harsher charges than white defendants for the same crime. The race of the victim can also impact sentencing, as crimes against white victims may result in harsher penalties for offenders, regardless of their race. This dynamic reflects deep-seated biases within the criminal justice system.

People of color often face less favorable plea deals than white individuals, leading to longer sentences and more significant criminal records. This disparity can perpetuate cycles of disadvantage and recidivism.

Data collected by various organizations, including the Bureau of Justice Statistics, reveal that racial minorities, particularly Black Americans, are overrepresented in incarceration rates and often serve longer sentences for the same crimes compared to white individuals, even when accounting for factors like crime severity and prior criminal history.

The acknowledgment of these disparities has led to growing calls for criminal justice reform, including initiatives aimed at addressing systemic racism in sentencing and law enforcement practices.

While not every case will fit this pattern, the broader statistical evidence suggests that white individuals benefit from more lenient treatment within the criminal justice system. This perpetuates existing inequalities and raises significant concerns about fairness and justice. Addressing these disparities remains a critical focus for policymakers, advocates, and researchers.

Analyzing these injustices reveals a consistent pattern: systemic racism continues to manifest in policing, capital punishment, and broader judicial practices. The end of public lynchings did not extinguish racial violence; it merely transformed into subtler, yet equally damaging, forms of control and terror. The alternative Modern policing, while ostensibly a protective force, often mirrors the racial hierarchies once enforced through the alternative lynching, keeping alive the vestiges of white supremacy.

Both lynchings and police killings expose the entrenched racism woven into the fabric of American society. Although lynchings were blatant acts of brutality, modern policing reveals an insidious reality of racial profiling and excessive force targeted at marginalized communities.

Furthermore, the death penalty frequently reinforces these disparities, as it predominantly impacts people of color.

The public justification of lynchings as a means to maintain social order has evolved; today, police killings are frequently framed within the narrative of public safety, though recurring instances of excessive force, particularly against unarmed individuals, challenge the validity of such claims. Similarly, capital punishment is often justified under the guise of justice, disproportionately affecting marginalized groups.

Movements advocating for justice reform have risen in response to these injustices, drawing connections between past and present. The Civil Rights Movement sought to dismantle the violent legacy of lynching, while contemporary movements like Black Lives Matter confront police brutality and call for changes to capital punishment laws.

Comprehensive reforms are critical to dismantle these entrenched systems.

Policy Reform: New legislation is essential to change policing practices, including bans on chokeholds, stricter rules on deadly force, and comprehensive de-escalation training for officers.

Accountability Mechanisms: Establishing independent investigations for police shootings and ensuring accountability can help rebuild trust in law enforcement. Utilizing body cameras and anonymized reporting can enhance transparency.

Community Engagement: Strengthening community-police relations through outreach initiatives can foster trust and accountability.

Ending the Death Penalty: Reassessing capital punishment and focusing on bias elimination or abolishing it altogether may signify a crucial step towards systemic justice.

Education and Awareness: Raising awareness of racial violence's historical and ongoing impacts through education can cultivate empathy and empower advocacy for change.

The troubling correlation between lynchings, police killings, and capital punishment highlights the systemic racism embedded within the justice system. While lynchings represent a violent chapter in American history, modern police violence and capital punishment reveal ongoing struggles over authority, race, and human rights. Understanding these connections is vital for fostering meaningful discussions and advancing social justice reform in America. We can work towards a more equitable and just society by addressing these intertwined issues through honest discourse and concerted action.

The People vs. Trump A Scenario to Unite for Justice and Accountability

The moment has arrived for individuals and groups to challenge Donald Trump and MAGA (Make America Great Again) officials in court. This isn't just about political disagreements; it's a fight for the rights of marginalized communities, including transgender individuals, people of color, immigrants, women, and LGBTQ+ individuals. Each of us can take part in this movement, bringing civil lawsuits against these officials for their harmful actions and statements. Remember, we must target the individuals, not just their positions, this makes them individually financially liable not our government. No one is above the law!

We must shine a light on the many ways our rights have been violated. For instance, the defamation suffered by marginalized communities can stem from false statements that hurt their reputations. Trans individuals often
face derogatory comments that aim to undermine their identities, while people of color experience racial slurs and harmful stereotypes that damage their social standing and mental health. Immigrants are frequently portrayed as threats, which can obstruct their lives and livelihoods. Women and LGBTQ+ communities also deal with

mischaracterization and insults that chip away at their dignity and sense of belonging. All of us must understand the importance of standing up against these injustices.

Human rights should be sacred, yet we see blatant violations every day. For example, policies that deny transgender individuals access to healthcare or safe spaces are not just misguided; they are violations of basic human rights. These policies create barriers that force individuals into situations that can be harmful, impacting their well-being and sense of security. People of color often bear the brunt of systemic racism and discriminatory practices, while immigrants frequently endure family separations and harsh detention conditions that strip away their dignity and sense of identity. Women's rights to healthcare, autonomy, and safety are perpetually threatened in hostile political climates. Discrimination against LGBTQ+ individuals, such as barring them from military service or basic services, further infringes upon their fundamental rights. When we take action against these abuses, we not only uplift those harmed but also affirm our collective commitment to justice.

We must also consider civil rights. Each person deserves equal treatment under the law, regardless of their race, gender, or sexual orientation. Many trans individuals face exclusion in various areas of life, including athletics and healthcare coverage. Communities of color frequently contend with racial profiling and unfair treatment within the justice system that disproportionately affects their day-to-day experiences. Immigrants often endure discrimination while seeking work and building lives in new communities, reinforcing narratives that unjustly paint them as outsiders. Additionally, justice for women often falls short, with inadequate protections leading to persistent issues of violence and harassment that undermine their rights and opportunities. It is imperative that we recognize these patterns of discrimination and work together to dismantle them.

Moreover, constitutional rights those enshrined in our nation's founding documents are also under siege. From discriminatory laws that target transgender individuals to practices that unfairly profile people of color, the erosion of constitutional protections is alarming. Immigrants navigating legal proceedings often face unjust treatment, as their rights can be overlooked in favor of a system that prioritizes speed over fairness. Reproductive rights are constitutionally protected, yet there are increasing efforts to roll those back, directly impacting women. Attempts to erase marriage equality threaten the rights of LGBTQ+ individuals established by the Supreme Court, raising concerns about the future landscape of civil liberties in our nation. Together, we need to safeguard these essential rights, advocating for a society where everyone can thrive without fear of discrimination or violence.

These lawsuits are not just essential; they are empowering. Each time a plaintiff wins a case against Trump or any MAGA official, it can have monumental implications for their financial future. With Trump's estimated worth in the billions, a successful lawsuit could reclaim funds taken from communities through harmful governance. Moreover, this action serves to inspire others to join the cause, signifying that citizens can demand justice and accountability, engaging in a movement that has the potential to create profound change. This isn't solely about reparation; it's about restoring dignity to individuals and entire communities that have been marginalized or battered by unfounded claims and systemic injustices.

Collective legal action has the power to reshape public perception of Trump and the MAGA movement. When enough people unify in the pursuit of justice, we send a powerful message to the political class and fellow citizens: accountability is non-negotiable. This isn't just about winning legal battles; it's about fostering a culture where justice, ethics, and integrity in governance are foundational values. The more individuals stand up and tell their stories, the more unique narratives emerge, painting a fuller picture of the struggles within our society and demanding the attention they deserve.

As we pursue these legal actions, we also spark crucial conversations around accountability that can redefine political narratives. If Trump's endorsement begins to lose its allure due to ongoing legal issues, potential Republican candidates may hesitate to associate themselves with him, reshaping the political landscape considerably. The implications of these legal battles can echo through political affiliations, causing rifts within the party and encouraging a broader discourse around accountability that can influence elections and policymaking.

So, how can you find an attorney willing to take on Trump and MAGA officials? Navigating the legal landscape can be daunting, especially when tackling such high-profile individuals. Here are some essential steps to guide you in your search for an attorney:

First, research specialized lawyers who focus on civil rights, defamation, or constitutional law. Many organizations and legal advocacy groups emphasize these areas, and they can connect you with experienced professionals who understand the complexities of cases against influential public figures. A specialized attorney will be able to navigate the intricacies of law, fighting for justice in ways that general practitioners may not.

Consult legal aid organizations that offer assistance to marginalized communities and individuals facing hardship. Organizations such as the ACLU, Lambda Legal, and the Southern Poverty Law Center not only have resources for obtaining legal representation but also advocate for justice and can direct you to attorneys with seasoned experience in holding powerful figures accountable. These organizations are committed to fighting for civil liberties and can often provide guidance and support to plaintiffs navigating the complexities of their cases.

Your local or state bar association may also provide referral services that connect individuals with attorneys based on their areas of expertise. This is a beneficial way to find reputable attorneys who understand the nuances of political litigation and have a successful track record with cases like yours. Establishing a connection with a qualified attorney can provide the necessary legal underpinning for your claims.

Networking within advocacy communities can also be incredibly useful. Connect with community organizations and advocacy groups that focus on civil rights and social justice. They likely have relationships with attorneys who are passionate about tackling the injustices faced by marginalized populations, making them an excellent resource for recommendations. These connective tissues within communities strengthen our collective resolve while providing critical support to those willing to take action.

Before you choose an attorney, consider scheduling consultations. Many attorneys offer free initial consultations to discuss your case. This is your opportunity to gauge their experience and willingness to take on cases against high-profile officials. Ask thoughtful questions about their past experiences with similar cases and their legal philosophy. Ensure that you feel comfortable and confident in their ability to fight for your rights.

Lastly, seek referrals from those who've been involved in similar legal battles or faced discrimination. Personal referrals can lead you to dedicated attorneys who are ready to take on challenging cases and understand the emotional and psychological toll these battles can have on individuals. Supportive networks often flourish within communities undergoing similar struggles, providing camaraderie in the pursuit of justice.

By employing these strategies, you can find an attorney who is not only capable but also passionate about the fight for justice and ready to take on the challenges posed by powerful political figures. With the right ally in your corner, you can effectively navigate the complexities of the legal system and make your voice heard.

We stand at a crossroads where we can redefine our political system. The legal avenues we pursue against Trump and his allies aren't just about individual accountability; they are about reinforcing fundamental democratic principles: that no one, regardless of their status, is above the law. Each case we take can shatter the illusions of impunity and highlight a pathway towards systemic change.

Imagine, a democracy where every citizen feels empowered to speak out against misconduct and hold their leaders accountable. Your involvement matters. When you engage in this movement, you amplify the voices of those who feel sidelined and create a more just society for all. The collective roar of voices united in seeking justice can resonate far and wide.

Let's harness our collective strength to tackle injustices head-on. Every lawsuit filed is a step toward a brighter future where democratic principles thrive. Join this fight for justice, ensuring that those in power know their actions have consequences. Your voice counts; stand up, take action, and be part of a movement that prioritizes accountability in our political systems.

The repercussions of holding powerful figures accountable extend far beyond the courtroom. By pursuing these legal actions, we champion a societal norm where authority is consistently checked and leaders must answer for their actions. This reinforces the foundation of democracy, where every citizen has the right to expect ethical leadership, and where the arc of justice bends toward accountability rather than impunity.

We can cultivate not just a demand for justice today but also inspire future generations to remain vigilant against political misconduct. This is our moment to shape a more equitable, just society—one lawsuit at a time. Each action we take ensures that our democracy remains vibrant and responsive to the needs of all its citizens. Join us, and let's pave the way for lasting change together. Together, we can reclaim our future and reinforce the very values our democracy stands for.

Only Lower-Income and Middle-Income Americans Should Be Able to Hold Elected and Appointed Offices

The principle of representation lies at the core of governance in any democratic republic.

We are witnessing an increasing presence of wealthy elites serving in and influencing political power, which has transformed our government into an oligarchy.

This growing oligarchy is overshadowing the voices of everyday citizens and undermining the representation of the average American.

To ensure a truly representative political landscape, we must advocate for a system where only qualified individuals from lower to middle-income backgrounds can hold elected and appointed offices.

This way, this would guarantee that representation reflects the financial realities faced by the majority of American citizens.

To foster authentic representation, candidates for these roles should adhere to specific income and investment guidelines.

One example is when Congress finds out about a merger because it needs congressional approval and the officials make purchases of stock purchases before the merger approval is made public which is considered insider trading and is illegal. So all elected officials and their circle of friends and family financials should be closely monitored to prevent and stop the insider trading, and they should be prosecuted because it is based on privileged information that Congress needs to evaluate.

A proposed maximum income limit could be set at twice the median household income (which was $82,685 in 2024). This would ensure that those in leadership roles are more aligned with the financial realities of their constituents.

There should be no minimum income requirement to hold office, allowing individuals from various economic backgrounds especially those in lower-income brackets to enter public service and contribute diverse voices to politics.

Furthermore, anyone leaving office who becomes extremely wealthy should be subject to investigation, as it would suggest that they acted illegally during their tenure.

Many elected officials from both parties engage in insider trading while in office. It is highly questionable how someone earning a salary of $170,000 a year could amass $150 million over a career, especially considering that even a 40-year tenure in Congress would total just $7 million in cumulative salary.

To strike a balance between experience and fresh perspectives, age requirements and term limits for elected and appointed officials should be implemented.

Being a politician should not be seen as a career choice; rather, it should be viewed as a temporary opportunity for service aimed at improving the lives of constituents not just enriching the politicians themselves. The success of elected officials must be aligned with, but not exceed, the well-being of their constituents.

For elected positions, a minimum age requirement of 25 years would allow individuals to gain life experience and the opportunity to attain a master's degree if they choose that educational path. While a college degree could be beneficial, it should not be mandated before individuals assume leadership roles. Additionally, establishing a maximum age limit of 72 could encourage younger voices and fresh ideas in governance.

House of Representatives: Members could serve a maximum of three terms (totaling six years) and receive a lifetime pension of 50% of their average elected salary.

Senate: Senators could serve a maximum of two terms (totaling 12 years) and be eligible for a lifetime pension of 50% of their average elected salary.

This structure would allow for a cumulative maximum service of 18 years in Congress (six years in the House and 12 years in the Senate) or until individuals reach their 72nd birthday, whichever comes first. Importantly, individuals would receive only one pension, regardless of the offices they have held. Transitioning to the presidency would provide a former member only with the presidential retirement salary.

Public office should fundamentally be viewed as a role of service to constituents rather than a platform for power or privilege. Elected officials must recognize their accountability to the voters who elected them and placed their trust in them. The mantra, "It's not my way; it's their way," should resonate deeply among those in power.

This shift in perception would require elected officials to genuinely listen to their constituents, engage in open dialogue, and prioritize the public's needs over their personal ambitions. The authority of elected and appointed officials derives from the consent of the governed, and their decisions should reflect the will of their communities—not the interests of themselves or special interest groups. The true measure of an elected official's effectiveness should be their ability to respond to and serve the needs of their constituents.

To ensure accountability, effective mechanisms must be established for holding elected officials responsible for their actions. An accessible and efficient process for removing an elected official, such as a recall election, is essential. This would allow voters to initiate votes of confidence or no confidence with minimal bureaucratic hurdles.

Currently, recall elections cannot be used to remove federal officials, including the President, in the United States. The U.S. Constitution does not provide for recall elections at the federal level. Federal officers, including members of Congress and the President, can only be removed through impeachment (for the President, Vice President, and other civil officers) or by expulsion by their respective houses (for members of Congress).

Implementing these measures would empower constituents to remove unresponsive or ineffective representatives, reinforcing the notion that elected officials must remain aligned with public interests and accountable to their constituents.

Nineteen states allow for the recall of state-level officials, including governors, while thirty-nine states permit recall elections at local jurisdictions, such as counties and cities.

In a democratic society, officeholders must represent the citizenry. All candidates for elected office should be American citizens to strengthen their connection to national values and responsibilities. However, birthright citizenship should not be a requirement for holding any elected office, except for the presidency.

Furthermore, since the United States has no official language, speaking English should not be a prerequisite for holding elected or appointed office. Similar to the UN, translation services could be provided. However, politicians should be able to understand and communicate effectively with their constituents. Fluency in multiple languages is beneficial and can help representatives connect with all segments of their communities.

By implementing standards such as maximum income limits, age thresholds, term limits, and citizenship requirements, we can create a political structure that genuinely reflects the populace. Elected officials who understand the challenges faced by their constituents are more likely to develop policies that serve the needs of the majority rather than the elite. Politicians who can relate to their constituents will likely advocate for equality and inclusivity, working to combat food insecurity and promote health and safety programs.

While qualifications and capabilities should ultimately dictate who holds elected and appointed office, prioritizing candidates from lower-income to middle-class backgrounds—combined with specific safeguards— can lead to a more representative and equitable political landscape. By focusing on leaders who embody the aspirations and struggles of the broader citizenry, we can strive for a government that truly serves the people's interests, fosters trust, enriches decision-making, and strengthens democracy. Let us reaffirm that public office is a position of service, dedicated to improving society rather than personal gain. It's time to redefine representation in our political institutions for a better future for all.

Rethinking the Southern Border: A Practical, Humane Approach to U.S. Immigration

Immigration at the southern border is a complex policy challenge, not a slogan. The United States is dealing with an overstretched system, narrow and outdated legal pathways, and a political conversation that often substitutes heat for light. A workable approach can do several things at once: maintain control at the border, uphold due process, and expand lawful channels that match today's economic and humanitarian realities.

The most immediate problem is administrative capacity. There are not enough asylum officers, immigration judges, or support staff to handle current caseloads. The immigration court backlog surpassed three million cases by late 2023, according to TRAC's analysis of federal data, and USCIS has carried a large affirmative asylum backlog—hundreds of thousands of cases, approaching a million by some recent counts. When decisions take years, uncertainty grows for everyone and incentives tilt toward irregular crossings.

Legal channels are also out of sync with demand. In 2019, the United States granted just over one million lawful permanent resident visas (green cards). Roughly twothirds were familybased when counting both immediate relatives of U.S. citizens and familypreference categories; about 14 percent were employmentbased; the rest were primarily humanitarian and diversity visas. More than half of the recipients adjusted their status from within the United States rather than arriving directly from abroad. Tight numerical caps and percountry limits have produced long queues. By the late 2010s, about one million workers and family members in the United States were caught in employmentbased green card backlogs, and roughly 3.6 million people abroad were waiting in numerically limited family or employment categories. For nationals of highdemand countries such as India, employmentbased waits can stretch a decade or longer.

Regulatory changes can improve processing and fairness at the margins, but the larger truth is hard to avoid: congressional reform is likely necessary to replace the patchwork we have with a coherent system that channels the constructive power of immigration rather than disrupting it.

Recent years show how much the executive branch can influence legal flows within existing statutes. During the pandemic, visa issuance abroad collapsed. From April to September 2020—the final half of fiscal year 2020—the State Department issued about 398,000 nonimmigrant visas worldwide, compared with more than 5.6 million in the same sixmonth span in 2016, a drop of roughly 93 percent. Even before COVID19, from January 2017 through February 2020, monthly nonimmigrant visa issuances averaged about 12 percent lower than in January 2013 through February 2016, with cumulative issuance down a little over 14 percent. Comparing total visas issued abroad during the Trump years through November 2020 with Obama's second term, independent analysts estimate roughly 418,000 fewer immigrant visas (about an 18 percent decline) and about 11.2 million fewer nonimmigrant visas (about a 28 percent decline), with pandemic restrictions doing most of the work.

Refugee admissions fell to modern lows after annual cuts to the refugee ceiling under the Refugee Act of 1980. Admissions dropped from 84,995 in fiscal 2016 to about 11,800 in fiscal 2020. The episode underscored how much discretion presidents have over legal immigration within broad congressional delegations.

Order at the border depends on credible, timely, and fair procedures. More staffing and technology at ports of entry, better appointment and casemanagement tools, and handson application help can redirect movement into lawful channels and away from irregular crossings. Early evidence from CBP One appointment systems and targeted parole programs suggests that when people can access real, timely pathways, unauthorized entries fall and screening improves.

Work authorization rules also matter. Asylum applicants generally must wait at least 150 days to apply for employment authorization and 180 days before eligibility to receive it. Shortening that time paired with strong antifraud measures would reduce exploitation, improve compliance, and shift costs off local governments by allowing people to support themselves sooner.

Demography is destiny here. The United States has an aging workforce and fertility below replacement, with the total fertility rate in recent years in the mid1.6 range. The Social Security workertobeneficiary ratio has fallen below three workers per retiree. A large body of research, including the National Academies' comprehensive assessment, finds that immigration on average complements most native workers, boosts productivity, and strengthens entrepreneurship and innovation. Fiscal effects vary by level of government in the short run, but over the long term immigrants and their children make net positive contributions, including payroll taxes that support Social Security and Medicare.

Labor market signals point in the same direction. Demand for seasonal and temporary workers has climbed: the State Department issued about 196,000 H2A visas for agricultural work in 2018, up from roughly 11,000 in 1996; H2B nonagricultural seasonal visas grew from about 12,200 in 1996 to nearly 98,000 in 2018, with Congress often authorizing supplemental numbers. Demand for highskilled talent is intense. Between 2008 and 2020, the annual H1B cap was typically reached within the first five business days. U.S. colleges and universities have enrolled more than 600,000 international students annually since 2008–2009, topping one million in several prepandemic years, yet many graduates face prolonged waits for permanent residence because of numerical limits and percountry caps.

Constraints have realworld consequences. The Semiconductor Industry Association has warned of shortages of technicians, computer scientists, and engineers. TSMC's Arizona project faced delays and brought in experienced technicians from Taiwan amid local workforce gaps, pushing mass production to 2025. Innovation trends tell a related story: recent studies find immigrants founded or cofounded a large share of leading U.S. AI companies, and international students make up a substantial majority of graduate students in AIrelated fields. As economist Madeline Zavodny and others have noted, absent continued net inflows of immigrants, the U.S. workingage population will shrink over the next two decades, leaving the country with millions fewer workers by 2040 than in 2022. Highprofile layoffs and debates over artificial intelligence do not change the basic arithmetic: the United States needs additional workers across the skill spectrum, and international migration is the only reliable source of growth in the workingage population in the near term.

The United States hosts the largest number of international migrants in the world is about 50.6 million as of 2020, roughly 15 percent of the U.S. population and about 18 percent of the global migrant stock. Arrivals span more than 200 countries and territories. From 2011 to 2020, the United States admitted roughly 10.3 million lawful permanent residents; Mexico remained a major origin, though its share has declined as flows diversified.

The foreignborn population tracked by the Census Bureau hovered around 44–45 million in the late 2010s and rose to roughly 46 million by 2022–2023 as legal entries rebounded from pandemic lows and net migration increased. No president fully "controls" how many people attempt to migrate. Push factors economic crises, authoritarian rule, violence, disasters, and publichealth shocks—drive movement, while smugglers and migrants adjust routes in response to perceived policy openings. Venezuela's collapse has displaced more than seven million people since 2015; many moved through the hemisphere seeking protection and work. Violence and insecurity in parts of Mexico and Central America, along with changing smuggling networks, have also shaped timing and composition. That is why durable management requires regional cooperation on protection, legal pathways, and enforcement against traffickers.

Immigration policy in the United States is made through overlapping authorities. Congress sets most of the durable rules; presidents exercise wide discretion over enforcement priorities, refugee ceilings, parole, and admissions within statute; and states are central to integration and public safety. The years since 2017 have highlighted both the reach and the limits of executive action. Pandemic proclamations and reduced refugee ceilings showed how admissions can swing. Meanwhile, statefederal conflicts—highprofile enforcement initiatives in Texas, litigation over barriers and razor wire, and disputes over the scope of state authority—illustrate the tensions built into a federal system.

In early 2024, a bipartisan Senate package that paired border and asylum changes with foreign aid drew support from a crossparty group of senators but stalled after opposition in the House and from influential national figures. The episode underscored the core point: lasting fixes require legislation, resources, and coordination across levels of government.

A few basics help keep the debate grounded. Noncitizens cannot lawfully vote in federal elections; doing so is a federal crime and can trigger severe immigration consequences. Multiple studies find immigrants are at least as lawabiding as nativeborn residents and, in many places, have lower rates of criminal conviction or incarceration. Immigrants pay taxes, contribute to GDP, and are overrepresented among founders of highgrowth firms and patent holders. None of this minimizes real pressures at the border or in receiving communities, but it does argue for evidence over alarmism.

The system is fragmented and slow to adapt. Compared with a framework that prioritizes economic contributions while safeguarding families and humanitarian obligations, current rules constrain growth and create avoidable backlogs. Some fixes are squarely within executive authority—modernizing processing, targeting smugglers, expanding proven casemanagement programs, and speeding lawful work authorization with strong integrity checks. But the scale of today's challenge makes the larger path clear. Congress will need to recalibrate visa numbers, update percountry limits, invest in adjudication capacity, and better align refugee and labor pathways with U.S. commitments and needs. That is how to restore order with dignity.

American immigration policy has cycled between openness and exclusion. The periods that worked best paired values with pragmatism: real legal pathways that fit economic reality, timely and fair adjudication, and a steady focus on public safety. That remains the right formula.

The United States can have both secure borders and a fair immigration system. Expand lawful avenues that people can actually use. Protect due process and adjudicate cases swiftly. Focus enforcement on real security threats and criminal networks. Work with partners in the region to address the conditions that drive displacement. Do those things, and the country will manage migration more effectively while staying true to its laws and its ideals.

The Minimum Wage Debate: Bridging the Gap to Economic Justice

The ongoing discussion around minimum wage and labor rights intersects with a variety of systemic issues affecting marginalized communities, including racial and xenophobic biases that distort public perceptions and policy. Currently, the federal minimum wage stands at $7.25, unchanged since 2009. This wage starkly contrasts with living wage standards across the United States, highlighting a significant gap that leaves many workers in economic hardship. For example, in Mississippi, the lowest estimated living wage is around $45,906 annually, translating to approximately $22 per hour. This inadequate wage not only fails to meet basic living standards but also perpetuates economic hardship, pushing many workers, disproportionately from marginalized backgrounds, into cycles of poverty.

The Living Wage Discrepancy,

Understanding the implications of the federal minimum wage reveals the stark realities faced by low-wage workers. At $7.25 an hour, a full-time worker, assuming 40 hours a week earns approximately $15,080 annually before taxes. For a single person, this equates to roughly $1,257 per month or $294 per week.

Challenges for single individuals and Families: Living on a minimum wage salary poses insurmountable challenges, particularly for individuals supporting families.

Housing: Rent for a modest apartment can easily exceed $700-$1,500 per month, consuming more than half of a minimum wage worker's income.

Food: A reasonable grocery budget might be around $200-$300 per individual monthly, leaving little for other necessities.

Healthcare: Without health insurance or Medicaid even basic medical care can be financially crippling.

Transportation: Public transit or car ownership introduces additional costs, further straining limited resources.

For parents and caregivers, financial constraints become even tighter, turning basic survival into an ongoing struggle.

Dependence on Welfare Programs:
An essential outcome of adopting a living wage would be a substantial reduction or near elimination of dependence on various welfare programs, including the Supplemental Nutrition Assistance Program (SNAP), Temporary Assistance for Needy Families (TANF), the Women, Infants, and Children (WIC) program, the Children's Health Insurance Program (CHIP), the Low-Income Home Energy Assistance Program (LIHEAP), housing assistance, and Medicaid. Many individuals earning a minimum wage currently rely on these programs to supplement their low incomes and provide for their families.

Research indicates that for every dollar increase in the minimum wage, public spending on welfare programs decreases, resulting in significant savings for taxpayers. Transitioning to a living wage could reduce welfare spending by tens of billions of dollars annually. If low-wage earners receive adequate compensation, the government could redirect those savings to address other pressing social needs.

Stereotypes and Misconceptions
The narratives surrounding low-wage jobs are often steeped in stereotypes that misrepresent the realities of the workforce. Public figures like President Donald Trump have suggested that immigrants are taking jobs from Black Americans, reinforcing harmful beliefs that characterize low-wage labor as primarily filled by non-native workers. This rhetoric distorts the reality of who works these jobs and fuels public anxieties about wage increases, creating a political environment resistant to necessary reforms.

The idea that the federal minimum wage should remain stagnant is supported by factions who believe that maintaining low wages keeps particular populations vulnerable and controllable a notion that echoes historical practices of exploitation. Comparisons have been drawn between the indignities faced by low-wage workers and slavery. While the conditions differ, the underlying theme of exploitation persists: the current wage structure serves as a means of economic bondage.

Proposing Solutions: Raising the Minimum Wage: To address these pressing issues, a foundational change in wage structures is crucial. One viable proposal is to establish a minimum starting pay of $15.00 per hour, not a living wage. However, this wage represents a significant step toward achieving a living wage for workers across the nation.

Implementing a Cost of Living Adjustment (COLA): In conjunction with raising the minimum wage, implementing a Cost of Living Adjustment (COLA) program is essential. This program, similar to the military's compensation framework, would provide additional funds to employees through checks or direct deposits, helping bridge the gap between earned wages and the lowest local living wage standards.

For instance, military wages are established based on rank and include support through the COLA, which ensures personnel can maintain an adequate standard of living irrespective of their location. This structured system could serve as a potential template for civilian wage policies that adapt to regional economic realities.

Addressing minimum wage and labor rights is not just about economic calculations; it is a matter of social justice and human dignity. The current federal minimum wage fails to reflect living realities, particularly for marginalized communities. By raising the minimum wage to $15.00 per hour and implementing a Cost of Living Adjustment, we can take significant steps toward dismantling the cycle of poverty and promoting economic equity.

The struggle to survive on $7.25 an hour not only perpetuates poverty but also underscores the urgent need for reform.

Comparing the economic constraints faced by today's low-wage workers to slavery highlights a discomforting truth: when work fails to provide a means of subsistence, it strips individuals of dignity and agency.

It is time to advocate for a wage structure that is not only fair but also upholds the fundamental rights of all laborers. Understanding these issues is paramount for fostering a more equitable society where every worker can thrive. Together, we can reframe the narratives surrounding labor, ensuring that all workers are afforded the dignity and respect they deserve in the workplace.

When those at or below the poverty level have to rely on outside assistance for food clothing and housing they are scapegoats for the middle and upper class who are getting the perks off of paying their staff one third of the poverty rate.

If that wasn't enough the upper and middle class demand huge tax breaks that require cutting the programs they rely on to cover their greed allowing them to pay below the minimum wage.

If the government raised the minimum wage to a living wage everyone would benefit. The lower wage earners would not need assistance and they would begin paying taxes. The government revenue from federal taxes would increase. The upper and middle classes would have loyalty and people would increase productivity.

Generational Prejudice

So to make this simple without reading the article:

Everyone practices Generational Prejudice. It is an acceptable behavior and trait in our society.

Resolution: Stop being a Dick to someone because of the year they were born. Please get to know the individual, what they know, who they are, and so on. Generation Prejudice cheats you out of most things you need and want to know.

To the moral failings of bigotry, we should add generational prejudice.

People should not be defined by the color of their skin, the faith tradition in which they were raised, whether their genotype is XX or XY, or the generation into which they were born.

The goal in learning about others is not to dismiss them but to get to know them – not just as members of some category or class, but as distinctive human beings who, given the opportunity, can likely defy our expectations.

If you had to name three characteristics of Millennials, Baby Boomers, or Gen Zers right now, you probably could.

However, your generalizations may be born mainly from prejudice.

They're not just unhelpful; they influence everything from how we perceive and treat our colleagues to how we design processes at work.

Generational Prejudice bears many similarities to other forms of discrimination, and its effects are no less pernicious. It stigmatizes a whole group of people simply by an accident of birth. Millennials (1981-2000) are typically characterized as me-first, self-absorbed, and technophilic. Gen Xers (1966-1980) are suspicious of authority, pampered, and operate with a sense of entitlement. Baby Boomers (1945-1965) are perceived to be the cause of all that is wrong today...

Likewise, the Traditionalists (before 1946), who until recently ran most such organizations, were said to be too risk-averse, linear and uncreative in their thinking, and excessively deferential to authority.

Generation Prejudices are dangerous in part because they can become a self-fulfilling prophecy, a false understanding of a situation that evokes attitudes and behaviors that cause it to become true.

Convinced that members of other generations just don't get it, seniors may fail to challenge junior colleagues in ways that could contribute to their professional growth.

Such prejudices can also short-circuit the sharing of perspectives between people of different generations, who might otherwise learn something valuable from each other that could enhance their work.

The notion that age tells us all we need to know about a person or group of people is dubious.

To be sure, a 15-year-old is likely more adept than a 55-year-old at texting or posting an entry on a social media site.

A 75-year-old is more likely to have military experience than a 25-year-old.

But such generalizations and prejudices gloss over far more interesting interpersonal differences in domains such as culture, life experience, temperament, and character. We cannot reliably predict that a member of any generation is more diligent, creative, or loyal than another simply by age.

Such generalizations are biased and invalidated all the time.

Allen Ginsberg, perhaps the best-known of the beat poets and the author of Howl, qualified as a Traditionalist.

Many of the most prominent figures in the rise of Silicon Valley, including Bill Gates and Steve Jobs, were Baby Boomers, a group supposedly reluctant to change and blamed for all the problems today.

To be human is to be tempted to categorize, pigeonhole, and have prejudiced beliefs against people, to adopt shortcuts that relieve us of the burden of really getting to know and understand those around us.

In the end, it represents a lamentable form of sloth. To save ourselves the trouble of finding out for ourselves, to justify our uneasy sense of self-worth, or to gorge on the forbidden fruit of presumed superiority and self-satisfaction, we pretend that highly heterogeneous people are all alike.

Gen X, which is marked by a resistance to sharing information, includes Twitter founder Jack Dorsey.

Generational Predjudices, who benefits from them, and why do we like to place people into buckets?

The year is 2005. The first cohort of Millennials is stepping into the workforce. And the business world has plenty to celebrate: The economy is booming, job offers are plentiful and competitive, and technology is advancing faster than ever.

The goal is to bring in fresh faces and new ideas and drop the old-fashioned ways and the people who initiated them.

It sounds like a youthful happily ever after. But there was a plot twist:

Report after report emphasized how many Baby Boomers and Gen Xers <u>needed to change</u> to accommodate this new generation of <u>lazy, entitled, and disloyal</u> workers and how these young folks would disrupt the workplace as we knew it.

The media latched on to these prejudices, reporting that <u>Millennials wanted more "me" time on the job</u>, <u>only took "yes" for an answer</u>, and let their parents assume a peculiarly <u>active role in their professional lives</u>.

As a result, company leaders and senior employees did change, <u>creating processes and policies based on these prejudices</u>. Ping-Pong tables and beer on tap became priorities, <u>constant feedback</u> the gold standard, and <u>work-life balance</u> more important than meaningful career progression.

We put things in buckets to make sense of them. According to <u>Michael Kramer</u>, former chair of the department of communication at the University of Oklahoma, "Humans naturally seek simplified explanations for their own and others' behavior through a process of sensemaking, especially during uncertain times. Constructing and adopting prejudices is one way of doing that."

Bobby Duffy, a professor and the author of <u>The Generation Myth: Why When You're Born Matters Less Than You Think</u>, agrees. "We like stories about who we are and who we're not, and we like to categorize everything into what it is and what it's not," he told us. These stories are appealing, especially when they're vivid and memorable, with labels and anecdotes behind them. "And that's certainly what's happened with generational prejudices," he added.

All of this makes us feel closer to the people of our generation.

We feel that when we are born matters because there is a sense of connection to our peers…They have gone through what we have gone through. It feels intuitive. And it works well as shorthand communication in headlines or when we want to summarize complex things in simple labels.

Companies that are nervous or unsure about leading a particular generation— particularly when the media is putting them on high alert — may rely on generational labels as shortcuts for engaging and attracting those workers.

Leaders sometimes use prejudices as scapegoats when something isn't working. "When you believe that it's not your fault as an employer — that it's just whatever generation you choose to blame that in your workforce and the employer feels placing unreasonable demands on them— they shift the blame onto that generation" instead of understanding and addressing the root issue.

Rosy retrospection plagues us. Cognitive psychologist Gordon Bower found that our memories are reconstructed when we recall them — a process prone to manipulation and errors. Various types of memory prejudices can affect our decision-making in both positive and negative ways. Rosy retrospection, or declinism, is one such bias: It refers to our tendency to minimize the negatives, leading us to view things more positively.

Coupled with generational prejudices, we feel the current situation is dreadful; clearly, whatever generation we blame is at fault and will change everything.

When we look for someone to blame, any cohort could conveniently fit the bill.

Generational stereotypes have created a cottage industry. From books to podcasts to consultancies, there are many lucrative reasons to assert that generational prejudices do, indeed, exist and are central to the workplace.

There is a whole industry around generations and each generation's prejudices.

Because managers believe they must adapt their approaches for different generation practices— and are unsure about how to do that — they often seek help that can provide insights and guidance. As a result, "companies go out and hire <u>generational prejudice experts</u> to come in and clean up intergenerational conflicts

It was not cheap. As of a few years ago, some consultants were <u>charging $20,000</u> to $30,000 per hour, and <u>Source Global Research</u> estimated that U.S. organizations spent $60 million to $70 million on <u>generational prejudice consulting</u> in 2015 alone. The long-term success of such efforts remains to be seen (we're still debating if <u>Millennials will ever get the workplace they want</u>). Meanwhile, generational prejudice consulting <u>related to Gen Z</u> has become popular. At the same time, Baby Boomers are receiving less attention because they are transitioning out of the workforce.

Is it so bad that companies try to leverage popular insights to win over every generation at work?

Well, yes. We're basing a lot of prejudicial generation practices and our decisions, a lot of policies, and a lot of approaches in the workplace on pretty shaky science.

It can negatively affect employees. A <u>LinkedIn poll</u> was posted asking people if being part of a generation of prejudice influences how they're treated at work. Sixty percent of respondents said it did.

How The Republicans Are Responsible For The Destruction of The American Economy

At one time, our currency was backed by silver and gold, and the US could not print currency or mint coins unless it had the gold and silver in the Federal Reserve to back them.

Our paper money used to have silver or gold certificates written across the top.

This system limited the amount of currency that could be produced. With fewer bills and coins in circulation, the value of our money increases. As a result, because a dollar holds significant value, products and services are sold at lower prices.

Circulation of Money indicates that when there are fewer bills and coins in circulation, the scarcity of the currency leads to an increase in its value. This is similar to the economic principle of supply and demand. When a commodity is scarce, its worth typically rises.

The value of Money means that a stronger dollar allows consumers to buy more with each currency unit. This increased purchasing power tends to lower prices for goods and services, as sellers adjust their pricing to the higher value of money.

Overall economic impact suggests that by limiting the amount of currency, this system can help maintain a stable financial environment and avoid the adverse effects of inflation, which causes prices to rise and the purchasing power of money to decrease.

A limited currency supply can increase the value per currency unit, allowing consumers to purchase goods and services at lower prices.

After Democrats won unified control of Congress and the presidency in the 1912 elections, President Wilson, Congressman Carter Glass, and Senator Robert Latham Owen crafted a central banking bill, the Federal Reserve Act, establishing a central banking system to stabilize the dollar's value.

The Federal Reserve Act created a national currency and a monetary system that could respond effectively to the stresses in the banking system and create a stable financial system. To create a national economic system and financial stability.

The Federal Reserve Act also provided many other economic functions and financial services, such as check clearing and collection for all members of the Federal Reserve.

With the passing of the Federal Reserve Act, Congress required that all nationally chartered banks become members of the Federal Reserve System.

In June 1917, the Democratic President and Congress passed significant amendments to the Act to enable monetary expansion to cover the expected costs of World War I.

The amendment allowed a more flexible definition of the gold backing the dollar currency in circulation. This relaxation de facto allowed less gold backing for each dollar note. It enabled the currency in circulation to double from $465 million to $1.247 billion just from June to December 1917.

The Federal Reserve was given control to regulate inflation, even though the government's control over such powers would eventually lead to controversial decisions.

Some of the most prominent implications of the Federal Reserve include the internationalization of the U.S. Dollar as a global currency and the impact of the perception of the Central Bank structure as a public good by creating a system of financial stability.

Under FDR, a Democrat, the international monetary system established after World War II was dubbed the Bretton Woods system after forty-four countries met in Bretton Woods, New Hampshire 1944.

The countries agreed to keep their currencies fixed (but adjustable in exceptional situations) to the dollar, which was fixed to gold.

Since 1958, when the Bretton Woods system became operational, countries settled their international balances in dollars, and U.S. dollars were convertible to gold at a fixed exchange rate of $35 an ounce.

The United States was responsible for keeping the dollar price of gold fixed and adjusting the supply of dollars to maintain confidence in future gold convertibility worldwide.

The Bretton Woods system initially operated as planned. Japan and Europe were still rebuilding their postwar economies, and demand for U.S. goods, services, and dollars was high.

The system seemed secure since the United States held about three-quarters of the world's official gold reserves.

Richard Nixon, a Republican, decided to delink the dollar from gold, which he announced without warning in August 1971. His action instantly remade the global monetary system.

With the ability to create unlimited currency and coins, inflation skyrocketed, and GDP plummeted.

This is why a nickel loaf of bread is now $4.

What the Republicans wanted was some way to devalue the dollar, but because it was pegged to gold, the administration couldn't do that.

Under Republican control, August 15, 1971, was the precise date on which America's singular dominance of the world economy ended.

Nixon, with the backing of the elected Republicans, decided that the dollar would no longer be backed by gold.

To cover up the aftermath, Richard Nixon imposed a 90-day wage-price freeze in the U.S. to curb inflation and a 10% tariff on all imports.

The Economic Rollercoaster, the price of goods and services, took a steep ride up and hasn't dipped much since.

So now, Federal Reserve notes can be made without backing other than a government promise.

In simple terms, the more money you print, the more currency is in circulation and the higher the inflation rate.

The more currency in circulation, the less value the currency has.

The Lower the value of money, the higher the cost of goods.

The lower the wages, the more currency drops per employed person.

The higher the inflation grows

The lower the wage is, the more significant the gap between the rich and the poor.

Now for the drastic changes

In 1981, "Reaganomics" was the most serious attempt by any administration since the New Deal to change the course of U.S. economic policy.

Trickle-down Economics was touted as an enormous economic booster for everyone. However, it was the most prominent political hoax ever perpetrated against everyone but the businesses and the elite.

Trickle Down Economics is such a flop that Social Security would be left alone

The changes to the federal tax code for the top one percent were much more substantial. The top marginal tax rate on individual income was reduced from 70 percent to 28 percent.

The corporate income tax rate was reduced from 48 percent to 34 percent.

Reagan eased or eliminated price controls on oil and natural gas, cable TV, long-distance telephone service, interstate bus service, and ocean shipping. This Is Why Gas Stays Around $4.00 A Gallon Today.

Banks were allowed to invest in a broader set of assets, and the scope of the <u>antitrust</u> laws was reduced. The major exception to this pattern was a substantial increase in import barriers.

The Reagan administration did not propose changes in the legislation affecting health, safety, and the environment, but it reduced the number of new regulations under the existing laws.

Woodrow Wilson (Democrat)

1916-1917 Tax Rate For The Highest Income 67%.

1918-1923 Wealthy Tax Rate 77%

Calvin Coolidge (Republican)

1924 46% Tax On The Rich

1925-1932 27% Tax On The Wealthy

Herbert Hoover (Democrat)

1933-1935 Tax on the rich 63%

FDR (Democrat)

1936-1943 Tax The Rich 79%

Harry Truman (Democrat)

1944-1959 Tax 94% on $200,000 and above.

JFK (Democrat), LBJ (Democrat), Nixon (Republican), Ford (Republican), Carter (Democrat)

1960-1980 Tax Rate For The Rich 70%

I bet you know what's coming next.

Reagonomics

Reagan (Republican)

1981 Wealthy Taxed 50%

1982-1990 Wealthy Paid 28%

George H.W. Bush (Republican)

1991-1992 Wealthy Tax Rate 31%

Bill Clinton

1993-2000 Wealthy Taxes Paid 39.6%

George Bush Jr. (Republican)

2001-2012 Rich Tax Rate 35%

Obama (Democrat)

2013-2017 Tax Rate For The Rich 39.6%

Trump (Republican)

2018-2023 Wealthy Tax Rate 37%

The tax rate on anyone making one million or more should never exceed 70%. All loopholes, deductions, and credits should be closed and removed.

After the deductions, loopholes, and credïts to which the rich are entitled are taken, there isn't much taxable income left. Some owe as little as $500, and a few owe nothing.

Has anyone else noticed that the poor and middle class do not qualify for many if there are any deductions?

Unless you consider EIC, People with kids get a deduction.

To sum it all up, Nixon, Reagan, and Trump destroyed the American Economy:

Nixon devalued the dollar, which caused inflation to go out of control.

Reagan, with a trickle-down, made the rich richer and the poor poorer, and started stealing from the Social Security reserve to replace the money the rich did not pay, and to meet the government budget needs

Trump repeated the trickle-down that made the rich richer and the poor poorer and again started stealing from the Social Security reserve to replace the money the rich did not pay and to meet the government budget needs

---

Corporate Greed Will Undermine And Destroy Any Democracy: Time To Hold The Elite Accountable

In a landscape marked by pervasive inequality and systemic issues, it has become increasingly clear that the burgeoning wealth of the elite demands scrutiny and concerted action.

As billionaires accumulate unprecedented wealth with over two trillion dollars enriched since 2019 largely through tax cuts benefiting the wealthy during the first Trump administration the question arises:

Why should we allow a select few to hoard wealth while the majority of the population struggles to make ends meet?

It's time to challenge our socioeconomic frameworks that enable this disparity and advocate for policies compelling the wealthy to contribute to the common good, addressing crises largely perpetuated by corporate greed all within a framework of democracy and equitable opportunity.

When individuals accumulate wealth exceeding the limits of what they and their descendants can utilize, a moral obligation emerges.

Billionaires to do business in the United States should be required to embody a sense of responsibility to society, particularly towards their employees and consumers, many of whom are often denied a living wage.

Instead of rewarding their workforce and contributing meaningfully to the community, too many wealthy individuals resort to union-busting tactics and corporate strategies designed to maximize profits at the expense of their staff. Price hikes and profit doubling can become the norm, resulting in a detrimental cycle that exacerbates socio-economic divides.

In discussions of wealth inequality, it's important to consider the significant financial disparities that define the landscape of the American economy.

While the term "monopoly" traditionally applies to market structures where a single entity dominates supply and pricing, the concentration of wealth among the elite can resemble monopolistic power in its effects on society.

Recent data highlights that the wealthiest segment of the population holds an overwhelming share of national assets.

The top 50% of earners in the United States control approximately $156 trillion, a figure that exceeds 88% of the country's total wealth.

This leaves the bottom 50%, which owns only about $4 trillion, in a markedly precarious position. Among these wealth holders, the top 1% or approximately 1.3 million households individually command nearly $49 trillion, representing about one-third of the entire national wealth.

This staggering wealth concentration underscores the difficulties faced by lower-income households in achieving upward mobility and financial stability.

While the elite do not fit the traditional governmental definition of a monopoly, their extensive financial resources yield considerable influence over economic policies and outcomes, potentially affecting market competition and living standards for the broader population.

Such disparities raise vital questions about the fairness and functionality of our economic system. They compel us to examine the mechanisms that facilitate this wealth accumulation and the implications it has for democracy and social equity.

True success in a democracy should not be defined solely by financial accumulation but by the positive impact, one can have on society.

A Responsible capitalist would achieve their financial goals and then redirect their efforts toward philanthropy and improvements in the lives of others.

However, many choose the path of political involvement with ulterior motives, pushing agendas that undermine the public interest. The emergence of billionaires, such as Donald Trump and Elon Musk, in politics demands vigilance; how can we trust individuals who have garnered immense wealth while promising to serve the public for a fraction of their earnings?

Unchecked corporate greed coupled with the overwhelming influence of the top 1% is not merely an economic concern it poses an existential threat to our democracy.

When wealth becomes concentrated in the hands of a few individuals or corporations, the fundamental tenets of democracy, equality, representation, and accountability are undermined. Elites wield disproportionate power over the political landscape, enabling them to manipulate democratic processes to their advantage.

As we witness figures like President Trump and Musk who blatantly defy court orders and constantly violate our constitutional rights since becoming prominent voices, their vast resources allow them to sway public opinion, influence legislation, and perpetuate a narrative that serves corporate interests.

This concentration of power erodes the diversity of voices essential for a functioning democracy. Political decisions increasingly reflect the whims of billionaires, sidelining the needs and concerns of everyday citizens.

Furthermore, the lack of accountability for such individuals fosters a cash-and-grab society. When wealth and influence go unchecked, the ethical boundaries that typically govern business operations blur.

Decisions made in boardrooms and with politicians prioritize short-term financial gain over the long-term health of communities and the environment.

This greed-driven mentality not only exacerbates economic inequalities but also cultivates a culture of cynicism and disengagement among the populace.

When citizens perceive that their voices and votes do not matter against the backdrop of unchecked corporate influence, trust in democratic institutions erodes, leading to increased polarization and instability.

This moment calls for a reevaluation of our economic priorities. For instance, consider that with $162.5 million, we could significantly address the nation's homeless crisis through innovative housing solutions. Moreover, ending hunger in the United States would only require approximately $25 billion, according to estimates from Joel Berg, CEO of Hunger Free America. This figure accounts for ensuring adequate nutrition for all Americans while also addressing related factors like poverty and unemployment.

Ending hunger would yield broader positive effects, such as reduced healthcare costs, improved educational outcomes, and increased economic productivity. A 2020 Hunger Report illustrates that the U.S. spends $160 billion annually on healthcare costs driven by food insecurities. This statistic underscores the urgent need for comprehensive solutions:

Investing in the well-being of citizens can lead to substantial savings for the healthcare system and strengthen the economy.

Critics often express concerns about assisting those in need, arguing that it is unfair to those who pay for their homes or basic needs. However, the reality is that stable housing and adequate nutrition help foster economic participation and consumerism. When individuals have a place to live and food to eat, they are more likely to invest in their communities, boosting local economies and creating a thriving middle class. In contrast, those without stable housing or access to nutritious food cannot contribute as they should leading to diminished purchasing power and a stagnating economy.

An essential aspect of addressing corporate greed and ensuring fair treatment for employees is the mandatory establishment of independent, outside unions that advocate for workers' rights.

These unions would play a crucial role in representing employees across all sectors, negotiating fair wages, and advocating for improved working conditions and benefits.

By being organized collectively, employees can exert pressure on corporations to recognize their rights and prioritize their well-being.

Outside unions can serve as powerful advocates for employees, enabling them to voice their grievances, negotiate for better standards of living, and hold their employers accountable.

This representation not only empowers workers but also helps to balance the power dynamics within companies, ensuring that employee interests are considered in decision-making processes.

When employees are collectively represented, businesses are compelled to acknowledge their needs, leading to a healthier workplace culture, increased productivity, and ultimately enhancing the overall economy as well.

Capitalists would not lose any money or profits by paying their employees a comfortable living wage. Paying a living wage would actually increase their profits.

The more expendable income workers have, the more buying power they gain, ultimately leading to a higher accumulation of wants and needs.

Increased purchasing power aligns with corporate interests, as satisfied consumers drive demand and boost profits. Yet the prevailing attitude among the wealthy often revolves around power and control rather than genuine consideration for the well-being of their employees.

Currently, only 56% of full-time workers in the U.S. are earning a living wage, while 44% struggle to cover their families' basic needs, according to the inaugural Dayforce Living Wage Index. This alarming statistic emphasizes the disconnect between corporate profits and employee welfare and highlights the urgent need for change in our compensation structures.

As active participants in a democracy, we hold significant power. One of the most effective ways to challenge the dominance of billionaires and abusive corporate practices is through strategic boycotts. Companies whose leaders are worth billions must be held accountable for their practices. By redirecting our purchasing power, we signal to these corporations that the public demands responsibility, equity, and ethical behavior. We must raise our voices against those who exploit the system for their gain while disregarding the struggles of everyday people. A concerted effort to boycott can serve as a robust statement against greed and push for systemic changes, urging lawmakers to create regulations that require the wealthy to give back.

By opting to support businesses that prioritize fair wages, ethical labor practices, and community investment, we can foster a marketplace that values integrity over sheer profit.

The simple act of choosing where to spend our money is a potent tool in shifting corporate behaviors. Collective action can create ripple effects, encouraging companies to adopt more socially responsible practices, lest they find themselves on the receiving end of consumer backlash.

The dangers of unchecked corporate greed and the influence of the top 1% cannot be overstated. As we grapple with crises stemming from economic inequality, environmental degradation, and erosion of democratic principles, we must advocate for policies compelling the wealthy to contribute to solutions, all within the framework of democracy.

By supporting independent unions that advocate for employee well-being and holding billionaires accountable through boycotts, we can pave the way for a fairer, more just society. Our collective action can dismantle the barriers erected by corporate greed and generate a new economic landscape where the wealth generated by society is shared more equitably.

The call for billionaires to give back isn't just a plea for fairness; it is a necessity for a sustainable future. Let us embrace a system that champions democratic values while ensuring that those at the top also do their part. A truly responsible capitalist should not merely seek profit but strive to elevate the very fabric of society. Together, we can demand a world where the wealthy use their resources to uplift others, truly embodying the principles of social responsibility and equity that are essential for building a better future for all.

Ending corporate greed and implementing laws that require corporations to reinvest a portion of their profits into society is essential, especially in light of the prevailing greed demonstrated by the top 1% of the population and its social consequences.

Government mandates aimed at curtailing corporate behavior would not only mitigate negative impacts, such as environmental degradation and wage stagnation, but would also promote consumer spending, ultimately benefiting the economy as a whole.

Regulating corporations and fostering a culture of social responsibility will help build public trust. When companies are held accountable and forced to visibly contribute to societal well-being, it enhances their reputation and encourages customer loyalty both of which are vital for long-term success and sustainability.

Investing in sustainable practices and community development can also spur innovation. Such investments not only address pressing societal challenges but can also lead to economic growth in emerging sectors, creating new job opportunities and fostering a healthier ecosystem.

Corporate greed is a leading contributor to income and wealth inequality. Enforcing regulations that mandate corporate investment in social programs can help level the playing field, reducing disparities and contributing to a more equitable society.

Requiring corporations to reinvest some of their profits into society through regulatory frameworks, as well as addressing tax obligations, is not merely a moral imperative; it is a necessary strategy for fostering a sustainable and equitable economy. It will also ensure we have a healthy operating and functional Democracy.

Holding businesses accountable for their actions and the roles they play in environmental degradation, income inequality, and public health issues will also restore faith in our elected officials by ensuring they serve their constituents rather than succumbing to financial influence.

We must ensure that the benefits of economic activity are shared broadly, leading to a healthier society, a secure Democracy, and a more resilient economy.

The condition of our Democracy today is that we are on the verge of a total collapse. Why? Just so that the greed and entitlement of 1.3 million people get their way, which is hoarding wealth, power, and control.

Ending Homelessness: A Comprehensive Approach for a Lasting Solution

Homelessness is a pressing issue that demands a multifaceted, coordinated approach. Many people experience the cycle of being unable to get a job without a stable home, and vice versa. To address this, we need a network of accessible addresses that also house active phone numbers, facilitating communication for those seeking employment and housing.

Essential services such as healthy food options and appropriate clothing are crucial in making a difference. A well-balanced diet, rather than one high in fat, starch, and cholesterol, is vital for improving overall health and employability. The age-old adage "dress for success" highlights the importance of presentability when seeking work opportunities.

Additionally, communities should provide private shower booths, even if you only offer cold water, spread throughout the city to help individuals maintain personal hygiene. This type of access can dramatically improve self-esteem and the chances of gainful employment.

Reflecting on personal experience from the 1980s, I faced a similar plight after being laid off and relocating to California. Lacking a home address hindered my ability to secure job interviews. Lacking a job kept me from securing a residence. Back then, cell phones weren't a thing, making it even more challenging to network for opportunities.

In a last-ditch effort, I used my last $40 to rent a mailbox, designating it with an apartment number. This provided me with an address I could use on applications. By parking near a payphone that accepted incoming calls, I established a makeshift home phone line. I utilized the public outdoor showers on the beach for bathing and washed clothes in the public restroom sinks.

Although the journey was difficult and took about eight months, I eventually secured employment and began the process of finding stable housing.

This story showcases the potential effectiveness of implementing comprehensive solutions to homelessness. Establishing systems that facilitate job training, mental health resources, and stable housing can empower individuals, helping them regain dignity and independence.

As communities work to create real change, incorporating job training programs and affordable housing initiatives will foster stability. Increasing access to healthcare ensures that individuals can prioritize their well-being. With collaborative efforts, we can also enhance availability for food security, reliable communication, and personal hygiene facilities.

Ending homelessness goes beyond momentary relief; it encompasses building pathways for individuals to thrive. When we recognize the challenges and invest in sustainable solutions, we can ensure that many, like the individual from the 1980s, can rebuild their lives and successfully re-enter society.

Scapegoated and Shortchanged

How Low-Income Families Are Punished by Policy, Business Practices, and Everyday Gatekeeping

Government assistance programs like SNAP, TANF, Medicaid, and housing support aim to help low-income individuals and families, but they are often criticized for perpetuating a system where large corporations can pay wages below a living standard. This dynamic can lead to workers relying on government aid to fill the income gap, effectively allowing corporations to boost profits by keeping labor costs low. As a result, taxpayers, including the middle class, bear the financial burden of subsidizing the cost of living for low-wage workers, which can contribute to ongoing poverty and economic inequality.

In a country where working full-time can still leave a family hungry or homeless, people who rely on assistance for food, clothing, or shelter are routinely cast as the problem rather than the predictable outcome of the problem.

Those earning minimum wage are scapegoated in political speeches, policed at checkout lines, and buried under paperwork at government offices all while many employers and policymakers quietly benefit from the very conditions that force these families to seek help in the first place. The result is a cycle: low wages push people to public programs, those programs are stigmatized and targeted for cuts, and the same low-wage model persists, subsidized by taxpayers and enforced by policy choices and institutional practices that keep assistance users perpetually looking for aid.

Plenty of people work hard and still can't make rent or buy enough food. They get help just to survive, then get blamed for needing it. Meanwhile, businesses and politicians benefit from the setup that keeps pay low. Taxpayers end up covering basics that paychecks should cover, and the system keeps repeating.

When wages don't meet basic needs, means-tested assistance backfills the gap, and a significant share of the economic benefit is captured by employers and asset owners, not the families forced to navigate stigma and red tape. The public pays twice: once at low retail prices achieved through suppressed labor costs, and again through taxes that fund the safety net. Meanwhile, assistance users are blamed for needing help that the system itself makes unavoidable.

When jobs don't pay enough, the government steps in. That help keeps workers alive but it also lets some companies keep wages low. We all pay for this in taxes, and then we're told to be mad at the people getting help instead of the low wages that made help necessary.

Assistance is not a moral failing; it is a predictable response to pay that lags far behind local costs. When employers offer wages that don't cover rent, food, transportation, childcare, and healthcare, workers turn to SNAP, Medicaid, housing vouchers, and tax credits to survive. That reliance is not rare or fringe. Most benefit recipients are often employed in essential roles in caregiving, retail, hospitality, logistics, and food service, where hours are unstable and schedules unpredictable.

Needing help doesn't mean someone did something wrong. If a job doesn't pay enough to cover basics like rent and food, people turn to programs like food stamps (SNAP), Medicaid, and housing help. Lots of folks on these programs are working, often in the jobs we all rely on, like caregivers, store workers, and delivery drivers, but their pay and hours are shaky.

Below-minimum pay also happens in practice. Wage theft, off-the-clock labor, misclassification, unpaid overtime, and legal loopholes keep effective wages below statutory floors with little risk to violators. Even when employers follow the letter of the law, a sub-living wage shifts basic labor costs onto the public: taxpayers buy groceries, fund healthcare, and help pay rent for workers whose paychecks don't stretch.

Some companies break the rules making people work off the clock, not paying overtime, or calling employees "contractors" to dodge benefits. Even when they don't break the law, paying too little means the public has to make up the difference through government programs.

This transfer is sizable. Analyses from the UC Berkeley Labor Center estimate that taxpayers spend well over $100 billion annually on major public programs supporting working families costs that, in a higher-wage equilibrium, would be borne by employers and customers rather than the public. Research on Medicaid and SNAP confirms that a large share of adult enrollees live in working households, especially in low-wage industries.

This isn't small change. Taxpayers spend over a hundred billion dollars a year helping working families because their jobs don't pay enough. Many adults on Medicaid or SNAP are in families where someone works, especially in lower-paying industries.

Public debate often fixates on the person with the EBT card instead of the pay stub that made the card necessary. Shaming benefits users disguises the structural math: if full-time work doesn't cover basic needs, assistance is a rational necessity. It also obscures who truly benefits. Low consumer prices and higher corporate margins are underwritten when taxpayers pick up the tab for workers' essentials. In this sense, safety-net programs function as a quiet subsidy to low-wage business models.

People get shamed for using benefits cards, but the real issue is paychecks that don't cover the basics. When taxpayers cover food and healthcare, it lets companies keep wages low and prices low. That's basically a hidden subsidy for low-wage business models.

Anti-fraud rhetoric further muddies the waters. While intentional fraud exists, many so-called "improper payments" arise from complex rules and administrative error not deceit by recipients. Yet the enforcement spotlight falls hardest on poor families, even as wage violations in the private sector go under-enforced.

Yes, fraud happens sometimes, but most "errors" are because the rules are complicated, not because people are cheating. Still, poor families are watched the closest while many companies breaking wage laws don't get caught or punished enough.

The cycle persists because policy is designed to keep it going. Powerful lobbies push for tax cuts skewed toward high earners and large corporations; the resulting revenue hole invites austerity that targets discretionary spending, including the very programs that stabilize low-wage households. Program rules often feature sharp "benefit cliffs," where a small raise or extra shift can trigger a disproportionate loss of food, housing, or healthcare support. Families are penalized precisely when they attempt to get ahead.

The rules are set up to keep the system as-is. Big interests push for tax cuts that mostly help the wealthy and big companies. Then, to "save money," we cut programs that help low-income families. On top of that, if someone gets a small raise, they can lose a big chunk of benefits all at once so trying to get ahead can actually set them back.

Meanwhile, enforcement gaps let wage theft and misclassification thrive. Scheduling volatility on-call shifts, last-minute changes, and insufficient hours forces workers to absorb hidden costs for childcare and transportation. The public then subsidizes the fallout through assistance. The system is tight where it burdens the poor and loose where it benefits firms.

Not enough is done to stop companies from underpaying or misclassifying workers. Unstable schedules make life and childcare harder and pricier. Then taxpayers cover the fallout with assistance. The rules are strict when they hurt poor people and loose when they help companies.

Beyond formal rules, ordinary gatekeeping compounds the harm. At grocery stores, benefits users face side-eye and extra scrutiny. In housing, voucher holders encounter denials or subtle steering, sometimes under the guise of neutral criteria. At work, employees who rely on public programs are shamed as "not pulling their weight," even when low pay and erratic hours are the actual culprits.

Every day life piles on. People using benefits get judged in stores. Landlords often turn away renters with vouchers. Workers who get help are shamed, even though low pay and messy schedules are the real problem.

Long waits, repetitive forms, hard-to-meet documentation demands, and frequent recertifications, act as a rationing tool, dissuading eligible families from accessing support. Scholars call this "administrative burden," and it functions as a hidden tax on time and dignity. Notably, wealthy beneficiaries of public largesse from mortgage-interest deductions to corporate tax incentives—rarely face equivalent scrutiny or hassle.

Getting help is made exhausting on purpose endless forms, long lines, and constant re-checks so fewer people stick with it. It's like a tax on your time and dignity. Meanwhile, richer people and big companies get tax breaks without this kind of hassle.

Taxpayers shoulder the cost when low wages force families onto public programs. Employers benefit from lower labor costs and turnover; consumers benefit from lower prices; and shareholders benefit from maintained margins. Assistance recipients many of them workers sustaining essential sectors absorb the stigma, instability, and bureaucratic friction.

We all pay for low wages through our taxes. Companies save money on pay and turnover; shoppers get cheaper prices; investors keep profits up. The people who need help are many working essential jobs who face stress, shame, and paperwork.

Some supports are explicitly designed as wage supplements. The Earned Income Tax Credit is effective at reducing poverty, but research shows that in markets where employers have hiring power, part of its value can be captured by firms via lower wage growth than would otherwise occur. In housing, evidence suggests that in tight markets some landlords capture part of voucher value through higher effective rents. These are not arguments against the programs' usefulness; they are reminders that without fair wages and competitive labor and housing markets, public benefits can be partially privatized by those with market power.

Programs like the Earned Income Tax Credit help a lot, but in places where bosses have more power, some of that benefit can end up helping companies instead of workers because wages don't rise as much as they should. With housing vouchers, in crowded rental markets, landlords can sometimes raise rents to capture some of the benefit. The programs still help but fairer wages and fairer markets would keep more of the benefits with families.

If the low-wage model is subsidized by the safety net, why do some upper-income interests push to cut it? Because weak, stigmatized assistance can still serve as a labor stabilizer while keeping workers insecure. The playbook is consistent: suppress wages and bargaining power, stigmatize the safety net to divide workers, keep support stingy and conditional, and reap the profits from a compliant, low-cost labor force. In this dynamic, the safety net is tolerated as a pressure valve, just enough to maintain labor supply, not enough to confer real bargaining power or security.

Why do some powerful people attack the very programs that help their business model? Because small, complicated, and stigmatized work helps keep workers desperate enough to accept low pay. The safety net is allowed to exist just enough to keep people working not enough to give them real leverage or stability.

Raise the wage floor to a local living wage and index it to inflation. This shifts the cost of labor back to firms and reduces dependence on means-tested programs.
Enforce existing labor laws. Crack down on wage theft, misclassification, and abusive scheduling that push effective pay below legal floors.

Smooth benefits cliffs. Gradual phase-outs, income averaging, and continuous eligibility prevent small raises from triggering large losses.

Support small businesses in transition. Temporary, targeted credits, technical assistance, and access to low-cost capital can ease adjustment while preserving jobs.

Strengthen worker voice and standards. Sectoral wage boards, transparent scheduling rules, and fair contracting reduce monopsony power and prevent subsidy capture.

Modernize administration with dignity. Simplify eligibility, reduce paperwork churn, and invest in outreach so supports function as bridges, not barriers.

We can fix this. Pay a true living wage and keep it updated with inflation. Enforce the laws we already have. Change benefits so people don't lose everything when they get a small raise. Help small businesses adjust during the change. Give workers a real voice and fair schedules. Make getting help simpler and more respectful.

Evidence from numerous minimum wage increases shows modest price effects, reduced turnover, improved morale, and productivity gains that offset part of the higher wage bill, with small to neutral employment effects at commonly enacted levels. Fewer families would need assistance; more low-wage workers would become net taxpayers; and public dollars could be targeted toward mobility-building investments like childcare, housing, and education.

Studies of minimum wage increases show prices don't jump much, workers stick around longer, morale and productivity go up, and jobs usually don't disappear. With better pay, fewer families need benefits, more people pay taxes, and we can invest public money where it builds a better future.

Assistance users are not the problem; they are the proof of a problem. When an economy is built on sub-living wages, the public is asked to backfill the basics and then asked to resent the people who need that help. That cycle does not serve the public interest. It props up low-wage business models, socializes their costs, and punishes the families who keep essential sectors running.

People who need help show us that wages are too low not that they're doing something wrong. The current setup makes the public pay for basics and then blames the poor. That protects low-wage business models and hurts the families we all rely on.

A living wage, stronger enforcement, and safety-net rules that avoid punishing progress would reduce reliance on assistance and restore a fairer alignment between who pays and who profits. Most importantly, these changes would shift the conversation from blaming those at the bottom to fixing the systems at the top that make help necessary.

If we pay a living wage, enforce fair pay, and fix benefits so a small raise doesn't wreck a family's budget, fewer people will need assistance. We'll match costs with profits more fairly—and we'll focus on fixing the system, not blaming people who are doing their best.

The Correlation Between Historical Lynchings, Modern Police Killings, and Capital Punishment in America

The concept of "blind justice," embodied by Lady Justice in her blindfold, is meant to signify a legal system that treats all individuals without bias. In practice, it is a white superiority justice system with an abundance of evidence revealing that systemic racism and societal bias have significantly shaped judicial outcomes across various facets, including arrest rates, sentencing, and access to legal resources.

The historical backdrop of lynching in the United States resonates in today's police killings, prompting critical conversations about race, justice, and societal values. Similarly, the application of capital punishment sheds light on ongoing racial disparities and systemic inequality within the justice system.

While lynchings, police violence, and capital punishment stem from different historical contexts, they collectively underscore persistent issues related to racial dynamics and reflect the lasting impact of white supremacy in America. Investigating these connections unearths historical continuities and exposes systemic flaws within the U.S. justice framework.

Between the late 19th century and the mid-20th century, the United States witnessed a harrowing wave of lynchings targeting Black individuals. The Equal Justice Initiative notes that more than 4,400 Black men, women, and children were lynched from 1877 to 1950, serving as instruments of white terror and social enforcement, particularly in the South.

In states like Mississippi, which recorded at least 579 lynchings from 1882 to 1968, these public spectacles not only incited severe violence but also illustrated community complicity in perpetuating racial terror.

Witness accounts reveal that many lynchings were performative, attracting large crowds, including members of law enforcement, who often treated these horrific acts as entertainment

Legal consequences for lynchers were virtually nonexistent, with a study by the NAACP indicating that between 1882 and 1968, fewer than 1 percent of these cases resulted in prosecution. However, a troubling statistic, it is higher than today when compared with modern police killing prosecution rates.

In the present day, modern police killings have garnered national scrutiny, with high-profile cases like those of George Floyd, Breonna Taylor, and Michael Brown igniting nationwide calls for reform. Current data reveal that Black individuals are significantly more likely to be killed by police than their white counterparts; for instance, the Mapping Police Violence database indicates that Black Americans are three times more likely to be victims of fatal encounters with law enforcement.

In 2021, over 1,058 people were killed by police, with approximately 25 percent of these individuals being Black, even though Black Americans make up only about 13 percent of the U.S. population. In 2022, this number increased to around 1,192, while for 2023, it indicates there have been 1,329 police killings. The year 2024 saw 1365 police killings. The rate of prosecution for police killings remains starkly low. A 2021 analysis by the Washington Post revealed that, since 2005, only about 2 percent of police officers involved in fatal shootings have been charged with a crime. Specifically, in 2021, out of over 1,058 police killings, only seven officers were arrested and convicted. In 2022, only five officers were convicted in connection with approximately 1,192 killings. As of 2023, 2 officers faced convictions concerning the over 1,300 killings, showcasing a conviction rate of roughly 0.17 percent for the current year.

The death penalty in the U.S. further complicates the narrative of racial bias and inequality. Since its reinstatement in 1976, there have been 1,632 executions, predominantly in a handful of states. Shockingly, around 47 percent of those exonerated after being wrongfully sentenced to death are Black, highlighting a glaring disparity in how justice is administered. Ignominiously, there have been documented cases of individuals executed who were later proven innocent, a sobering reminder of the irrevocable nature of capital punishment.

Examining the timing of executions reveals an unsettling pattern: Black individuals in certain jurisdictions face swifter executions than their white counterparts. Additionally, studies indicate that the race of the victim dramatically influences whether a defendant receives the death penalty, with crimes against white victims resulting in harsher sentences. The disproportionate number of people of color among those executed—over 70 percent since 1976—further amplifies the urgency for reform.

Specific states have been identified as executing Black individuals at a faster rate.

Texas accounts for approximately 37% of all executions since 1976, with Black individuals representing about 35% of those executed in the state.

In Florida, about 40% of those executed are Black, despite African Americans making up roughly 13% of the state's population.

Georgia has seen about 57% of those executed since 1976 being Black, showcasing a significant racial disparity.

In Virginia, approximately 48% of those executed have been Black, reflecting substantial racial imbalances.

Alabama presents a particularly stark picture, with nearly 60% of those executed being Black.

In Mississippi, about 80% of those executed since 1976 have been Black individuals, demonstrating extreme racial disparity in its application of the death penalty.

The assertion that white individuals often receive more lenient sentences than people of color for similar crimes is supported by various studies and statistics regarding racial disparities in the U.S. criminal justice system. Research has shown that white individuals typically receive lighter sentences compared to their Black or Hispanic counterparts for similar offenses.

A study by the U.S. Sentencing Commission found that, on average, Black male offenders received sentences that were 19.1% longer than those of white male offenders for similar crimes.

Numerous studies indicate that racial bias can influence judicial outcomes, including charging decisions, sentencing lengths, and the likelihood of receiving plea deals.

Black defendants are often more likely to face harsher charges than white defendants for the same crime. The race of the victim can also impact sentencing, as crimes against white victims may result in harsher penalties for offenders, regardless of their race. This dynamic reflects deep-seated biases within the criminal justice system.

People of color often face less favorable plea deals than white individuals, leading to longer sentences and more significant criminal records. This disparity can perpetuate cycles of disadvantage and recidivism.

Data collected by various organizations, including the Bureau of Justice Statistics, reveal that racial minorities, particularly Black Americans, are overrepresented in incarceration rates and often serve longer sentences for the same crimes compared to white individuals, even when accounting for factors like crime severity and prior criminal history.

The acknowledgment of these disparities has led to growing calls for criminal justice reform, including initiatives aimed at addressing systemic racism in sentencing and law enforcement practices.

While not every case will fit this pattern, the broader statistical evidence suggests that white individuals benefit from more lenient treatment within the criminal justice system. This perpetuates existing inequalities and raises significant concerns about fairness and justice. Addressing these disparities remains a critical focus for policymakers, advocates, and researchers.

Analyzing these injustices reveals a consistent pattern: systemic racism continues to manifest in policing, capital punishment, and broader judicial practices. The end of public lynchings did not extinguish racial violence; it merely transformed into subtler, yet equally damaging, forms of control and terror. Modern policing, while ostensibly a protective force, often mirrors the racial hierarchies once enforced through lynching, keeping alive the vestiges of white supremacy.

Both lynchings and police killings expose the entrenched racism woven into the fabric of American society. Although lynchings were blatant acts of brutality, modern policing reveals an insidious reality of racial profiling and excessive force targeted at marginalized communities. Furthermore, the death penalty frequently reinforces these disparities, as it predominantly impacts people of color.

The public justification of lynchings as a means to maintain social order has evolved; today, police killings are frequently framed within the narrative of public safety, though recurring instances of excessive force, particularly against unarmed individuals, challenge the validity of such claims. Similarly, capital punishment is often justified under the guise of justice, disproportionately affecting marginalized groups.

Movements advocating for justice reform have risen in response to these injustices, drawing connections between past and present. The Civil Rights Movement sought to dismantle the violent legacy of lynching, while contemporary movements like Black Lives Matter confront police brutality and call for changes to capital punishment laws.

Comprehensive reforms are critical to dismantle these entrenched systems.

Policy Reform: New legislation is essential to change policing practices, including bans on chokeholds, stricter rules on deadly force, and comprehensive de-escalation training for officers.

Accountability Mechanisms: Establishing independent investigations for police shootings and ensuring accountability can help rebuild trust in law enforcement. Utilizing body cameras and anonymized reporting can enhance transparency.

Community Engagement: Strengthening community-police relations through outreach initiatives can foster trust and accountability.

Ending the Death Penalty: Reassessing capital punishment and focusing on bias elimination or abolishing it altogether may signify a crucial step towards systemic justice.

Education and Awareness: Raising awareness of racial violence's historical and ongoing impacts through education can cultivate empathy and empower advocacy for change.

The troubling correlation between lynchings, police killings, and capital punishment highlights the systemic racism embedded within the justice system. While lynchings represent a violent chapter in American history, modern police violence and capital punishment reveal ongoing struggles over authority, race, and human rights. Understanding these connections is vital for fostering meaningful discussions and advancing social justice reform in America. We can work towards a more equitable and just society by addressing these intertwined issues through honest discourse and concerted action.

Medicare-for-All: Transforming American Healthcare for a Healthier Future

The ongoing debate over Medicare-for-All (MFA) has emerged as a pivotal topic in reshaping the American healthcare landscape, driven by the urgent need for affordable and accessible healthcare solutions.

Advocates argue that implementing a single-payer system could not only secure universal healthcare for all citizens but also yield substantial financial benefits for families.

However, despite growing public support, the proposal has yet to pass, largely due to powerful opposition from entrenched interests, including insurance companies, lobbyists, and the political establishment.

A transition to MFA would significantly reduce profits for private insurers, curtail lobbyist influence, and diminish campaign contributions that many politicians rely on to fund their electoral efforts.

These stakeholders have mounted robust campaigns against MFA, fearing that its implementation could disrupt the lucrative healthcare market that currently prioritizes profit over patient care.

This comprehensive analysis delves into the multifaceted implications of a Medicare-for-All model, leveraging extensive research and data available up to 2023.

From anticipated savings in insurance premiums and out-of-pocket expenses to the promise of universal coverage, this exploration aims to present a detailed assessment of how MFA could revolutionize healthcare in the United States while navigating the complex landscape of political resistance and vested interests.

Reduced Premiums
One of the most critical aspects of the Medicare-for-All proposal is the anticipated reduction in insurance premiums for American households.

Analyses from institutions such as the Political Economy Research Institute suggest that average households could save approximately $2,400 annually in premiums due to the elimination of private insurance.

The shift from multiple private insurance plans to a single-payer system removes the middle layer of private healthcare, which tends to incur high administrative costs.

Medicare's operations are much more streamlined, with lower overhead, allowing savings to be redirected toward patient care rather than administrative bureaucracy.

Lower Out-of-Pocket Expenses
Currently, many Americans face significant out-of-pocket expenses, such as high deductibles and co-pays that can make healthcare access financially burdensome.

In a Medicare-for-All system, the elimination of these costs is a focus, leading to projected savings ranging from $1,000 to $5,000 annually.

The complete removal of deductibles and co-pays means individuals would not face unexpected financial burdens when seeking necessary care, resulting in greater access to preventive services and reduced barriers to treatment.

Universal Coverage
With over 29 million people currently uninsured and even more underinsured in the U.S., a universal coverage model like Medicare-for-All promises to eliminate out-of-pocket costs for all necessary medical services.

For those who currently lack adequate healthcare access, estimates suggest that they could save between $1,500 and $3,000 annually, which factors in enhanced access to medical care that can lead to improved health outcomes.

The implementation of such a system would also reduce uncompensated care, which is costly for taxpayers who frequently subsidize emergency services for uninsured individuals.

Healthcare Access Improvement
The principle of improved access to healthcare is inherently tied to any universal healthcare plan.

By enabling broader access to routine check-ups and preventive screenings, emergency room utilization would likely decline.

Analyses indicate that reducing emergency room admissions alongside increased preventive care can result in meaningful savings for the healthcare system.

Although the figure of $24 billion in potential savings may feel generalized, various studies support the argument that a proactive approach to healthcare could significantly lessen overall healthcare spending.

Economic Impact
Advocates of Medicare-for-All assert that transitioning to this system could reduce national healthcare spending by an estimated $600 billion to $1 trillion annually.

These projections stem from analyses conducted by reliable organizations like the Urban Institute and the Center for American Progress.

By eliminating insurance company profits, unnecessary administrative costs, and systemic inefficiencies prevalent under the current model, a single-payer system has the potential to foster a more efficient distribution of healthcare resources ultimately contributing to substantial savings.

Furthermore, these significant savings could theoretically bolster economic activity, as the funds that would have otherwise gone into healthcare costs are reallocated to consumption, savings, or investment.

This reallocation has the potential to improve overall disposable income, subsequently leading to increased wages and job creation in other sectors of the economy, thereby enhancing the overall economic landscape.

Comprehensive Coverage
A key feature of the Medicare-for-All initiative is its promise of comprehensive coverage that meets the health needs of all individuals.

Under this system, all essential services including preventive, hospital, vision, dental, and mental health care would be fully covered.

This positions Medicare-for-All as a marked improvement over the current landscape, where coverage may vary widely, leaving patients vulnerable to significant medical bills for services deemed non-essential by private insurers.

Tax Adjustments and Redistribution
While the savings for individuals are a significant part of the conversation, it's also essential to examine the tax implications of a Medicare-for-All framework.

To support the funding necessary for such a comprehensive system, the government would need to adjust revenue collection through progressive taxation measures.

Interestingly, while higher-income buyers may face increased taxes, many low- to middle-income families are expected to see a net reduction in overall healthcare spending.

By profoundly simplifying the structure of healthcare financing, individuals could be relieved of premiums and out-of-pocket costs that currently consume a significant portion of household budgets.

Economic Impact and Job Creation
The transition to a Medicare-for-All model may also impact jobs in the economy positively, especially within the healthcare sector.

While there may be a decrease in administrative jobs tied to private insurance companies, the overall demand for healthcare services is likely to grow, necessitating new hires in hospitals, clinics, and supportive roles.

A healthier population, empowered by better access to care, could foster increased productivity across various sectors, further contributing to economic growth.

Policy Considerations and Challenges
Bear in mind that while these savings sound beneficial, the transition to such a system involves substantial policy considerations, potential tax adjustments, and political debates that affect how these savings are realized.

The exact outcomes may differ based on the specific structure of the Medicare-for-All program implemented, as well as regional healthcare dynamics and cost-of-living variations across the U.S.

The complexity of these considerations underscores that while the theory behind Medicare-for-All is promising, its practical implementation will require nuanced policy development to ensure equity and efficiency.

The Medicare-for-All proposal offers a transformative opportunity to revamp the American healthcare system notably, presenting substantial potential savings for voters through lowered premiums, reduced out-of-pocket expenses, and comprehensive coverage.

By emphasizing universality and financial accessibility, advocates argue that such a system could enhance healthcare access while ensuring a healthier population overall.

As a deeper understanding of these issues is developed through ongoing research and analysis, both public opinion and legislative objectives may evolve regarding the potential implementation of a Medicare-for-All structure.

In summary, achieving projected savings of approximately $1.9 trillion annually entails a cumulative effect of cost reductions across multiple facets of the healthcare system, including premium reductions, lower out-of-pocket costs, and increased administrative efficiency, ultimately making healthcare a fundamental right accessible to all Americans.

To cover the cost of Medicare For All the following would need to happen:

To cover the cost of Medicare-for-All, a multifaceted funding strategy would need to be employed. Increasing the Federal Insurance Contributions Act (FICA) tax rate from 6.2% to 9% would significantly enhance the revenue pool dedicated to healthcare funding.

This adjustment could substantially increase the funds available to support a universal healthcare system. However, alone, this increase in FICA would not be sufficient to fully cover the projected costs of such a program, which has been estimated by various analyses to exceed $30 trillion over ten years.

To effectively bridge this gap, additional funding sources would need to be identified:

Including increased income taxes on the top 10%. Raising income tax rates on the highest earners could yield substantial revenue. For instance, implementing higher marginal tax rates for individuals making over $400,000 could ensure that the wealthiest individuals contribute a fairer share towards the public healthcare system.

Corporate tax increases could serve as another source of funding. Corporations often benefit from a healthy workforce; hence, their contribution to Medicare-for-All could be justified as a reciprocal benefit to ensure their employees are healthier and more productive.

Additionally, higher taxes on wealth and capital gains can provide more revenue.

Adjusting tax structures to increase rates on capital gains and implementing wealth taxes can ensure that those who have accumulated wealth contribute equitably.

Other tax revenue options could include increasing taxes on tobacco and sugary beverages and potentially introducing financial transaction taxes.

Each of these could generate revenue while also promoting public health initiatives.

While raising the FICA tax to 9% would bolster the healthcare funding pool, the cumulative effect of these measures would be essential to adequately finance a Medicare-for-All program.

Such a comprehensive system would result in a healthier population, ultimately benefiting the economy and businesses alike, thus justifying the expectation that the top 10% of earners should contribute their fair share.

Overall, a socially equitable funding approach is critical not just for meeting budgetary needs, but also for ensuring public support and enhancing the impact of a universal healthcare system.

Fact-checking notes indicate that various analyses, including studies by the Political Economy Research Institute (PERI), estimate the cost of a Medicare-for-All program to exceed $30 trillion over ten years, though estimates vary widely based on assumptions and methodologies used. The current employee portion of the FICA tax is 6.2% for Social Security and 1.45% for Medicare, totaling 7.65%. The proposal to increase the FICA tax by 2.8% to 9% refers specifically to the income earner's part and aligns with efforts to improve the funding base for Medicare.

Corporate taxation is an essential consideration in comprehensive funding strategies, as businesses benefit from a productive workforce. Currently, the capital gains tax rate is typically lower than standard income tax rates, leading to proposals for tax reform aimed at equity.

This information encapsulates both the mechanics of funding a Medicare-for-All program and some pivotal points of broader tax policy discussions in the U.S.

The Three Trillion Dollar Question! Who Stole The Social Security?

The Social Security system has served as a cornerstone of financial security for millions of Americans since its inception.

Designed to provide various forms of assistance primarily to retirees, disabled individuals, and survivors of deceased workers.

Social Security has historically maintained a surplus intended to fund future benefits, especially in light of projected demographic shifts.

The stability of this surplus has been called into question over the decades, particularly following significant changes in fiscal policies during the Reagan and Trump administrations.

Before the 1983 amendments to the Social Security Act, the system operated with a surplus that was strategically accumulated, and invested into U.S. Treasury bonds, to prepare for the impending shortfall anticipated with the retirement of the baby boomer generation.

Born between 1946 and 1964, this cohort represented the largest demographic bubble in American history and was expected to place unprecedented demands on the Social Security system as they reached retirement age.

By the early 1980s, Social Security had amassed approximately $70 billion in reserves, an amount that would continue to grow as payroll taxes and U.S. Treasury bond dividends, outpaced benefit payouts.

This surplus was critical, allowing the program to absorb fluctuations in the ratio of workers to beneficiaries, which would later be skewed as the baby boomer generation entered retirement.

In the early 1980s, under President Reagan, significant changes were made to the tax code, with a focus on supply-side economics and substantial tax cuts directed primarily at wealthier Americans and corporations, also known as trickle-down economics theory.

These policies were touted as a means to stimulate economic growth. However, the tax breaks led to major shortfalls in federal revenue, necessitating the use of Social Security surpluses to balance other budgetary deficits.

The 1983 Social Security amendments sought to rectify projected imminent shortfalls by increasing payroll taxes and gradually raising the retirement age.

However, alongside these measures, the environment fostered by the administration encouraged unsustainable fiscal policies that diverted funds away from essential social programs, ultimately weakening the long-term viability of Social Security.

Rather than the surplus remaining intact for the intended purposes, funds were secretly used to conceal broader budget deficits, leading to a depletion of resources that were originally allocated for future beneficiaries.

Fast forward to the Trump administration, which further exacerbated the situation through the Tax Cuts and Jobs Act of 2017.

This legislation, largely benefiting the wealthy and corporations, reduced federal revenues while making it even more challenging to maintain social safety nets like Social Security.

By the time Trump left office, estimates indicated that the Social Security and Medicare Trust Funds faced critical challenges, with projections showing a decline in reserves from approximately $7 trillion to around $2.9 trillion—far less than what would be necessary to fulfill the program's obligations to future beneficiaries.

The political landscape surrounding Social Security has increasingly become contentious. Many critics argue that the funds were effectively "stolen" from the program, not through direct theft, but through policies brought by Reshan and Trump, that undermined its long-term sustainability.

These policies transferred wealth to the affluent under the guise of economic growth, leading to a question of equity. The wealth accumulated by a select few was prioritized over investments in critical social programs designed to uplift the broader population.

Now, as calls arise from some MAGA Republicans to reform or even eliminate Social Security, the program faces potential threats that echo historical injustices.

MAGA Republicans who gave the 2 trillion tax cut to the rich, and profited from policies that weakened the program now propose dismantling it, potentially abandoning millions of Americans who rely on these benefits for basic living expenses in retirement.

The depletion of the Social Security surplus and the diminishing reserves are not merely numbers; they represent real future hardships for millions of Americans.

The policies enacted by past administrations have led to significant funding discrepancies, leaving the program vulnerable to cuts and reforms that could eliminate critical support.

To safeguard the future of Social Security, advocates for social equity must unite to challenge policies that neglect the welfare of the working class while prioritizing the interests of the wealthy few.

Addressing these disparities and advocating for comprehensive reforms will be essential to restoring the integrity of a system that many depend upon for their livelihoods.

The current discourse surrounding Social Security requires a renewed emphasis on the principles of equity and fairness.

As the nation grapples with questions of taxation, social welfare, and economic growth, it is incumbent upon citizens and policymakers alike to ensure that support systems are preserved, equitable, robust effectively designed to meet the needs of future generations and uphold the social contract envisioned by the program's founders.

In this discourse, the imperative remains clear: MAGA Republicans need to put the funds back where they got it from. Social Security is not merely a program; it is a lifeline. As such, it deserves our unwavering commitment to ensure that it remains intact and fully funded for those who will rely on it in the decades to come.

____

How The Republicans Are Responsible For The Destruction of The American Economy

At one time, our currency was backed by silver and gold, and the US could not print currency or mint coins unless we had the gold and silver in the federal reserve to back them.

Our paper money used to have silver or gold certificates written across the top.

This system limited the amount of currency that could be produced. With fewer bills and coins in circulation, the value of our money increases. As a result, because a dollar holds significant value, products and services are sold at lower prices.

Circulation of Money indicates that when there are fewer bills and coins in circulation, the scarcity of the currency leads to an increase in its value. This is similar to the economic principle of supply and demand. When a commodity is scarce, its worth typically rises.

The value of Money means that a stronger dollar allows consumers to buy more with each currency unit. This increased purchasing power tends to lower prices for goods and services, as sellers adjust their pricing by the higher value of money.

Overall economic impact suggests that by limiting the amount of currency, this system can help maintain a stable financial environment and avoid the adverse effects of inflation, which causes prices to rise and the purchasing power of money to decrease.

A limited currency supply can increase the value per currency unit, allowing consumers to purchase goods and services at lower prices.

After Democrats won unified control of Congress and the presidency in the <u>1912 elections</u>, President Wilson, Congressman <u>Carter Glass</u>, and Senator <u>Robert Latham Owen</u> crafted a central banking bill, the Federal Reserve Act, establishing a central banking system to stabilize the dollar's value.

The Federal Reserve Act created a national currency and a monetary system that could respond effectively to the stresses in the banking system and create a stable financial system. To create a national economic system and financial stability.

The Federal Reserve Act also provided many other economic functions and financial services, such as check clearing and collection for all members of the Federal Reserve.

With the passing of the Federal Reserve Act, Congress required that all nationally chartered banks become members of the Federal Reserve System.

In June 1917, the Democratic President And Congress passed significant amendments to the Act to enable monetary expansion to cover the expected costs of World War I.

The amendment allowed a more flexible definition of the gold backing the dollar currency in circulation. This relaxation de facto allowed less gold backing for each dollar note. It enabled the currency in circulation to double from $465 million to $1.247 billion just from June to December 1917.

The Federal Reserve was given control to regulate inflation, even though the government control over such powers would eventually lead to controversial decisions.

Some of the most prominent implications of the Federal Reserve include the internationalization of the <u>U.S. Dollar as a global currency</u> and the impact of the perception of the Central Bank structure as a public good by creating a system of financial stability.

Under FDR, a Democrat, the international monetary system established after World War II was dubbed the Bretton Woods system after forty-four countries met in Bretton Woods, New Hampshire 1944.

The countries agreed to keep their currencies fixed (but adjustable in exceptional situations) to the dollar, which was fixed to gold.

Since 1958, when the <u>Bretton Woods system became operational</u>, countries settled their international balances in dollars, and U.S. dollars were convertible to gold at a fixed exchange rate of $35 an ounce.

The United States was responsible for keeping the dollar price of gold fixed and adjusting the supply of dollars to maintain confidence in future gold convertibility worldwide.

The Bretton Woods system initially operated as planned. Japan and Europe were still rebuilding their postwar economies, and demand for U.S. goods, services, and dollars was high.

The system seemed secure since the United States held about three-quarters of the world's official gold reserves.

Richard Nixon, a Republican, decided to delink the dollar from gold, which he announced without warning in August 1971. His action instantly remade the global monetary system.

With the ability to create unlimited currency and coins, inflation skyrocketed, and GDP plummeted.

This is why a nickel loaf of bread is now $4.

What the Republicans wanted was some way to devalue the dollar, but because it was pegged to gold, the administration couldn't do that.

Under Republican control, August 15, 1971, was the precise date on which America's singular dominance of the world economy ended.

Nixon, with the backing of the elected Republicans, decided that the dollar would no longer be backed by gold.

To cover up the aftermath, Richard Nixon imposed a 90-day wage-price freeze in the U.S. to curb inflation and a 10% tariff on all imports.

The Economic Rollercoaster, the price of goods and services, took a steep ride up and hasn't dipped much since.

So now, Federal Reserve notes can be made without backing other than a government promise.

In simple terms, the more money you print, the more currency is in circulation and the higher the inflation rate.

The more currency in circulation, the less value the currency has.

The Lower the value of money, the higher the cost of goods.

The lower the wages, the more currency drops per employed person.

The higher the inflation grows

The lower the wage is, the more significant the gap between rich and poor.

Now for the drastic changes

In 1981, "Reaganomics" was the most serious attempt by any administration since the New Deal to change the course of U.S. economic policy.

Trickle-down Economics was touted as an enormous economic booster for everyone. However, it was the most prominent political hoax ever perpetrated against everyone but the businesses and the elite.

Trickle Down Economics is such a flop that Social Security would be left alone

The changes to the federal tax code for the top one percent were much more substantial. The top marginal tax rate on individual income was reduced from 70 percent to 28 percent.

The corporate income tax rate was reduced from 48 percent to 34 percent.

Reagan eased or eliminated price controls on oil and natural gas, cable TV, long-distance telephone service, interstate bus service, and ocean shipping. This Is Why Gas Stays Around $4.00 A Gallon Today.

Banks were allowed to invest in a broader set of assets, and the scope of the antitrust laws was reduced. The major exception to this pattern was a substantial increase in import barriers.

The Reagan administration did not propose changes in the legislation affecting health, safety, and the environment, but it reduced the number of new regulations under the existing laws.

Woodrow Wilson (Democrat)

1916-1917 Tax Rate For The Highest Income 67%.

1918-1923 Wealthy Tax Rate 77%

Calvin Coolidge (Republican)

1924 46% Tax On The Rich

1925-1932 27% Tax On The Wealthy

Herbert Hoover (Democrat)

1933-1935 Tax of the rich 63%

FDR (Democrat)

1936-1943 Tax The Rich 79%

Harry Truman (Democrat)

1944-1959 Tax 94% On $200,000 and above.

JFK (Democrat), LBJ (Democrat), Nixon (Republican), Ford (Republican), Carter (Democrat)

1960-1980 Tax Rate For The Rich 70%

I bet you know what's coming next.
Reagonomics

Reagan (Republican)

1981 Weathy Taxed 50%

1982-1990 Wealthy Paid 28%

George H W Bush (Republican)

1991-1992 Wealthy Tax Rate 31%

Bill Clinton

1993-2000 Wealthy Taxes Paid 39.6%

George Bush Jr. (Republican)

2001-2012 Rich Tax Rate 35%

Obama (Democrat)

2013-2017 Tax Rate For The Rich 39.6%

Trump (Republican)

2018-2023 Wealthy Tax Rate 37%

The tax rate on anyone making one million or more should never exceed 70%. All loopholes, deductions, and credits should be closed and removed.

After the deductions, loopholes, and credits to which the rich are entitled are taken, there isn't much taxable income left. Some owe as little as $500, and a few owe nothing.

Has anyone else noticed that the poor and middle class do not qualify for many if there are any deductions?

Unless you consider EIC, People with kids get a deduction.

To sum it all up, Nixon, Reagan, and Trump destroyed the American Economy:

Nixon devalued the dollar, which caused inflation to go out of control.

Reagan, with a trickle-down, made the rich richer and the poor poorer, and started stealing from the Social Security reserve to replace the money the rich did not pay, and to meet the government budget needs

Trump repeated the trickle-down that made the rich richer and the poor poorer and again started stealing from the Social Security reserve to replace the money the rich did not pay and to meet the government budget needs.

Understanding the Political Evolution of the Republican and Democratic Parties

To grasp the complexities of today's American politics, it is essential to examine the evolution of the Republican and Democratic parties, particularly their changing ideologies regarding civil rights and social justice over the past two centuries. This analysis provides valuable insight into the current political landscape and the various factions within each party, highlighting how historical contexts inform modern ideologies.

The Democratic Party was founded in 1828 and, historically, during the 19th century, it supported slavery and resisted civil rights reforms following the American Civil War. Its ties to the Ku Klux Klan and its active endorsement of Jim Crow laws serve as stark examples of its reliance on intimidation and violence to maintain control over the Black population in the South. However, beginning in the late 1870s, the party began a gradual transformation aimed at broadening its constituency. This marked the early migration of conservative Democrats to the Republican Party, which started as a slow trickle.

The shift toward a more active government role in economic affairs gained significant momentum during the 20th century, particularly with the New Deal programs initiated by Franklin D. Roosevelt (FDR), which aimed to address the economic disparities wrought by the Great Depression.

However, it is crucial to recognize that, despite their positive impacts, many of these programs exhibited significant racial prejudices and inequalities. For instance, policies such as Social Security and the Civilian Conservation Corps often excluded African Americans and other people of color from participation, reflecting and reinforcing existing social hierarchies. The implementation of these programs frequently favored white, working-class citizens while systematically marginalizing communities of color.

The complexities of race became even more pronounced during World War II. FDR's declaration of war highlighted a paradox in American democracy: while the nation fought against fascism abroad, it turned a blind eye to injustices at home. The forced internment of over 120,000 Japanese Americans two-thirds of whom were U.S. citizens serves as a stark reminder of this contradiction. These individuals were uprooted from their homes and placed in concentration camps, driven by wartime hysteria and racial prejudice rather than any evidence of disloyalty. This brutal chapter exemplifies how wartime policies often reflect prevailing racial dynamics, resulting in the marginalization of specific ethnic groups.

The legacies of these historical injustices continue to resonate in contemporary American politics. Racial dynamics persist in various forms, including systemic inequalities in housing, education, healthcare, and employment.

Discriminatory policies, voter suppression efforts, and the ongoing debates over immigration and civil rights reveal how deeply rooted racial biases can shape political discourse and policy decisions.

The demographic shifts in the United States, combined with an increasingly diverse electorate, have sparked tensions that expose the underlying racial divisions in American society. As such, understanding the historical context of racial injustices, including those faced during the New Deal and World War II, is essential for addressing current disparities and moving toward a more equitable society.

The 1960s witnessed a significant transformation in American society and politics, particularly under the leadership of John F. Kennedy and Lyndon B. Johnson. Migration patterns among African Americans intensified during and after Franklin D. Roosevelt's presidency, fueled by the search for better economic opportunities and civil rights, and this trend continued in the wake of the elections of Kennedy and Johnson.

Kennedy advocated for civil rights as a moral imperative and played a pivotal role in proposing the Civil Rights Act of 1964, although it was ultimately Johnson who secured its passage after Kennedy's assassination. Additionally, Kennedy's efforts in civil rights were marked by his support of desegregation initiatives and his famous address on civil rights in June 1963, where he framed the struggle for equality as a fundamental American issue.

Johnson's civil rights agenda was robust; he signed the landmark Civil Rights Act of 1964 and the Voting Rights Act of 1965, which aimed to eradicate racial discrimination and secure voting rights for African Americans. These measures prompted many white Southern Democrats to realign with the Republican Party, perceiving the Democratic Party's commitment to civil rights and inclusivity as a departure from their traditional values.

Over the decades, the Democratic Party evolved from its agrarian roots into a platform that embraced inclusivity and equity, gaining support from a diverse coalition advocating for civil rights, LGBTQ+ rights, and environmental reforms. This transformation reflected broader social changes and contributed to the party's current identity as a champion of diverse causes.

The Affordable Care Act (ACA), enacted in 2010, aimed to expand health insurance coverage to millions of uninsured Americans. Despite its intention to lower healthcare costs and improve access to healthcare services, the ACA faced significant political backlash surrounding its implementation, including numerous attempts at repeal by Republican opponents.

Internally, the Democratic Party encountered challenges due to rising divisions over the Vietnam War and subsequent economic policies. These divisions created discontent among working-class voters, many of whom felt that the Democratic Party was no longer adequately representing their interests.

Founded in the 1850s primarily as an anti-slavery movement, the Republican Party initially championed the rights of African Americans. However, by the mid-20th century, the party began to devolve away from this progressive stance. During the post-World War II era, several Republicans adopted platforms emphasizing individual freedom, smaller government, and resistance to federal intervention, particularly concerning civil rights.

The 1960s were pivotal, marked by the rise of figures like George Wallace, a prominent segregationist whose political campaigns explicitly advocated for segregationist policies and white supremacist views. During this era, the Republican Party developed the "Southern Strategy," particularly under Richard Nixon. This strategy aimed to appeal to white voters in the South who were resistant to the Civil Rights Movement and desegregation.

While Nixon and other Republicans did not openly endorse white supremacy, the Southern Strategy capitalized on existing racial tensions and indirectly benefited from racist sentiments for political gain. This environment solidified a conservative ideology centered around limited government and states' rights, prompting many who believed in these tenets to leave the Democratic Party in droves and join the Republican ranks.

Between 1965 and 2015, the Democratic Party successfully implemented several landmark policies that sought to promote social welfare. The Great Society programs aimed to eliminate poverty and racial injustice, significantly impacting education, healthcare, and civil rights. The 1996 Personal Responsibility and Work Opportunity Reconciliation Act restructured welfare programs, fundamentally altering how assistance was dispensed and promoting work as a key component of welfare, though it led to controversial debates regarding its effectiveness in poverty reduction.

Key developments, such as the passage of the Civil Rights Act of 1964, were supported by many Republicans but highlighted the growing ideological rift within the party, as many Southern conservatives migrated toward the GOP. Those who believed in equality left the GOP and joined the ranks of the Democratic Party.

Ronald Reagan's presidency (1981-1989) emphasized tax cuts for the wealthy, deregulation, and a strong anti-communist foreign policy, enabling the Republican Party to build a coalition of fiscal conservatives, social conservatives, and national defense hawks.

In the 1990s and early 2000s, Republicans increasingly emphasized issues such as law and order, economic deregulation, tax reductions for the wealthy, and limiting immigration. The party's platform began incorporating the perspectives of religious conservatives, integrating moral and ethical dimensions into its policies. This evolution often positioned the GOP as a champion of traditional values against perceived liberal excesses.

Things changed significantly for the Republican Party in 2015 with the emergence of the MAGA Republicans, marking a departure from traditional GOP principles. Speculation has arisen that the MAGA movement may have effectively ended the traditional Republican Party. Critics argue that MAGA is neither conservative nor committed to small government, nor does it uphold the party's historical association with law and order.

Under Donald Trump's leadership, this faction has utilized populist and nationalist rhetoric that resonates with disenchanted voters, particularly among the working class. Trump's presidency heralded an era of openly confrontational politics characterized by a rejection of established norms and increased polarization.

Critics contend that this shift has led the GOP toward extremism, raising questions about the party's commitment to democratic republican principles and civil discourse.

Today's Republicans are often criticized for promoting pro-white and anti-civil rights sentiments while attempting to claim historical civil rights achievements as part of their narrative. This disconnect leads to discussions about authenticity and accountability within the party's political identity. The struggle to reconcile the party's past with its current values has further entrenched divisions within the GOP, making it challenging for moderate voices to navigate the political landscape.

Under Donald Trump's leadership, this faction has utilized populist and nationalist rhetoric that resonates with disenchanted voters, particularly among the working class. Trump's presidency heralded an era of openly confrontational politics characterized by a rejection of established norms and increased polarization.

Critics contend that this shift has led the GOP toward extremism, raising questions about the party's commitment to democratic republican principles and civil discourse.

Today's MAGA Republicans are criticized for promoting pro-white sentiments and opposing civil rights while attempting to co-opt historical civil rights achievements as part of their narrative.

This disconnect leads to discussions about authenticity and accountability within the party's political identity. The struggle to reconcile the party's past with its current values has further entrenched divisions within the GOP, making it challenging for moderate voices to navigate the political landscape.

One notable observation in today's political climate is the similarity between MAGA Republicans and the original Democrats at their inception, both parties sometimes shift their strategies or messaging in response to criticism or policy shortcomings.

This phenomenon often involves rebranding efforts that allow them to distance themselves from unpopular positions, even though they continue to hold that position secretly. Yet they will always overlook the need for genuine accountability and reform.

For example, as issues such as systemic racism and climate change become more prominent, the MAGA Republican Party will attempt to reposition itself without addressing the underlying problems that contribute to systemic inequities. This lack of accountability raises important questions about the long-term political health of the party and its commitment to genuinely representing the interests of the MAGA constituents.

The evolution of the Democratic and Republican parties reflects profound ideological changes driven by social movements and shifting voter demographics. Understanding these dynamics provides insight into the motivations behind current political strategies and the ongoing challenges each party faces today. As the political landscape continues to evolve, the Democratic Party adapts and evolves to societal changes.

In contrast, the Republican Party appears to be focused on returning to past ideals, which suggests a resistance to change. This situation could potentially lead to new alliances and party structures, reminiscent of historical transformations.

With Donald Trump's re-election after Biden served between his first and second terms, Trump is considered a lame-duck president because he cannot legally serve again.

As a lame-duck president with millions of supporters, Trump's primary focus has allegedly been on leveraging power over those who refuse to comply with his demands, by bending the knee and kissing the ring.

Trump is accused of selling favors and accepting substantial bribes from countries known for their nefarious reputations.

For instance, he has verbally accepted a $400 million plane from Qatar, a country that supports International terrorism and Hamas, as a personal gift, which raises legal concerns.

Trump also signed a multi-billion-dollar deal with Saudi Arabia in exchange for political favors, such as lifting sanctions against the Syrian ruler, who is an ally and friend of the Saudi Prince with whom Trump negotiated.

Trump has defied judicial rulings against him and has been disregarding the legislative branch by terminating cabinet positions or laying off hundreds of thousands of government employees without congressional permission.

He has also dismissed personnel at the Department of Justice for performing their duties during the previous administration.

Donald Trump has done what he has falsely accused the Democratic Party of doing which is to weaponize the DOJ, FBI, and other agencies to serve his interests rather than those of the public.

Donald Trump and the MAGA movement have significantly reshaped the Republican Party, steering it away from its traditional values and platform.

The party's current direction characterized by divisive rhetoric and extreme loyalty to Trump has alienated moderate Republicans and independents who once found common ground within the party.

Trump's influence has overshadowed longstanding conservative principles, prioritizing personal allegiance over party philosophy.

Given this transformation, it seems unlikely that the traditional Republican Party can return to its former stance without a fundamental rebranding.

A new name and a more inclusive platform may be necessary to attract a broader base and regain the trust of voters who value unity and bipartisan cooperation. Without significant changes, the party risks becoming further entrenched in a polarized political landscape.

Evolution of America's Migration Policy

From the colonial period through the Industrial Revolution, the Roaring Twenties, the Great Depression, and up to today, radical swings in migration policy have had their connections to earlier debates and policies.

86 million people immigrated to the United States between 1783 and 2019.

Immigrating into the United States has changed radically over the years; the politics surrounding those changes have remained contentious.

The United States possesses an incoherent immigration process with outdated program objectives.

Let's review the history of U.S. Immigration Practice, including the legal controversies that empowered Congress with its immigration plenary power and the historical policy decisions that still guide the U.S. immigration system.

From the colonial period through the Industrial Revolution, the Roaring Twenties, the Great Depression, and up to today, radical swings in immigration practice have had their connections to earlier deliberations and policies. It's important to understand how the immigration program got to this point because many of the same debates keep recurring.

Britain fiercely protected citizenship by limiting naturalization and forcibly populating its colonies with criminals and other social pariahs that the British government deemed undesirable. Naturalization was economically essential because only British citizens, known as "subjects," could own real estate and bequeath it to their heirs under English common law.

Britain's unwillingness to naturalize immigrants relegated most of its alien residents to a legal position called "denizen," similar to the Athenian metic (a foreign resident of Athens). This gave them limited economic rights. Their political rights were reduced. This likewise placed restrictions on bequeathing their estates under English common law.

European countries discouraged the internal migration of their citizens, they typically encouraged moving skilled workers to the new world without encouraging naturalization. European authorities also advocated migration to their colonies and colonial governments offered quick naturalization, land grants, and debt relief.

In North America, the British Crown's desire to settle its colonies caused it to ignore the lax naturalization processes in the colonies, which granted immigrants the rights of Englishmen within the territories in which they lived. Eventually, however, in 1700 Parliament limited the colonies' ability to grant naturalization and other group rights because it believed that the colonial naturalization policies weakened English citizens' trading positions.

Thereafter, many colonies relied on local naturalization and grants of citizenship until the Parliament passed the Plantation Act of 1740 to ease the colonial naturalization process and spur settlement.

The Pact created a uniform naturalization system that granted new, non-Catholic colonial settlers. English naturalization after seven years of residency. Also, contingent upon a religious test, a pledge of allegiance, and proof of Christian belief to which some people, such as Jews, were exempt.

Individuals arrived in the British colonies via two unique paths. It forced some to immigrate, either through transport or slavery, while others came voluntarily. "Transportation," a criminal term for involuntary immigration, allowed Britain to expel its social undesirables, convicts, and others to populate its North American colonies. Criminals sentenced to death could either choose transportation or hanging, and so mandatory immigration was a popular choice, since death was the only punishment for a felony conviction under English common law.

The 1717 Transportation Act granted English courts the ability to sentence convicts to transportation, thus streamlining the process. The courts could effectively banish convicts for up to 14 years and turn them into indentured servants. Before the American Revolution, Britain transported about 50,000 convicts to the American colonies. While colonists opposed transportation, the colonies could not prevent the changing residence of British subjects who were exempted from many colonial immigration restrictions.

The largest population of forced migrants to North America was not criminals from Britain, but 388,000 African slaves.

Slavery differed from the other forced migrations as, unlike the cases of convicts, there was no possibility of earning freedom.

African slaves and their descendants have comprised a substantial part of the population in the British colonies and the United States since the 1600s, but thinking of slaves as immigrants stretches the imagination of that word to its breaking point. Enslavement was an experience so radically different from what was experienced by other migrants that the story of slavery does not fit into this paper's narrative.

The allure of cheap land, high wages, and the freedom of conscience drew people who migrated to the colonies of their own volition in British North America. Many of these individuals financed their passage by entering indentured servitude contracts.

At the end of their contracts, they would discharge the indentured servants with a small amount of cash and skills, and sometimes land on the new continent. During the 1700s, a significant share of Europeans coming to British North America were indentured servants.

While the colonies had an open-door immigration policy to attract immigrants, some colonial cities along with some towns still regulated immigration by barring the entry of the poor, applying head taxes, and using banishment. However, these small and heterogeneous colonial communities were less meticulous than European governments in enforcing their immigration requirements and generally granted equal rights to accept foreigners. For example, Massachusetts applied its requirements against pauperism equally to all members, regardless of citizenship status. Other states extended voting rights to immigrants and, sometimes, to "servants, Africans, aliens, Jews, and Common sailors."

In 1755, Great Britain realized the colonial population had surpassed one million residents. This worried England.

So, in 1763, Britain prohibited colonists from settling the land gained from France during the Seven Years' War and subsequently curtailed colonial naturalization authority in 1773.

Great Britain's actions infuriated the New World, so they complained about them in the Declaration of Independence, charging King George III with preventing "the population of these States; for that purpose, obstructing the Laws for Naturalization of Foreigners; refusing to pass others to encourage their migrations hither and raising the conditions of current appropriations of Lands."

The New World population had increased to roughly 2.2 million residents at the start of the American Revolution.

They shaped the immigration policy through many legal issues that were addressed during the early days of the American Republic. Citizenship was one of the earliest issues that American politicians grappled with.

Three fundamental concepts underlie U.S. citizenship law, and their relative importance shifts depending on the needs and the norms of the era.

The first is jus soli, the right of the soil, so those born on U.S. land are automatically granted citizenship.

The second is jus sanguineous, the right of blood, so those born to U.S. residents in other countries automatically earn U.S. citizenship under most conditions.

The third is pledged allegiance, whereby those who civically commit to the United States become U.S. residents.

It related pledged allegiance to the concept of naturalization, the process by which an immigrant voluntarily moves to the United States and swears allegiance to the government to fully enter American political life through citizenship.

Immediately after issuing the Declaration of Independence, the Founders thought that pledging allegiance would confer citizenship through consent.

This approach diminished the new country's reliance on jus soli and jus sanguineous. It is unsurprising that during the American Revolution, when the American Founders feared the British would punish their disloyalty with death, loyalty trumped one's birth country or bloodline as a matter of importance.

Thus, a pledge of allegiance was the ticket to receive the full panoply of political rights in a new and struggling nation.

The colonies were made up of three groups.

Former British nationals supported the revolution and became American citizens.

British citizens still supported the British regime and were developed into enemy aliens.

Plus a dreary middle ground of fair-weather residents.

After the war, former loyalists and those in the murky middle prompted the U.S. government to view citizenship as "both a matter of place of birth and one of consent.

The Constitution enumerates other powers that are inherent to a sovereign, but the Founders did not include immigration as one of them.

The Constitution gave Congress the power to establish a uniform rule of naturalization in Article I, Section 8, and made immigrants eligible for all federal offices except the presidency and, later, the vice presidency.

In 1789, almost 10 percent of all members of the House of Representatives and the Senate were foreign-born, compared to just 3 percent in 2021.

The Constitutional Convention decided to grant the federal government authority over naturalization.

Making it easy and allowing the banishing of criminals and immigrants, also denying entry to the poor, and even attempting to ban entire races.

The U.S. population was ethnically and racially heterogeneous in 1790.

Congress passed the Naturalization Law of 1790, extending citizenship to free white people of excellent character who had lived in the United States for two years and took an oath of allegiance.

The order excluded indentured servants, non-whites, and slaves from naturalization.

Despite these exclusions, the Naturalization Act of 1790 was arguably the most liberal naturalization order to date, as it created a short and uniform path to citizenship that lacked gender requirements, religious evaluations, skills assessments, or country of origin requirements.

Congressional representatives were not satisfied with the Naturalization Law of 1790 because they feared that a large foreign-born population with voting rights could undermine national security, especially when the United States faced the prospect of war.

Congress passed the Naturalization Statute of 1795. The new operation increased the residency requirement for naturalization to five years and added a clause requiring prospective citizens to declare their intention to naturalize three years before doing so.

Notably, the Naturalization Act of 1795 held a religious and moral subtext that changed "respectable character" to "useful righteous character."

Again, because of fears, Congress passed a series of bills in 1798, collectively known as the Alien and Sedition Acts. This expanded the federal government's involvement in immigration policy.

Together, these laws subjected aliens to the threat of national surveillance, and arbitrary arrest and granted a new power to the president to deport immigrants via decree. Notably, these acts increased the residency period for naturalization to 14 years and required that prospective citizens declare their intent to naturalize five years before doing so.

During the congressional debate, a partisan schism arose over whether foreigners had rights under the Constitution.

Democratic-Republicans argued noncitizens possessed all rights under the Constitution because it often used the words "people" or "persons" rather than "citizens."

James Madison denounced the idea that noncitizens didn't have rights under the Constitution and maintained that even if they did, the government would still not have absolute authority over them.

Congressional representative also decried that deportation by presidential decree violated the Fifth and Sixth Amendments.

Although these acts empowered the federal government, much of the Alien and Sedition Acts expired by 1801. In 1802, Congress passed the Naturalization Law of 1802, which reverted the residency qualifications for naturalization to five years.

Today's immigrants who entered on student visas, adjusted to H1B visas, and then earned green cards may stay longer for citizenship, but they do not mandate those wait times as they arise from a combination of different legal requirements.

After the 1800 election, both parties courted the support of the approximately 250,000 European immigrants who arrived between 1783 and 1815.

By 1819, economic depression and the worry that Britain might ship their poor to the United States tempered Congress's pro-immigration position. While Congress lacked an enumerated power under the Constitution to control immigration.

In 1819 Congress, underhandedly regulated immigration by calling it for safety by limiting the number of passengers that a ship could carry based on its tonnage.

Still in 1819, the legislation lowered the carrying capacity of traveler ships and increased the price of travel, consequently reducing the number of poor immigrants who could afford passage. The bill still required ship captains to provide a traveler manifest to customs officials that allowed the federal government to track immigration flows for the first time.

Expansion of the Federal Government along with the Second and Third Wave was part of the Second and Third Wave.

When the U.S. population was over 12 million, the next wave of immigrants began arriving.

Most newcomers in this second wave relied on credit or family remittances to pay for their passage to the United States. These funding methods caused the number of indentured servants to decline and nearly disappear.

Foreign developments,!such as the Irish Potato Famine, beginning in 1845, and the European political revolutions of 1848, helped push settlers to the United States.

Overall, foreign and domestic conditions increased the quantity of settlers from 599,125 during the 1830s to 1,713,251 during the 1840s.

During the Antebellum Era, settlers were mainly German, Irish, English, Canadian, and French.

Natural-born citizens worried about these foreigners because of wage competition, immigrants' use of outdoor relief (welfare consumed outside of institutions), and other welfare programs, and the religious dichotomy between the current Catholic immigrants and the native-born Americans, who were primarily Protestant. Nativists were more concerned that Catholic immigrants would oppose slavery.

In New York City, 51% of the people were foreign-born, while in California, over 63% of the state was foreign-born in 1855.

Immigration sentiments spawned the American Party, also called the Know-Nothings, in the 1850s. The party's central goal was to increase the residency period for naturalization to 21 years. The party's popularity subsided after immigration slowed in 1855.

Despite the slowing of settlers reducing the flows, between 1820 and 1860 the 30 plus years there was a long wave of immigrants that altered U.S. demography, increasing the foreign-born population to 13.2 percent by 1860.

When the Civil War began in 1861, demand for workers in war industries increased. To fill the void, pro-immigration Republicans sought to discredit nativists. President Abraham Lincoln contended that "our immigrants are one of the principal replenishing streams which are appointed by Providence to repair the ravages of an internal war and its waste of national strength and wealth."

Congress passed both the Homestead Act in 1862 and the Act to Encourage Immigration in 1864, also known as the Contract Labor Act.

The Homestead Act offered territory grants to both U.S. citizens and immigrants who were eligible for naturalization and who would settle and develop the land for five years.

The last consequential immigration law passed during Lincoln's presidency was the Contract Labor Act of 1864, which allowed private employers to recruit foreign workers, pay their transportation costs, and contract their laborers.

The Lincoln administration had a longer-term effect on American immigration policy when it appointed Anson Burlingame as the U.S. Minister to China in 1861.

Burlingame negotiated the Burlingame-Seward trade treaty with China in 1868. Recognizing the "mutual advantage of the free migration and emigration of their colonists," the Burlingame-Seward Treaty ensured Chinese citizens had the right to emigrate and enter the United States.

The treaty didn't secure naturalization rights for Chinese settlers, it secured their ability to migrate, which had been illegal under Chinese law.

The U.S. government negotiated a treaty where the major provision required the Chinese government to allow immigration to the United States. As a result, Chinese foreigners joined an increasing flow that pushed the U.S. foreign-born population up to about 14.4 percent of the total in 1870.

When the Civil War concluded, Congress set about reforming the naturalization law to be consistent with the end of slavery.

However, Congress members disagreed on how far they should extend the rights afforded by naturalization.

The Naturalization Decree of 1870 only granted naturalization rights to "refugees being free white individuals, and to immigrants of African nativity and people tof African descent." This Act excluded the naturalization of Native Americans and Asians, as they were not eligible for emancipation.

The Fourteenth Amendment, which stated that "all persons born or naturalized in the United States, and subject to the jurisdiction thereof, are citizens of the United States. The State, wherein they live," prohibits birthright citizenship for the descendants of Chinese immigrants.

The federal government held this position until the Supreme Court ruled otherwise in the 1898 United States v. Wong Kim Ark decision.

In response to growing anti-Chinese sentiment nationwide, and especially in California, Congress passed the Page Act of 1875. These restrictions violated the Burlingame-Seward Treaty.

The Page Act restricted the immigration of Chinese contract laborers, convicts, and many Chinese women, most of whom were the wives of male workers, on the spurious grounds that they were prostitutes.

Throughout the 1870s, the federal government adopted and began enforcing many state-level restrictions that had been on the books for decades but were rarely enforced.

Congress also passed the Immigration Act of 1882 and the Chinese Exclusion Law in the same year. The former bill introduced a $0.50 federal head tax on each alien passenger to fund immigration enforcement.

Although the Chinese Exclusion Law of 1882 only required a 10-year ban on Chinese laborers, Congress extended this ban through 1943.

While the Supreme Court initially ruled that the states had the jurisdiction to regulate immigration, it expanded the federal government's immigration jurisdiction over time. For example, the Supreme Court found, in the case of Corfield v. Coryell (1823), that "[c]commerce with foreign nations, and among the several states, can mean nothing more than the intercourse with those nations, and among those states, for trade.

The Supreme Court did not consider free immigrants to be articles of commerce, so they were not subject to federal regulation.

Similarly, the Supreme Court's 1837 New York v. Miln ruling noted that "persons are not the subjects of commerce, and not being imported goods, they do not fall within the reasoning founded upon the construction of a power given to Congress to regulate commerce and the prohibition of the states from imposing a duty on imported goods."

Thus, states could pass measures discriminating against and excluding various kinds of immigrants, reaffirming the lack of federal jurisdiction.

Twelve years later, the Supreme Court's rulings in the Passenger Cases struck down countless state laws that restricted immigration because they interfered with the commerce clause and federal jurisdiction over taxation and indirect regulation of foreigners.

By 1875, the Supreme Court's Henderson v. Mayor of New York ruling struck down a New York state law that required both a bond for ship captains and an immigrant fee because it infringed on Congress's power to regulate commerce.

Here, the Justices noted that the right to regulate commerce ended when the passengers landed in the United States.

In the 1884 Head Money Cases, the Supreme Court decided Congress had "the authority to pass a law regulating migration as a part of the commerce of this country with foreign nations" and overrode state immigration policies.

Many of these cases expanded Congress's authority. They were minor encroachments relative to the Supreme Court's decision in Chae Chan Ping v. the United States in 1889.

Prompted by a provision of the Chinese Exclusion Act, the Supreme Court determined Congress had an extra-constitutional plenary power over immigration based on the "fact of sovereignty" rather than any specifically enumerated authority.

Even though the Constitution explicitly enumerates other powers that are unquestionably a "matter of sovereignty," such as regulating international commerce, raising an army, and declaring war.

In the Court's opinion, Justice Stephen Field recounted California's constitutional convention, which had found that "the presence of Chinese laborers had a baneful effect upon the material interests of the state, and upon public morals; that their immigration was in numbers approaching the character of an Oriental invasion and was a menace to our civilization."

They reasoned that the United States had the power to "preserve its independence, and give security against foreign aggression and encroachment," such as Chinese migration.

The Supreme Court's decision created a "constitutional oddity" that subsequently decreased judicial oversight of immigration law.

Understanding Social Security Without All Of The Rhetoric

Social Security is designed to be self-sustaining, primarily funded through payroll taxes that generate a surplus. This surplus is then invested in Treasury bonds, creating a significant asset pool. Critics argue that some politicians, particularly from the Republican Party, have used these Social Security funds as collateral for various spending projects, essentially masking them under the guise of Social Security revenues.

Such actions contribute to the federal deficit by diverting funds from their intended use for Social Security, allowing for increased discretionary spending without adequate transparency.

This practice raises ethical concerns and has sparked discussions about the long-term viability of the program and fiscal responsibility.

The debate surrounding Social Security often gets mired in political rhetoric, particularly from conservative factions. Analyzing this issue requires a clear understanding of what Social Security represents, how it functions, and the implications of proposed changes to the program.

Social Security is a social insurance program established in 1935 to provide economic security for the elderly, disabled, and survivors of deceased workers.

It is primarily funded through payroll taxes collected under the Federal Insurance Contributions Act (FICA). Employees and employers each contribute 6.2% of wages to the Social Security Trust Fund, totaling 12.4% for employees' wages. Self-employed individuals pay a combined rate of 12.4% (which includes both the employee and employer share).

As of recent data, the Social Security Trust Fund has a reserve of approximately $2.9 trillion. It's important to note that while Treasury bonds are held in trust as assets for future obligations, the characterization of "collateral" in connection with spending projects is misleading. These funds are intended to be preserved for Social Security benefits, and the use of surplus funds for other expenditures indeed raises concerns about the program's long-term

This trust fund is crucial, as it ensures the program can continue paying benefits even during periods when expenditures exceed revenues from payroll taxes. Social Security is structured to be self-sufficient and is not designed to contribute to the federal budget deficit.

Many conservative politicians and commentators have perpetuated the narrative that Social Security contributes to the national deficit, suggesting that it requires significant reforms or even cuts. This portrayal is fundamentally misleading. Social Security operates distinctly from the general budget; it is not part of the discretionary spending that contributes to the federal deficit, and its funding mechanism is separate from general tax revenues.

While Social Security itself is stable for the foreseeable future, debates often conflate it with discussions about Medicare and Medicaid, which face funding challenges due to rising healthcare costs.

The conflation of these separate programs can lead to misconceptions, reinforcing a narrative that paints Social Security in a troubled light when that is not the case.

Social Security serves as a critical lifeline for millions of Americans. Approximately 65 million beneficiaries depend on these payments, including retirees, disabled individuals, and survivors of deceased workers. For many, Social Security represents a significant portion of their retirement income, helping to alleviate poverty among older adults. In fact, without Social Security benefits, it is estimated that the poverty rate for seniors would increase substantially.

Social Security is vital for maintaining the economic stability of the middle class. It allows individuals to retire without fearing destitution and contributes to overall economic health by providing a steady stream of income to consumers, who in turn spend it on goods and services.

Proposals from conservative lawmakers, often under the guise of reform, have included suggestions to privatize Social Security or reduce benefits. Such measures pose significant risks, including exposing retirees to the volatility of the stock market and undermining the guaranteed income that Social Security provides.

The push for cuts or privatization disproportionately affects younger generations, Generation Alpha, Generation Z, Millennials, and Generation X, who supply the majority of the Social Security revenue and are relying on Social Security to provide a safety net in their retirement.

While there are legitimate concerns about the long-term financial viability of the program, the focus should be on reforming the funding structure through means such as raising the payroll tax cap, which currently applies only to earnings up to a certain threshold. Increasing this cap could enhance the program's solvency without diminishing benefits.

The MAGA movement, which has gained a foothold in the Republican Party, often emphasizes populist themes that resonate with working-class voters. While this movement includes criticism of the "establishment," it can also perpetuate confusion regarding Social Security, framing it as a burden rather than a benefit.

One of the more concerning aspects of the MAGA movement is its tendency to foster distrust in government institutions, including social safety nets like Social Security. This skepticism can lead to support for politically motivated changes that threaten the program's core function as a guaranteed source of income for millions.

The discussion surrounding Social Security should focus on its merits, foundational structure, and the importance of preserving its integrity as a self-sustaining program.

Mischaracterizations that link Social Security to the national deficit are not only factually inaccurate but also undermine the program's vital role in American society.

The focus should be on enhancing the program, ensuring it remains funded and viable for future generations, rather than diluting or dismantling it under misleading pretenses. Constructive dialogue is essential to combat misinformation and advocate for policies that protect and strengthen Social Security while reflecting a commitment to economic stability and security for all Americans.

An Economic Civil War Would Break Trump, MAGA Leaders Elected and Appointed, Along With Those Who Voted MAGA

Trump, MAGA, MAGA Leaders, and MAGA Elite decide policies, laws, and budgets based on how much money they can pocket.

We can hit them where it hurts, and because of their hate, greed, and ignorance, they have already taken us 2/3rds of the way there.

We proved this on Saturday, June 14, 2025, during the "No Kings Day" protest, with 5 million people coming out to show force for one day.

We need at least 18.9 million people to make a difference. Anyone over sixteen who's working should commit to a national work walkout. You have to commit because it doesn't have an end date. The fewer participants, the longer it will take.

If we could get momentum going and if I get a vote on the start date, I would pick January 6, 2026, as our Economic Civil War or our Financial Insurrection starts. There are two reasons: one, to take the date back from MAGA insurrectionists, and two, if MAGA responds negatively on that date, it would reinforce the fact that MAGA is anti-democracy and anti-First Amendment for everyone; it would only apply to MAGA.

As the stakes rise in this economic civil war, the implications extend beyond immediate policy debates. The potential disruption threatens to reshape national discourse, unravel economic stability, and redefine the very fabric of American society.

This will help the Pro Democracy, Pro Democratic Republic, and Pro Constitution Advocates explore the dynamics igniting this struggle, examine the societal consequences of a nationwide strike, and delve into how collective action and organized labor could usher in a transformative chapter in American history, one that advocates for equitable economic practices and reclaims power for the working people. If you work for or do business with anything MAGA, cease any exchange of dollars, business, or communication. We go dark with MAGA, regardless of who they are, family, friends, employer, employee, and everything in between.

In a deeply polarized America, the political landscape has been dramatically reshaped by the rise of the MAGA (Make America Great Again) movement, championed by President Donald Trump. Trump's tenure is driven more by a quest for power and personal gain than by genuine concern for the interests of the American people.

Trump is selling his signature, executive orders, pardons, our military, and our country to the highest bidder. His only goal is to be the wealthiest man in the world because he is a little fish in the big billionaire pond. If he doesn't reach his goal by January 6, 2029, he will try for a third term and sacrifice even more of our country.

At the heart of this conflict lies a stark power struggle, as MAGA seeks to maintain its grip on political influence and fill its pockets while a new and vocal growing coalition of individuals that are Pro Democracy, Pro Democratic Republic, and Pro Constitution Advocates is among the populace and growing, and will not negotiate our demands for economic justice and social equity.

A pivotal flashpoint in this unfolding drama was the recent mass protests during "No Kings Day." Over 10 million American Voters and non-voters from various sectors mobilized and took to the streets to express their frustrations with policies benefiting the wealthy elite and violating civil rights and human rights at the expense of marginalized communities.

This demonstration served as a potent symbol of deep-seated dissatisfaction, highlighting the profound economic divide between traditionalist voters primarily from rural and working-class backgrounds and urban communities advocating for progressive reforms.

It is crucial to recognize that much of the agricultural and ranching workforce has been drastically diminished recently due to policies implemented under the MAGA movement.

Farms and ranches have lost the majority of their staff as a direct result of stringent immigration policies and anti-immigrant sentiment that has characterized Trump's MAGA administration.

The mistreatment and dehumanization of immigrants, notably those who often form the backbone of our economy, has transformed the agricultural landscape, leading to significant labor shortages. By treating immigrants like animals by rounding them up and corralling them, the MAGA movement has created a toxic environment that not only affects those immigrants directly but also has severe economic repercussions across the country. We have little or no tourism in 2025. Without sufficient labor, many farms, ranches, and other agricultural professions struggle to maintain production levels, leading to food scarcity and unsustainable prices in certain regions.

At the same time, Trump's tariffs have inflicted additional damage to the economy, leading to increased costs on imported goods and destabilizing key industries. While intended to protect American jobs, these tariffs have paradoxically heightened economic pressure on domestic businesses that rely on global supply chains. The intertwining of labor shortages and trade tariffs could catalyze a rapid economic breakdown, demonstrating that the mechanisms for disrupting the status quo are already in place.

Throughout American history, mass labor actions have significantly influenced their times' political and economic contexts.

A few notable examples include the 1934 Minneapolis Teamsters Strike, which disrupted local commerce and galvanized the labor movement, leading to enhanced union recognition and labor protections, and the 1981 PATCO Strike, where air traffic controllers attempted a mass walkout, ending in severe governmental backlash and exemplifying the risks associated with striking while highlighting the complexities of labor relations.

These historical events serve as reminders of the potential for collective action to reshape societal norms and political realities, but they also underscore the significant risks involved.

We can do the same, but on a much grander scale. We have something our past didn't have: technology, an organized network, and the means to stop what we are doing long enough for MAGA to know we are the ones running this country all along. We may have been passive, but we have had enough, and without our permission, MAGA has no power.

Imagine where those workers who oppose MAGA, in various industries to the billionaires financing anti-Trump initiatives, coordinated a nationwide mass walkout from our jobs, irrespective of any MAGA employers' stances on the contentious issues surrounding this political movement.

As employees abandon their posts, MAGA businesses, tiny and medium-sized enterprises, will face immediate operational paralysis.

The financial consequences will be devastating to anyone and anything MAGA with cash flow dwindling or stopped and productivity halted; many MAGA businesses including Trump's ventures would struggle to survive, some will immediately fall into bankruptcies and without a complete staff to operate the MAGA following employees will suffer job losses which will further exacerbate the economic downturn MAGA and its stooges created when the decided to attack immigrants of color.

We can and will pull this off the MAGA downfall, which will escalate rapidly. The agriculture sector, already teetering on the brink due to staff shortages and rising costs, and exacerbated by tariffs, would be among the hardest hit. Without the immigration labor force to harvest crops, and when somewhere between 18 and 90 million citizens stop their work, the MAGA political train will immediately run out of steam.

If everyone who is anti-MAGA walked out past the sidewalk and sat on the curb, so you are legal and MAGA can not have you cited or arrested for trespassing, at the same time. It will have an immediate impact on the private sector and government agencies. All food supply chains would cease immediately, resulting in price inflation and further strife in communities already feeling the burden of economic struggle.

Mass blackouts and the closing of oil refineries, chemical plants, and nuclear power would not be monitored, police, Fire, and rescue would cease, airlines would be grounded, the Internet would go offline, and phone service would stop. Anything MAGA that's open to the general public, such as clothing stores, supermarkets, car dealerships, banks, universities, public schools, and every government office, to name a few.

Moreover, this collective economic paralysis would have cascading effects on local and state governments, which rely heavily on revenue from sales and income taxes. As local businesses close their doors, municipalities would see a sharp decline in tax collections, leading to budget shortfalls that might force governments to implement drastic austerity measures, cutting essential services and laying off public employees.

With the current economic climate already strained, a sizable disruption will push the economy toward a temporary Depression that can be corrected when everything and everyone MAGA has been flushed from our democracy. Our Democratic Republic Government has been restored, and our Constitution is enforced. This includes freezing all of the Assets of anything and anyone MAGA.

We will succeed if we take the first step. I know it works because this is not my first time being in a small group demanding change while surrounded by 2 million MAGA followers. Back then, we just called them what they are, RACIST BIGOTS.

Everyone, regardless of age or what workforce you're part of, who is anti-MAGA, has to come together for a temporary layover.

We have to remember that MAGA is barely 30% of our adult population, and they are not all registered voters, even though they are vocal.

The timeline for addressing the challenges posed by a mass walkout could vary dramatically based on numerous factors, including the duration of the walkout, public support, and corporate responses to the situation.

A walkout lasting just a few days to weeks would produce immediate repercussions. Still, an extended strike could lead to more pronounced and lasting damage to MAGA businesses and the economy. Striking workers need to rally public support from those who agree but are unwilling to take risks and walk out. It's up to all of us, regardless of what position we choose to take, to maintain momentum, as media narratives could sway public opinion, potentially galvanizing broader coalitions opposing MAGA and demanding transformative political action.

MAGA companies would quickly seek to replace absent workers, but I believe it will fail because of the MAGA Cult Followers demographic. I am not pointing that out just as a dig; the reality is that not all reds are MAGA, but not all MAGA are red. Most MAGA strongholds are Red States, with little or no financial resources to make up the loss. Red states are highest in unemployment, lowest in education, lowest in skilled workers, and most MAGA followers only know manual labor; they don't have to work hard at it. Again, I'm not saying as a dig. Just common sense, why would we have millions of immigrants as farm, ranch, cleaning, kitchen, and orderlies if the uneducated MAGA were willing to work? The MAGA would have to sink billions into alcohol and drug rehab, and years for them to see any return. Again, it's not to be hateful, look at the demographics.

Overall, if everyone opposed to MAGA did just one hard push all at once, our efforts would lead to a permanent reshaping of the labor market.

MAGA would have to invest billions, and it would take years for its business to implement automation and find companies willing to outsource labor to manufacture its products. Thus, we might become a lasting legacy of prolonged worker protests.

The notion of a mass walkout against the MAGA movement may seem radical, but the potential implications for the economy and the political landscape are substantial. If we can get an organized walkout to unfold, it could set off a chain reaction of events that would redefine the balance of power in American politics.

The political ramifications of such a mass walkout could be equally significant. Media outlets would inevitably spotlight the walkout, garnering national and worldwide attention and potentially swaying public opinion in favor of the strikers.

Suppose we can get a large portion of the populace not willing to walk out but empathizing with those walking out. In that case, it will pressure political leaders to reconsider their stance on the MAGA movement and promote policy changes that align with the demands of the dissenting workers.

The government's response would be crucial. Local, state, and federal entities might pursue urgent legislative measures to address workers' grievances, possibly resulting in an increased focus on workers' rights and labor agreements. Suppose political leaders perceived the economic consequences as a genuine threat to their power, where the vast majority called for political change. In that case, they might galvanize efforts to confront the MAGA movement head-on.

Ultimately, the path toward removing every trace of MAGA from government would depend on the resilience of those opposing it and the broader societal response to the turmoil induced by the walkout.

Given the existing vulnerabilities in agriculture, exacerbated by labor shortages and the damaging impacts of tariffs, it does not take much to spark significant unrest or distrust in the current administration.

Whether it leads to genuine reform or spirals into political upheaval remains a question that underscores the deep divisions inherent in contemporary American life and the ongoing struggle for an equitable future free from the overreach of power and greed.

As this economic civil war intensifies, the narrative emerges of resilience and determination among advocates for change. It epitomizes a broader battle for the soul of America, a fight against entrenched inequities perpetuated by an elite few. Suppose the burgeoning movement can transform its initial momentum into a sustained campaign. In that case, it can spark significant unrest that challenges prevailing economic policies and compels confrontation with systemic grievances regarding labor rights, economic inequality, and social justice.

The outcome remains uncertain, but the stakes are undeniably high, as the nation stands at a crossroads: a time for profound transformation or continued division. American society's horizon may be contingent upon how effectively the people's collective will can disrupt the status quo, reshaping economic policy and the political landscape, and ultimately breaking the MAGA movement's hold on power.

We have two options: this or whether to learn Spanish or French. History dictates, and Trump has shown his hand. If we don't do something, we will go to war as an aggressive nation. NATO will not aid us, they will rally around the invaded, and we will lose all dictators will lose and ask Germany what happened to their country when the war ended. For 40 years, a wall divided families, and they lost their right to govern the two countries they had become for decades. Ask the Middle East what happened after they lost WWI, and look at what has happened to all the little countries they became.

I'm guessing that when we lose, Mexico will get back all of the land we stole, and Canada will make us eat crow as they decide what's left of our country. I'm referring to Canadian provinces with the blessing of the United Kingdom. Or maybe to piss Trump off give the rest of our country to the indigenous people of the Americas. That will take the USA full circle.

America's Complex Role on the Global Stage: Can a Nation Exhibit Narcissism?

It is important to note that from the time the first Anglo colony was established in North America, a troubling trend began one that the United States continues to find acceptable: the exploitation, annexation, and annihilation of nations and continents of color.

This trend initiated with the systematic plundering and nearly caused the extinction of the indigenous peoples of the Americas. As if that wasn't far enough, the U.S. continued to exploit, plunder, and pillage the very peoples of the African continent, considering the actual demographic of Africans a commodity for exploitation.

Despite the colonies in the Americas proclaiming themselves a promoters and advocates of democracy, the U.S. does not have clean hands and is responsible for starting the animosities toward the US by nations and the continent of color in America's history.

The United States' treatment of nations of color beyond its borders including the people of color within its own borders speaks to a legacy of systemic aggression that has persisted since the inception of its first colony.

Our nation refuses to hold itself accountable, failing to admit its wrongdoing. Instead, it often doubles down and portrays itself as a victim, claiming unprovoked attacks necessitate retaliation whenever nations or continents of color rise against the injustices they endure. This mentality of defending its interests under the guise of democracy perpetuates the cycle of unrest and resentment.

For a young country compared to others, the United States frequently approaches international relations with a paternalistic attitude, attempting to impose its values on other nations. This mindset reflects a failure to learn from history and to emulate the democratic practices of older civilizations that have thrived for millennia. The U.S. has exploited nations of color since its inception, a practice that continues to shape its foreign policy and international relations. As a result, America's democracy now teeters on the brink of collapse.

A significant number of countries harbor deep resentment toward the United States, stemming from this troubling history of exploitation. The U.S. has appropriated land, resources, and governance for its benefit, particularly targeting nations of color. Notably, approximately 90% of countries adversely affected by U.S. policies fall into this category.

The following eight nations exemplify the complex and often damaging relationship the U.S. has fostered through its various forms of exploitation or intervention:

Puerto Rico: The relationship between Puerto Rico and the United States is fraught with historical, political, and economic tensions that contribute to resentment among many Puerto Ricans. Since becoming a U.S. territory in 1898, Puerto Rico has lost its sovereignty and operates under U.S. governance without full rights. Puerto Ricans are U.S. citizens but cannot vote in presidential elections and have no voting representation in Congress, leading to feelings of political marginalization. Furthermore, U.S. policies, such as the Jones Act, have adversely affected the island's economy, exacerbating issues like the recent debt crisis and contributing to a pervasive sense of economic exploitation and neglect. Culturally, many Puerto Ricans feel a loss of identity due to the imposition of American norms and values, alongside facing discrimination in mainland America. This complex dynamic fuels calls for either statehood or independence—a multifaceted grievance that illustrates the disconnect between Puerto Rico and the U.S. mainland.

Venezuela: The complex relationship between the United States and Venezuela is marked by long-standing resentment fueled by a series of interventions, economic sanctions, and perceived political meddling. Historically, the U.S. has intervened in Latin America under the pretext of promoting democracy and stability, but many Venezuelans view these actions as imperialistic. This includes U.S. support for various opposition groups during tumultuous times, notably during Hugo Chávez's presidency when the U.S. was perceived as backing a coup attempt in 2002. Such interventions fostered a narrative of the U.S. as a neocolonial power attempting to control Venezuela's political landscape, galvanizing nationalism and anti-American sentiment among both the populace and the government. Furthermore, economic sanctions targeting Venezuela's oil sector—the backbone of its economy—have exacerbated the nation's economic woes and contributed to a humanitarian crisis. Many Venezuelans blame these sanctions for widespread shortages of basic goods, food, and medicine, viewing them as punitive measures that deepen the suffering of ordinary citizens rather than encourage reform. This perception of U.S. interference has entrenched resentment and unified a national identity against what is seen as an external oppressor, deepening the rift between the two nations.

Cuba: Long-standing animosity between the U.S. and Cuba is rooted in the U.S. embargo and interventions in Cuban affairs. After Fidel Castro came to power in 1959, Cuba sought assistance from the U.S., but the latter's refusal to aid the island unless it aligned with American interests significantly contributed to Cuba's shift toward communism. The U.S. response included the embargo that economically isolated Cuba, escalating hostilities, and prompting Castro to turn to the Soviet Union for support. This realignment not only solidified Cuba's communist regime but also deepened anti-American sentiments within the country. The U.S. interventionist policies and economic sanctions pushed Cuba into the arms of a superpower willing to provide the aid and support that the U.S. denied, illustrating how U.S. actions can directly shape the political landscape of other nations. This historical context highlights the complexities of U.S. foreign policy and its unintended consequences on international relations.

Panama: Panama's animosity toward the United States has historical roots deeply embedded in its complex relationship with U.S. involvement in its sovereignty, particularly concerning the Panama Canal. The U.S. played a pivotal role in Panama's separation from Colombia in 1903, subsequently gaining control over the Canal Zone. This control was formalized through the Hay-Bunau-Varilla Treaty, which many Panamanians perceived as inequitable and forced upon them. For most of the 20th century, the U.S. exercised significant political and military influence in Panama, leading to resentment toward American interventionism. The Canal, a symbol of U.S. dominance, was critical to Panamanians, who felt that their land and resources were being exploited without fair compensation or respect for their sovereignty. This legacy fostered humiliation and anger exacerbated by U.S. military actions and political machinations, including support for the oppressive regime of Manuel Noriega. Noriega's eventual fall from grace led to the U.S. invasion of Panama in 1989, resulting in extensive casualties and damage, deepening distrust of American motives. Many Panamanians continue to harbor bitterness toward American policies, viewing them as exploitative and damaging to their national identity.

Honduras: Resentment and hostility toward the United States in Honduras can be traced back to a tumultuous history of U.S. involvement in political affairs, particularly the backing of military coups that subverted democratic processes. One glaring example is the 2009 coup that ousted President Manuel Zelaya, who had initiated progressive reforms aimed at addressing social inequality and poverty. The U.S. response to the coup was perceived as tacit approval, as it did not take immediate action to restore Zelaya's leadership. This complicity entrenched distrust toward the U.S. among many Hondurans, who see American influence as undermining their sovereignty and democratic institutions. Additionally, economic exploitation linked to U.S. corporate interests has contributed to resentment, as American companies in agriculture and textiles have often employed exploitative labor practices with inadequate wages. This perception of the U.S. as a nation that exploits local resources fosters feelings of injustice, contributing to a cycle of resentment that affects diplomatic relations.

Mexico: Mexico's animosity toward the United States is rooted in colonial history, territorial disputes, and economic disparities. The Mexican-American War (1846-1848) dramatically reduced Mexico's territory, fostering a deep-seated resentment toward the U.S. Policies that maintain cycles of dependency and underdevelopment contribute to poverty and violence in Mexico, which are often oversimplified in American discourse focused on cartel violence. Many Mexicans view U.S. actions as imperialistic, undermining their sovereignty and exacerbating domestic challenges.

Syria: The United States' actions in Syria have significantly contributed to deep-seated distrust and hostility toward America among many Syrians. Historically, the U.S. has supported Israel in its conflicts with

Syria, fostering animosity due to perceived imperialistic tendencies. During the Syrian Civil War, the U.S. intervened by backing various rebel groups, including those affiliated with extremist factions, which many saw as direct interference in Syria's sovereignty and governance. This military involvement was perceived as exacerbating the conflict rather than promoting stability, particularly as U.S. airstrikes targeted both ISIS and government forces, leading to civilian casualties and destruction of infrastructure. The consequences of U.S. sanctions and military actions have resulted in widespread suffering among the Syrian populace. The Caesar Act, aimed at crippling the Syrian regime, has further complicated the humanitarian crisis, inflicting economic pain on ordinary citizens rather than solely the governing elite. The lack of a comprehensive approach that represents the diverse voices of the Syrian population in peace negotiations has also bred resentment, solidifying a narrative that the U.S. prioritizes its strategic interests over the welfare of the Syrian people. As a result, many Syrians view the U.S. not as a promoter of democracy but as an imperialist entity that fuels suffering and instability.

Korea: America's need to dominate and control the political landscape after World War II significantly contributed to the animosity toward the United States in Korea. Following the end of the Japanese occupation, rather than supporting Korea's bid for independence, the U.S. and the Soviet Union chose to divide the nation along the 38th parallel. This move was not driven by an understanding of Korean aspirations for self-determination but rather by the superpowers' desire to establish military strongholds in the region. The division artificially imposed by foreign powers created deep divides within Korea and led to the establishment of two antagonistic regimes: a communist dictatorship in the North guided by the USSR and an authoritarian government in the South propped up by the U.S. Ultimately, this failure to honor the Korean people's desire for unity and autonomy sowed seeds of discontent and hostility toward the U.S. as a colonial participant in their ongoing struggle. In the years that followed, America's actions in Korea were largely dictated by the context of the Cold War, where containing communism became a critical objective. The U.S. chose to back

Syngman Rhee, an anti-communist leader whose regime was marred by authoritarianism and corruption, further alienating the population. The U.S. arrogance and disregard for the Korean perspective resulted in increased instability, which contributed to the outbreak of the Korean War. Throughout this conflict, U.S. military intervention was less about supporting Korean independence and more focused on asserting control in the region, fueling the animosity that had already begun festering post-WWII. The desire to dictate the narrative of democracy, coupled with a lack of genuine engagement with the Korean populace, not only jeopardized the possibility of a cohesive Korean state but also led to profound, lasting repercussions that have shaped U.S.-Korean relations to this day.

At the heart of these issues lies a deeply ingrained attitude of American exceptionalism, which conveys the belief that the U.S. has both the right and obligation to intervene in the affairs of other nations. This mindset often disregards the historical contexts and complexities of foreign societies, leading to poorly conceived policies that exacerbate existing tensions. Nations like Iran and Cuba perceive American cultural and political imposition as a form of imperialism, fostering resentment and resistance.

The impacts of U.S. interventions, economic sanctions, and diplomatic failures have left an enduring imprint on Iranian society and continue to stoke animosity. Historical U.S. interventions—most notably the 1953 coup—have fostered a narrative of external control that resonates in Iranian society today. Ongoing economic sanctions have significantly impacted the Iranian economy and civilian population, leading to widespread hardship. Critics argue that these sanctions exacerbate anti-American sentiment and hinder diplomatic resolutions.

In Cuba, the U.S. refusal to assist the nation post-revolution unless it adhered to American interests pushed the country toward communism and aligned it more closely with the Soviet Union, leading to a deep mistrust of U.S. intentions. The ongoing embargo has isolated Cuba economically and fueled resentment, illustrating the complexities of U.S. foreign policy and its unintended consequences.

The inability to constructively engage with both Iran and Cuba highlights the need for a shift in U.S. foreign relations. Acknowledging and addressing historical grievances is crucial for improving U.S.-Iran and U.S.-Cuba relations and ensuring a more collaborative atmosphere. By shifting to a partnership model that emphasizes collaboration and respect for national sovereignty, the U.S. can lay the groundwork for long-term stability. Engaging in people-to-people connections and understanding local political contexts can help mend relations at a grassroots level. Constructive engagement requires consistent and open dialogue, highlighting the need for back-channel communications, cultural exchanges, and Track II diplomacy initiatives. Policies grounded in empathy and understanding can mitigate conflicts, recognizing the unique historical, cultural, and political contexts that shape Iranian and Cuban societies.

Identifying shared values such as economic cooperation, regional stability, and the fight against extremism can become a foundation for dialogue between the U.S. and Iran, and Cuba. A peaceful U.S.-Iran relationship has implications beyond bilateral ties; stability in these countries can contribute to broader regional stability, impacting global issues like energy security, migration, and counterterrorism. Through critical reflection and a commitment to empathetic engagement, we can address the root causes of animosity and strive toward a more peaceful future.

Such a transformation would not only enhance ties with both nations but also positively influence the international community, paving the way for a more collaborative and peaceful world. By recognizing past mistakes associated with its engagements in nations like Mexico, Puerto Rico, Honduras, Venezuela, Syria, and Korea, while promoting policies centered on empathy and constructive engagement, the U.S. can foster a more stable relationship with those it once exploited. Ultimately, this could lead to a renewed chapter characterized by collaboration rather than coercion, benefiting both nations and the wider international community.

____

By Dehumanizing People of Color Makes Viewing Immigrants of color as Disposable

I plan to highlight the critical issue of how immigrants are often stripped of their humanity through derogatory language, harmful stereotypes, and negative media portrayals. This dehumanization process reduces individuals to mere statistics or caricatures, making it easier for society to justify mistreatment and accept oppressive policies. When viewed as less than human, immigrants are subjected to unjust policies, social division, and mental health issues, contributing to a troubling narrative that has historical parallels across various marginalized groups.

From the very founding of the United States, immigrants of color, including people who were forced to relocate to be sold into slavery, Indigenous peoples; were not considered American citizens until June 2, 1924, and have faced mistreatment at the hands of the federal government and Anglo citizens. This treatment has been shaped by various presidential policies and public perceptions that transcend party lines. While all forms of abuse are grievous, the levels of brutality can vary significantly, revealing a chilling pattern in American history.

At the heart of this issue is a complex interplay between national security, undocumented immigration, and the treatment of marginalized communities, particularly people of color (POC). A closer examination of modern U.S. presidential decisions, from Gerald Ford to Donald Trump, reveals a distressing evolution that paved the way for the establishment of the Guantanamo Bay detention facility and highlighted the xenophobic national security tactics used to justify the dehumanization of immigrants.

During Franklin D. Roosevelt's presidency, immigrants of color, including Asian Americans, faced significant challenges and discrimination. While the New Deal aimed to alleviate economic hardships during the Great Depression, many programs excluded or marginalized these communities, often influenced by racial biases. The bombing of Pearl Harbor in 1941 exacerbated the situation for Japanese Americans, leading to the forced internment of around 120,000 individuals, most of whom were U.S. citizens, based on perceived national security threats. This period highlighted the intersection of economic strife, racial prejudice, and wartime hysteria, impacting the lived experiences of immigrants of color in the United States.

Gerald Ford navigated a challenging landscape in the post-Vietnam War era as he confronted a significant influx of Vietnamese refugees following the fall of Saigon in April 1975. While his administration facilitated the resettlement of approximately 130,000 Vietnamese through programs like Operation Frequent Wind, the reception of these immigrants was mixed. Many Americans were sympathetic to the plight of the refugees, recognizing their connections to the U.S. war effort. However, others expressed negative sentiments, fueled by fears of economic competition, cultural differences, and lingering resentment over the war. These factors contributed to a segment of the population that viewed the newcomers with suspicion, leading to social tension and resistance to their integration. This period highlighted the complexities of immigration policy in the U.S., marked by both humanitarian efforts and challenges related to public opinion towards immigrants.

During the presidency of Jimmy Carter, the U.S. faced significant challenges regarding immigration and human rights, particularly in the context of the Cuban boat crisis in 1980. This crisis arose when thousands of Cubans took to the sea in small boats, fleeing political repression and economic difficulties in Cuba. Many sought asylum in the United States, leading to a surge of Cuban immigrants arriving on Florida's shores. At the same time, U.S. support for anti-communist regimes in Latin America, particularly in countries like El Salvador, resulted in widespread human rights violations, forcing individuals to flee and seek refuge in the U.S. While Carter aimed to promote human rights, the realities of foreign policy often led to contradictions, contributing to systemic inequalities faced by immigrants of color and challenging efforts to address their needs within U.S. immigration policy.

Ronald Reagan's presidency marked a turning point in U.S. immigration perception, largely influenced by the prevailing anti-communist sentiment of the time. Reagan's administration employed tough rhetoric that increasingly framed immigrants as potential criminals, reflecting broader anxieties about national security and social stability. This shift in narrative contributed to a changing public perception of immigration, leading to more stringent policies and attitudes towards newcomers. The climate of fear surrounding immigration laid the groundwork for extreme counterterrorism measures that emerged in subsequent years, as policymakers and law enforcement sought to address perceived threats. Thus, Reagan's presidency played a pivotal role in shaping the discourse around immigration, influencing how immigrants were viewed within the context of national security.

After the attacks on September 11, 2001, George W. Bush faced immense pressure to address a perceived national security crisis. This urgency led to the establishment of the Guantanamo Bay detention facility in 2002, intended to securely detain terrorism suspects, but it also highlighted legal ambiguities surrounding detention practices. The remote location of Guantanamo resulted in a lack of oversight, contributing to serious human rights violations, including allegations of torture and inhumane treatment.

In this post-9/11 context, the routine detention of individuals without trial raised significant concerns, particularly for Muslim individuals and other suspects of color who were disproportionately targeted. Guantanamo became a site where legal protections were circumvented, raising issues of dehumanization and mistreatment of detainees from racial and ethnic backgrounds often associated with terrorism. The political climate and public sentiment following 9/11 further reinforced this troubling narrative, as immigrants of color faced increased scrutiny and stigmatization. This framing persisted through subsequent administrations, influencing immigration policy and the treatment of marginalized communities.

Public sentiment and the political climate following 9/11 significantly shaped narratives surrounding immigrants of color and national security. Guantanamo became emblematic of broader efforts to frame immigrants of color as potential threats.

This narrative evolved through subsequent administrations, including that of Donald Trump, which notably impacted immigration policy.

Under the Trump administration, national security concerns were emphasized as the focus, and false narratives of immigrants of color in ways that many criticized as fostering persecution and the eradication of immigrants by promoting them as criminals, murderers, mental hospital escapees, and sex offenders.

One controversial policy Trump implemented during his first term was the family separation policy at the southern border, which involved the separation of children from their parents with no process in place to reunite them. This policy sparked widespread backlash as images and reports of the separations drew attention to the human rights implications.

Additionally, Trump's administration utilized the Guantanamo Bay detention facility for the detention of undocumented immigrants, reflecting ongoing tensions between U.S. ideals of justice and human rights and the realities of its immigration policies. In 2025, early in his second term, Trump declared a national emergency related to immigration at the southern border, citing concerns over security, drug trafficking, and an influx of migrants. This declaration enabled the use of federal funds for border security initiatives, including the continuation of border wall construction and the deployment of the National Guard to support enforcement efforts. The administration's approach combined various national security measures, raising complex questions about immigration policy and the treatment of individuals at the border.

Guantanamo Bay has been a focal point for criticism regarding the treatment of detainees, particularly in the context of national security policies. The facility has faced scrutiny for a range of issues, including a lack of oversight, restricted access for legal representatives and family members, and allegations of mistreatment and torture. These conditions raise serious questions about accountability and transparency, with critics arguing that the lack of external oversight has enabled abuses and a culture of impunity.

The use of military personnel for domestic law enforcement purposes is constrained by the Posse Comitatus Act of 1878, which limits the involvement of federal military forces—including the National Guard, when not under federal control—in law enforcement activities on American soil. While state governors have the authority to deploy the National Guard for emergencies, the involvement of federal personnel must align with legal standards and respect civil liberties. This legal framework necessitates that administrations balance enforcement actions with the obligation to protect human rights, particularly when addressing vulnerable populations such as immigrants.

In this context, critics have argued that the Trump administration's policies, including the family separation policy and the handling of detainees, demonstrated a lack of regard for human rights norms. The discourse surrounding these actions often becomes polarized, invoking debates about foundational values such as justice, compassion, and the rule of law.

Another significant concern is related to habeas corpus, a legal principle that protects individuals from unlawful detention. Detainees at Guantanamo have faced considerable challenges in obtaining writs of habeas corpus, which have hindered their ability to contest the legality of their detention. This situation raises alarms about the infringement of fundamental rights enshrined both in the International Covenant on Civil and Political Rights (ICCPR) and the U.S. Constitution.

The classification of detainees as "enemy combatants" has also led to the denial of protections typically afforded under the Geneva Conventions, designed to ensure humane treatment in conflict situations. These conditions illustrate a broader pattern that raises concerns about the alignment of U.S. practices at Guantanamo with essential principles of international human rights law, highlighting the necessity for reform to meet both domestic and international obligations.

The combination of legal maneuvering, reduced oversight, political calculations, and newly established detention practices culminates in a facility that reflects the complexities and prejudices of contemporary American governance. This situation underscores the urgent need for a reevaluation of policies, necessitating a more nuanced and fact-based discourse around immigration and national security, as well as a deeper understanding of the complexities involved in addressing issues related to organized crime and terrorism.

In recent times, with Trump's re-election campaign in 2024, the impact on immigration discourse has intensified. The decision to reopen Guantanamo to house undocumented immigrants reinforces the portrayal of these individuals as criminals or threats to national security. Such narratives not only contribute to the dehumanization of immigrants of color but also highlight an ongoing struggle for justice and humanity within American policy and society.

Why the Great Democracy Experiment Is Failing And How To Fix It!

The Enduring Legacy of Donald Trump's Presidency

Trump's goal has been to be remembered as a significant figure in the history of the United States, regardless of whether that legacy is viewed in a positive or negative light. Much like a child seeking attention, he seems to prioritize visibility and recognition over the nature of his popularity.

The impact of Donald Trump's presidency on American society and its international standing has been profound and complex. Throughout his tenure, several policy decisions have introduced substantial challenges at both domestic and global levels. Notably, the withdrawal from significant international agreements and changes in domestic policies affecting essential services have marked a shift towards prioritizing national interests over global cooperation and welfare. These actions have led to uncertainty and potentially increased human suffering.

Addressing the aftermath of these policies and rebuilding relationships will require sustained efforts from future generations. Emphasizing collaboration, inclusivity, and sustainability is essential to progress toward a more stable and equitable future. By actively re-engaging with the global community, reinforcing domestic cohesion, and restoring essential services, the U.S. can work towards repairing its reputation and fostering a more harmonious international and domestic landscape.

The policies affecting healthcare, food security, and humanitarian aid have had profound effects on human life, including the potential loss of tens of millions of lives.

Healthcare: The Trump administration's efforts to roll back Medicaid coverage impacted approximately 17 million people. Without access to necessary healthcare, there is a risk of preventable illnesses going untreated, potentially leading to increased morbidity and mortality. Studies have shown that a lack of healthcare can significantly reduce life expectancy and raise mortality rates, particularly among vulnerable populations. Research suggests that losing healthcare can lead to millions of premature deaths, especially among low-income individuals who lack alternative forms of coverage.

Food Assistance (TANF and SNAP): Reductions in Temporary Assistance for Needy Families (TANF) and the Supplemental Nutrition Assistance Program (SNAP) affected 11 million people, limiting their ability to secure basic nutrition. Food insecurity is linked to numerous health problems, including malnutrition, compromised immune function, and increased risk of chronic diseases. Estimates indicate that food insecurity can elevate mortality rates, particularly among children and the elderly. Access to adequate nutrition is crucial for children's development and academic performance.

Education and Free Lunch Programs: Ending free lunch programs for poor students can exacerbate educational disparities and affect millions of children. Proper nutrition is vital for cognitive development and learning. A lack of adequate meals can lead to poorer academic performance, which has long-term implications for economic mobility and health outcomes. Studies indicate that food insecurity can negatively impact students' concentration, behavior, and academic achievements, potentially leading to lifelong consequences.

Foreign Humanitarian Aid: Ending foreign humanitarian aid will have global repercussions, affecting millions in need of basic services like food, medical care, and shelter. Such reductions can exacerbate conditions in regions already suffering from poverty, conflict, and natural disasters. Humanitarian aid is often a lifeline for vulnerable populations, and its absence can lead to worsened health outcomes, increased mortality, and prolonged crises. International organizations have highlighted the critical role aid plays in saving lives and stabilizing regions.

While Hitler was in power, between 60-80 million people lost their lives, 50 million of whom were civilians. We have no war, but civilian loss of life worldwide while Trump is president will number in the tens of millions. The loss of life will surpass the concentration camps. Most of the loss of life will be in third-world nations since we ended humanitarian aid.

Healing political polarization and repairing international relations, as well as addressing social and economic inequalities, could require three generations (60 years) or more of sustained efforts. To fully address the impacts, especially concerning climate change, it may take ten or more generations (200 years or longer) given the scale of environmental setbacks.

The presidency of Donald Trump is characterized by significant policy changes across various sectors. As we examine these changes, it's important to understand both their immediate effects and their potential long-term impacts. This article delves into eight critical areas influenced by Trump's administration and explores the complexities involved in addressing these impacts over time.

Environmental Policy: The Trump administration withdrew the United States from the Paris Agreement and rolled back over 100 environmental regulations. Notably, it reduced restrictions on carbon emissions from industrial sources and eased protections for endangered species. The impacts include increased greenhouse gas emissions, contributing to global warming, while reduced protections can lead to biodiversity loss and disrupted ecosystems. Reversing such environmental damage could take 30 to 50 years, depending on the success of international cooperative efforts and advances in clean energy technologies.

Increased Greenhouse Gas Emissions: The withdrawal is likely to lead to a continuation of policies that allow for higher carbon emissions, exacerbating climate change.

Global Temperature Rise: Without U.S. participation in the Paris Agreement, efforts to limit global warming may falter, resulting in more severe climate impacts.

Biodiversity Loss: Eased regulations can lead to habitat destruction and more species at risk, disrupting ecosystems and threatening food security.

Climate Change Feedback Loops: Higher emissions contribute to feedback effects like ice melt, which can further accelerate global warming.

Economic Costs: Increased climate-related disasters can strain infrastructure and lead to significant economic losses.

Public Health Risks: Reduced air quality and pollution can lead to health crises, increasing healthcare costs, and impacting communities.

International Relations and Leadership: The U.S. losing credibility as a leader in climate negotiations can hinder global cooperation on environmental issues.

Future Policy Challenges: Future generations may face difficulties in reinstating credibility and negotiating meaningful climate agreements.

Judicial Appointments: Trump appointed over 200 federal judges, including three Supreme Court justices who shifted the judiciary to a more conservative stance. These lifetime appointments influence decisions on a wide range of issues, including reproductive rights, healthcare, and immigration. Decisions reflecting conservative legal interpretations can persist for decades, affecting legislation and civil liberties. Judicial philosophy shifts are slow, lasting 30 to 40 years unless changes in political control lead to a rebalancing of the judiciary.

Political Polarization: Trump's presidency exacerbated existing political and social divisions, amplifying partisan tensions and impacting public discourse. This polarization is evident in the increased partisanship in Congress and heightened social conflicts. Polarization leads to legislative gridlock, reduced bipartisan cooperation, and increased social unrest. Healing such divisions could take 20 to 40 years, requiring efforts in education reform, political engagement, and grassroots movements to foster dialogue and understanding.

International Relations: The "America First" policy altered traditional U.S. alliances as the administration renegotiated key trade agreements and challenged NATO's role, among others. This shift affected global diplomatic dynamics and trade relationships. Strained relationships with allies can impact global trade systems and international security. Restoring international trust might take 10 to 20 years, contingent on consistent foreign policy and diplomatic outreach from subsequent administrations.

Social Policies: Trump's immigration policies, including the termination of DACA and family separations, had profound impacts on immigrants and their families, affecting millions of lives. Increased fear and instability among immigrant communities, potential labor shortages, and social tensions due to these measures. Addressing these impacts involves legal reforms and social integration initiatives over a span of 20 to 30 years.

Economic Policies: Economic strategies such as tax cuts, protectionist tariffs, and deregulation aimed to stimulate growth but also increased the federal deficit and intensified income inequality. While tax cuts provided short-term economic boosts, they contributed to long-term budget deficits and exacerbated wealth disparities. Implementing corrective measures could take 10 to 20 years, involving strategic tax reforms and targeted economic policies to address inequality.

Healthcare: Efforts to dismantle the Affordable Care Act led to uncertainties in healthcare markets and access challenges for millions of Americans. Increased premiums, reduced coverage options, and heightened instability in the insurance market. Significant healthcare reform could require a decade of legislative effort and policy innovation to ensure stable and affordable coverage for all.

Education: Policies favoring school choice and reduced federal oversight impacted public education funding and expanded the educational achievement gap. Disparities in education quality and access, particularly affecting low-income and marginalized communities. Comprehensive education reform could take 15 to 20 years to implement, demanding increased investment in public education and shifts in policy at the federal and state levels.

Undoing or mitigating the impacts of the Trump administration's policies involves addressing multiple complex and interrelated issues. The timelines for recovery are estimated and depend heavily on future political leadership, societal engagement, and economic conditions. As the U.S. navigates these challenges, informed dialogue and active participation are crucial in shaping a sustainable future.

The long-term effects anticipated from the political polarization exacerbated during Trump's administration are significant and multifaceted, impacting various aspects of American society and governance. Here are some key potential outcomes:

Legislative Gridlock: Increased polarization can lead to persistent legislative stalemates, where bipartisan cooperation becomes rare. This gridlock can hinder the passage of essential legislation on critical issues such as healthcare, infrastructure, and climate change, ultimately stalling progress on policies that address pressing societal needs.

Erosion of Democratic Norms: Heightened polarization may contribute to a decline in respect for democratic norms and institutions. As partisan loyalty takes precedence over civic duty, there may be increased acceptance of anti-democratic behaviors, such as voter suppression or challenges to election results, undermining the integrity of the electoral process.

Social Fragmentation: Political polarization can exacerbate social divisions, leading to the entrenchment of communities along partisan lines. This fragmentation can diminish social cohesion and trust among individuals from different political backgrounds, making constructive dialogue and compromise more challenging.

Increased Political Violence: The rise in politically charged rhetoric and divisive narratives can lead to heightened tensions and potentially increase the risk of political violence. Instances of extremism and politically motivated attacks may become more common as individuals feel compelled to act on their beliefs.

Alienation and Disengagement: Many individuals may become disillusioned with the political process and disengage from civic participation, feeling that their voices are not represented. This alienation can lead to lower voter turnout and reduced involvement in community and political organizations, further entrenching polarization.

Impact on Governance: Polarized environments can lead to ineffective governance, where elected officials focus more on party loyalty than on collaboration and problem-solving. This can result in a lack of effective responses to national crises, such as public health emergencies or economic downturns.

Generational Effects: The current state of polarization may shape the political attitudes of younger generations, who may grow up in an environment marked by division and conflict. This could lead to a cycle of polarization that persists as new voters carry their experiences and beliefs into adulthood.

Diminished Global Standing: As political polarization affects the U.S. ability to present a unified front on international issues, it may weaken the nation's global standing. Allies may become uncertain of U.S. commitments, impacting international agreements and cooperation on global challenges such as climate change and security.

Long-Term Political Realignment: The enduring effects of polarization may lead to a realignment of political parties and ideologies. As factions within parties become more pronounced, new political movements or parties may emerge, further complicating the political landscape and potentially leading to instability.

Polarization of Media and Information: The media landscape may become increasingly polarized, with outlets catering to specific ideological perspectives. This can create echo chambers where individuals are exposed only to information that reinforces their beliefs, further entrenching polarization and reducing the likelihood of encountering diverse viewpoints.

Addressing these long-term effects will require concerted efforts from political leaders, civil society, and citizens to promote dialogue, understanding, and cooperation across partisan lines. Fostering a culture of engagement and respect for democratic processes will be crucial in mitigating the impacts of polarization on the future of American democracy.

Dehumanizing People of Color Leads to Viewing Immigrants of Color as Disposable.

We all know that an executive order was signed to remove DEI standards and terminate those who fit DEI guidelines

I plan to highlight the critical issue of how immigrants, particularly those of color, are often stripped of their humanity through derogatory language, harmful stereotypes, and negative media portrayals. This process of dehumanization reduces individuals to mere statistics and caricatures, making it easier for society to justify mistreatment and accept oppressive policies.

When people of color are perceived as less than human, they become susceptible to unjust policies, social division, and mental health issues. This troubling narrative mirrors historical patterns of marginalization experienced by various groups throughout history.

From the time we established the first colony in what would become the United States, immigrants of color including those who were forcibly relocated to be sold into slavery and were not granted citizenship until July 9, 1868, as well as Indigenous peoples who were not considered American citizens until June 2, 1924, making them immigrants in their homeland.

The historical trajectory of dehumanization can be traced back to colonial America, where Indigenous populations were viewed as obstacles to progress and prosperity, leading to their displacement and genocide. Slaves were treated and traded like livestock.

In the 19th and 20th centuries, groups such as Irish, Italian, and Chinese immigrants faced similar dehumanization through derogatory rhetoric that positioned them as subhuman, justifying discriminatory laws and practices. This historical precedent illustrates that disturbing patterns of racism and xenophobia are not just contemporary issues but have deep roots and are bred into American society. Making us the most restrictive and prejudiced that's supposed to be the freest country in the world.

These marginalized groups have and still continuously face mistreatment at the hands of the U.S. federal government and its Male Anglo citizens.

This mistreatment has been shaped by various presidential policies, false narratives, and public perceptions that transcend party lines. While all forms of abuse are grievous, the levels of brutality can vary significantly based on which party is in power and controls Congress revealing a chilling pattern throughout American history.

At the heart of this issue is a complex interplay of rhetoric and propaganda promoting perceived breaches in national security, undocumented immigrants as rapists, sex offenders, murderers, and terrorists causing the mistreatment of marginalized communities, particularly people of color (POC). A closer examination of modern U.S. presidential decisions, from Franklin Delano Roosevelt and Gerald Ford to Donald Trump, reveals a continuous distressing evolution that paved the way for the establishment of the Guantanamo Bay detention facility and underscores the xenophobic national security tactics used to justify the dehumanization and disposal of immigrants.

During Franklin D. Roosevelt's presidency, immigrants of color, including Asian Americans, faced significant challenges and discrimination. While the New Deal aimed to alleviate economic hardships during the Great Depression, many programs excluded or marginalized these communities, often influenced by racial biases.

The bombing of Pearl Harbor in 1941 exacerbated the situation for Japanese Americans, leading to the forced internment of around 120,000 individuals, most of whom were U.S. citizens, based on perceived national security threats. This period highlighted the intersection of economic strife, racial prejudice, and wartime hysteria, impacting the lived experiences of immigrants of color in the United States.

Gerald Ford navigated a challenging landscape in the post-Vietnam War era as he confronted a significant influx of Vietnamese refugees following the fall of Saigon in April 1975. While his administration facilitated the resettlement of approximately 130,000 Vietnamese through programs like Operation Frequent Wind, the reception of these immigrants was mixed. Some Americans were sympathetic to the plight of the refugees, recognizing their connections to the U.S. war effort.

Most expressed negative sentiments, fueled by hate, fears of economic competition, and cultural differences, Americans would incite violence because of lingering resentment over the war. These factors contributed to a large segment of the population that viewed the newcomers with suspicion, leading to social tension, violence, vandalism, and resistance to integration. This period highlighted the complexities of immigration policy in the U.S., marked by both humanitarian efforts and challenges related to public opinion toward immigrants.

During the presidency of Jimmy Carter, the U.S. faced significant challenges regarding immigration and human rights, particularly in the context of the Cuban boat crisis in 1980. This crisis arose when thousands of Cubans took to the sea in small boats, fleeing political repression and economic difficulties in Cuba. Many sought asylum in the United States, leading to a surge of Cuban immigrants arriving on Florida's shores. At the same time, U.S. support for anti-communist regimes, usually dictators, in Latin America, particularly in countries like El Salvador, resulted in widespread human rights violations, forcing individuals to flee and seek refuge in the U.S.

While Carter aimed to promote human rights, the realities of foreign policy often led to contradictions, contributing to systemic inequalities faced by immigrants of color and challenging efforts to address their needs within U.S. immigration policy.

Ronald Reagan's presidency marked a significant turning point in U.S. immigration perception, largely influenced by the prevailing anti-communist sentiment of the time. Reagan's administration employed tough rhetoric, propaganda, and false stereotypes that increasingly framed all immigrants of color as criminals, reflecting broader anxieties about national security and social stability.

This shift to the right in immigration narratives has contributed to a changing attitude and public perception of immigrants as threats to the

American way of life. Leading to more exclusionary stringent policies and attitudes towards newcomers. MAGA Republican rhetoric has deemed all immigrants as criminals so we must close our borders.

After the attacks on September 11, 2001, George W. Bush faced immense pressure to address a perceived national security crisis. This urgency led to the establishment of the Guantanamo Bay detention facility in 2002, intended to securely detain terrorism suspects, but it also highlighted legal ambiguities surrounding detention practices. The remote location of Guantanamo resulted in a lack of oversight, contributing to serious human rights violations, including allegations of torture and inhumane treatment, and the disappearance of individuals' names from the prisoner list.

In this post-9/11 context, the routine detention of individuals without trial raised significant concerns, particularly for immigrants of color who were disproportionately targeted. Guantanamo became a site where legal protections were circumvented, raising issues of dehumanization and mistreatment of detainees from racial and ethnic backgrounds who are disposable even when they aren't associated with terrorism.

The political climate and public sentiment following 9/11 further reinforced this troubling narrative, as immigrants of color faced increased scrutiny and stigmatization. This framing persisted through subsequent administrations, influencing immigration policy and the treatment of marginalized communities.

Public sentiment and the political climate following 9/11 significantly shaped narratives surrounding immigrants of color and national security. Guantanamo became emblematic of broader efforts to frame immigrants of color as potential threats.

This narrative evolved through subsequent administrations, including that of Donald Trump, which notably impacted immigration policy.

Under the Trump administration, national security concerns were emphasized as the focus, and false narratives of immigrants of color in ways that many criticized as fostering persecution and the eradication of immigrants by promoting them as criminals, murderers, mental hospital escapees, and sex offenders. One controversial policy Trump implemented during his first term was the family separation policy at the southern border, which involved the separation of children from their parents with no process in place to reunite them. This policy sparked widespread backlash as images and reports of the separations drew attention to the human rights implications.

Additionally, Trump's administration utilized the Guantanamo Bay detention facility for the detention of undocumented immigrants, reflecting ongoing tensions between U.S. ideals of justice and human rights and the realities of its immigration policies. In 2025, early in his second term, Trump declared a national emergency related to immigration at the southern border, citing concerns over security, drug trafficking, and an influx of migrants. This declaration enabled the use of federal funds for border security initiatives, including the continuation of border wall construction and the deployment of the National Guard to support enforcement efforts. The administration's approach combined various national security measures, raising complex questions about immigration policy and the treatment of individuals at the border.

Guantanamo Bay has been a focal point for criticism regarding the treatment of detainees, particularly in the context of national security policies. The facility has faced scrutiny for a range of issues, including a lack of oversight, restricted access for legal representatives and family members, and allegations of mistreatment and torture. These conditions raise serious questions about accountability and transparency, with critics arguing that the lack of external oversight has enabled abuses and a culture of impunity.

The use of military personnel for domestic law enforcement purposes is constrained by the Posse Comitatus Act of 1878, which limits the involvement of federal military forces—including the National Guard, when not under federal control—in law enforcement activities on American soil. While state governors have the authority to deploy the

National Guard for emergencies, the involvement of federal personnel must align with legal standards and respect civil liberties. This legal framework necessitates that administrations balance enforcement actions with the obligation to protect human rights, particularly when addressing vulnerable populations such as immigrants.

Critics have argued that the Trump administration's policies, including the family separation policy and the handling of detainees, demonstrated a lack of regard for human rights norms. The discourse surrounding these actions often becomes polarized, invoking debates about foundational values such as justice, compassion, and the rule of law.

Another significant concern is related to habeas corpus, a legal principle that protects individuals from unlawful detention. Detainees at Guantanamo have faced considerable challenges in obtaining writs of habeas corpus, which have hindered their ability to contest the legality of their detention. This situation raises alarms about the infringement of fundamental rights enshrined both in the International Covenant on Civil and Political Rights (ICCPR) and the U.S. Constitution.

The classification of detainees as "enemy combatants" has also led to the denial of protections typically afforded under the Geneva Conventions, designed to ensure humane treatment in conflict situations. These conditions illustrate a broader pattern that raises concerns about the alignment of U.S. practices at Guantanamo with essential principles of international human rights law, highlighting the necessity for reform to meet both domestic and international obligations.

The combination of legal maneuvering, reduced oversight, political calculations, and newly established detention practices culminates in a facility that reflects the complexities and prejudices of contemporary American governance. This situation underscores the urgent need for a reevaluation of policies, necessitating a more nuanced and fact-based discourse around immigration and national security, as well as a deeper understanding of the complexities involved in addressing issues related to organized crime and terrorism.

In recent times, Trump's re-election campaign in 2024, made an impact on immigration discourse. The decision to reopen Guantanamo to house undocumented immigrants reinforces the portrayal of these individuals as criminals or threats to national security. Such narratives not only contribute to the dehumanization of immigrants of color but also highlight an ongoing struggle for justice and humanity within American policy and society.

The climate of fear we planted and harvested from our past has laid the groundwork for not seeing individuals, dehumanizing, and making people of color disposable we can carry out mass deportations and sentence many to prison because we labeled immigrants as extreme terrorists passing measures that have emerged, as policymakers and law enforcement sought to address perceived threats. Thus, Reagan's presidency played a pivotal role in reshaping the discourse around immigration, and unjustly influencing how immigrants of color were viewed within the context of racism, bigotry, and national security.

Will end with this one note: MAGA Republicans and Trump are complaining about the federal debt and want to shut down entire cabinets that help people. However, they are expanding Gitmo to house 30,000 immigrants and they are willing to spend $13.5 million per year on each detainee at Guantanamo Bay. So at full capacity that's $405 billion per year.

Now ask yourself," Where is this money coming from and where is it going?"

Blindly following orders, even those from a high-ranking official, does not grant immunity from accountability. The price of such compliance can be the loss of personal freedom. While Congress established Immigration and Customs Enforcement (ICE) to enforce immigration laws, the agency has faced accusations from civil liberties groups, courts, and human rights organizations of violating the Constitution and breaking federal laws. These allegations involve unlawful searches and seizures, denial of due process rights, inhumane detention conditions, and discriminatory enforcement practices.

Critics allege that ICE has violated the Fourth Amendment, which protects against unreasonable searches and seizures, through tactics such as conducting raids without proper warrants and detaining individuals without probable cause. Unlike a judicial warrant signed by a judge, ICE often uses administrative warrants issued by its own officials. Courts have found that agents violated the Fourth Amendment by using these warrants to forcibly enter homes without consent or a proper judicial warrant. ICE has issued detainers that lead to prolonged detention without a signature from a neutral judge or a prompt judicial hearing, a practice a 2020 Ninth Circuit Court of Appeals ruling found violated the Fourth Amendment. Federal courts have ruled that agents cannot stop individuals based solely on factors such as race, ethnicity, or language. In raids, including those at worksites, ICE has been accused of unlawfully detaining U.S. citizens and lawful permanent residents and using excessive force.

The Fifth Amendment guarantees due process rights to all "persons" in the United States, not just citizens. Critics say ICE has repeatedly disregarded these protections. Allegations include deporting immigrants before they have a meaningful chance to appeal their case or arresting people at courthouses, undermining the legal process. Advocacy groups report that individuals in detention face systemic barriers to preparing their cases, including a lack of access to phones, mail, and legal documents, making it nearly impossible to access legal counsel. ICE has unlawfully detained and sometimes deported U.S. citizens, at times ignoring proof of citizenship. In August 2025, several members of Congress demanded an investigation into these cases, citing incidents involving children and cancer patients.

Immigrants and watchdog groups have reported poor and inhumane conditions at detention centers, which they argue violate the Eighth Amendment's prohibition on cruel and unusual punishment. A June 2024 report reviewing deaths in ICE custody found that 95% of documented deaths between 2017 and 2021 were likely preventable with adequate medical care. ICE's frequent and excessive use of solitary confinement, even for individuals with serious medical and mental health conditions, has been called torture by some human rights groups and falls short of the agency's own standards. Individuals in custody have reported lengthy lockdowns due to understaffing, unsanitary living conditions, and neglect. The government's own inspectors have found facilities with "barbaric" and "negligent" conditions.

Beyond constitutional issues, ICE has been accused of violating statutes and human rights norms. Under the "zero tolerance" policy, the government separated thousands of migrant children from their parents at the U.S. border. An investigation by the DOJ Inspector General found that department leaders underestimated the policy's effects and failed to properly track families, causing long-term harm. ICE has been accused of racial profiling and targeting communities of color through tactics such as aggressive workplace raids. The American Civil Liberties Union has also highlighted how some partnerships with local law enforcement under the 287(g) program have empowered racist behavior. Legal advocates have sued ICE for implementing enforcement policies that they say unlawfully strip humanitarian protections from crime victims and subject them to detention and deportation.

The Role of Patience and Prudence in a Democratic Judicial System

In a democracy, the judiciary serves as a cornerstone of justice, upholding the principles of fairness, equality, and due process. When individuals assume the roles of judge, jury, and executioner, whether metaphorically in positions of influence or literally within the legal system, it underscores the importance of a balanced approach to justice. An effective judicial system is not driven by haste or bias, but by a careful, deliberate examination of the facts at hand.

One key lesson often emphasized in democratic societies is the importance of waiting for all evidence to surface before making a judgment. The integrity of a democratic judicial system relies heavily on the patience and thoroughness of its legal professionals. They must diligently gather evidence and conduct comprehensive interviews with all parties involved. This process ensures that decisions are informed and judgments are rendered with the fullest insight into a situation.

The danger of acting on the testimony of a single, potentially manipulative source cannot be overstated. History and numerous legal precedents remind us of the risks of hasty conclusions. Individuals versed in manipulation may present a convincing yet ultimately deceptive narrative. As such, the courts must exercise extreme caution, distinguishing between truth and manipulation through critical analysis and cross-examination.

It is incumbent upon the judiciary to learn from past experiences. If patterns emerge where certain types of individuals consistently mislead or manipulate the system, the court must adapt and account for these tactics. This adaptation does not imply prejudice against individuals but highlights the need for heightened scrutiny and a robust mechanism to protect the integrity of the legal process.

Indeed, ignoring these lessons can have grave consequences. Should the courts fail to address manipulative tactics appropriately, the administration of justice could suffer. Outstanding cases may recur, each potentially more severe than the last, undermining public trust in the judicial system. Thus, the judiciary must remain vigilant, continually refining its processes and strategies to address deceit while maintaining a commitment to fairness and justice.

Ultimately, democracy requires the judicial system to serve not just as a mechanism of punishment, but as a bastion of fairness and a model of patience. Those in positions of judicial power must exercise their authority with wisdom and restraint, ensuring that justice is not only done but seen to be done by all members of society. By doing so, the judiciary safeguards the principles of democracy and reinforces the social contract that binds the community together.

Democracy in Action: How Sanctions Reflect Global Unity Against Aggression

In today's interconnected world, democracy extends beyond borders, shaping global responses to crises. A striking example of this is the way democratic nations have responded to Russia's invasion of Ukraine, showcasing a powerful, non-military method that aligns with democratic ideals: economic sanctions.

While the United States and European nations have chosen to avoid direct military conflict, they have rapidly mobilized to impose a diverse array of financial sanctions intended to severely impact Russia's economy. This strategy demonstrates the influence and speed with which democratic alliances can act. By restricting Russia's access to crucial foreign currencies like the dollar and euro, freezing assets of Russian banks, and cutting off access to the SWIFT financial messaging system, these democracies are applying heavy pressure on an aggressor without resorting to warfare.

Moreover, countries like Japan and even neutral Switzerland have joined the sanctions, signaling a rare and powerful global coalition. This unity illuminates the collective strength democracies hold when they coordinate efforts against violations of international law and peace.

Russia, in response, has tried to mitigate the economic damage by hiking interest rates and leveraging foreign reserves—reserves that are largely inaccessible due to sanctions. The Russian government's aggressive economic responses highlight the significant pressure sanctions impose, further proving their effectiveness as a tool of diplomatic and economic warfare.

For the Russian populace, however, these sanctions translate into economic hardship, illustrating a tragic byproduct of global diplomacy where ordinary citizens bear the brunt of their government's actions. This underlines a critical point about the nuances of democracy; it seeks to balance action against wrongdoers while minimizing harm to innocents—a challenge in any international conflict.

Globally, the sanctions have potential ripple effects. With Russia and Ukraine being major players in commodities such as oil, gas, and agriculture, these actions have already led to rising global prices, thus affecting economies worldwide. Democracies must navigate these economic shifts while maintaining internal support for sanctions, a testament to the complex interplay between domestic and foreign policy in democratic governance.

Corporations have also taken a stand, with firms like BP withdrawing investments from Russia. This corporate action not only reflects ethical stances but also emphasizes democracy's multifaceted nature, where public sentiment and corporate responsibility intertwine with governmental policies.

In this context, the sanctions serve as a testament to democracy's potential as a peacekeeping and justice-seeking entity. They represent a form of democratic consensus, a collective statement against aggression, underlining the values of dialogue, crisis management, and non-violent resolution at the international level. This seminal moment could redefine the dynamics of international conflict resolution, showcasing how democracies can unite to defend global peace and justice without direct conflict.

Ultimately, amidst the complexities and hardships, these sanctions remind the world of the enduring power of democratic unity and the shared responsibility to uphold international law and order, proving that democracy extends far beyond domestic governance, it is a global force for good.

Addressing Domestic Violence: A Democratic Imperative for Lasting Change

In the quest for a truly democratic society, addressing domestic violence is a vital undertaking that demands a comprehensive and multifaceted approach. Such efforts focus on protection, accountability, and cultural transformation, ensuring that every individual can live without fear of harm.

At the heart of a democratic response is the need to overhaul existing laws. Current penalties must be revised to reflect the true severity of domestic violence, moving beyond minimal fines to enforce significant consequences. This could include mandatory counseling and the possibility of incarceration for repeat offenders. By implementing such legal reforms, a democratic society sends a clear message: the protection of victims and the pursuit of justice are paramount.

Supporting victims is equally essential. Democracies should prioritize funding for shelters, hotlines, and counseling services, giving survivors the resources they need to find refuge and rebuild their lives. Crucially, the financial burden of abuse must not fall on victims; they require assistance to regain their independence and well-being without economic strain.

Education plays a pivotal role in shifting societal attitudes. Investing in public education programs that promote respect, equality, and non-violent conflict resolution can help change cultural norms. By engaging schools, communities, and media outlets, democracies can create environments where violence is not tolerated, fostering a culture of empathy and understanding.

Judicial reform is critical to this effort. Training judges, police, and legal professionals is necessary to ensure domestic violence cases are handled with sensitivity and urgency. Special units within police forces and courts can focus on these cases, offering expertise and prioritizing victim safety and justice.

Empowering women is fundamental to achieving meaningful change. Democracies must work towards increasing women's representation in politics and leadership roles, fostering economic independence, and dismantling patriarchal norms that often underpin domestic violence. By promoting equal opportunities and amplifying women's voices, society moves closer to lasting, positive change.

Community involvement is another crucial element. By encouraging community engagement in addressing domestic violence, it becomes a collective issue, not just a private one. Democratic societies should promote programs that support victims and rehabilitate offenders, helping to create a culture where violence is universally condemned.

Ultimately, tackling domestic violence within a democracy involves leveraging legal, educational, and social reforms to build a society where every individual is protected, valued, and free from harm. This holistic approach aims not only to address immediate concerns but also to drive long-term cultural change, reinforcing the democratic ideals of equality, justice, and human dignity for all.

———————————————

America's Facade Of Democracy and Equality Exposed

Pulling Back the Curtain and Exposing the Dark Underbelly of the United States Practice in Regards to Diplomacy

America's Complex Role it Plays on the Global Stage: Can a Nation Exhibit Narcissism?

The United States publicly praises democracy, civil rights, human rights, and the principle that all men are created equal; however, privately, we often overlook these ideals. Not only are we complicit in global injustices, but we frequently initiate the discord. In reality, much of the hostility and hatred toward America and its citizens stems from our government's initial interactions with various countries, including their demographics and the resources at stake.

It is important to note that from the time the first Anglo colony was established in North America, a troubling trend began that the United States continues to find acceptable. Whether out of habit or an inability to change, we are not only complacent but also actively participate in atrocities, both foreign and domestic: the exploitation, annexation, and annihilation of people of color, along with entire nations and continents.

This trend was initiated with the systematic plundering, pillaging, and stealing of land from the Indigenous American people, acting as though we were the first to occupy this continent and treating them as if they were not human. We set out to systematically annihilate and nearly cause the extinction of the Indigenous peoples of the Americas, who had occupied this land for thousands of years.

As if that weren't far enough, the U.S. continued to exploit, plunder, and pillage the very peoples of the African continent, considering this human demographic a commodity of our own. Our arrogance and failure to recognize them as human only compounded these injustices.

Despite proclaiming itself a promoter and advocate of democracy, the U.S. does not have clean hands and is the root cause of hostility and animosity toward the United States through its treatment, actions, and interactions with nations of color, continents of color, and people of color throughout its history.

The treatment of nations of color beyond our borders and the people of color within America's own borders speaks to a legacy of systemic aggression that has persisted since the inception of its first colony.

To perpetuate these hostilities toward the USA, the United States has never held itself accountable and continues to refuse to admit its wrongdoing. Instead, it often doubles down and portrays itself as a victim, claiming that attacks are unprovoked and necessitate retaliation whenever nations or continents of color rise against the injustices they endure. This mentality of the U.S., claiming it is defending its interests under the guise of democracy, perpetuates a cycle of unrest and resentment.

The United States frequently approaches international relations with a paternalistic attitude, attempting to impose its values on other nations. This mindset reflects a failure to learn from history and to emulate the democratic practices of older civilizations that have thrived for millennia. The U.S. has exploited nations of color since its inception, a practice that continues to shape its foreign policy and international relations. As a result, America's democracy now teeters on the brink of collapse.

Numerous countries harbor resentment toward America and its citizens due to a long history of exploitation, in which we have taken their people as commodities, along with their land, resources, and governance, for our gain. Notably, around 90% of these nations are countries of color.

Remarkably, the United States has never formally acknowledged these transgressions or made any meaningful reparations, including to the indigenous peoples or to the descendants of captives possessed by our citizens. Most within the American public have largely remained silent on the need to address these injustices.

This persistent arrogance and reliance on intimidation can only lead us so far. Since the beginning of humankind, when oppressed people reach their breaking point, they will inevitably react, regardless of the consequences they may face.

At the heart of this issue lies a deeply ingrained attitude of American exceptionalism, which holds that the U.S. not only has the right but also the obligation to intervene in the affairs of other nations.

This mindset often disregards the historical contexts and complexities of foreign societies, leading to poorly conceived policies that exacerbate existing tensions.

Due to America's arrogance and its feelings of entitlement to anything the globe has to offer, many countries, including Iran, perceive American cultural and political imposition as a form of imperialism, fostering resentment and resistance.

The fact that the U.S. is willing to impose its values at the expense of others' dignity only deepens international divides and hostilities, hindering progress toward mutual understanding and cooperation with countries and continents of color.

Most countries of color have voiced sentiments similar to those of Iran.

While Iran is a focal point due to its current prominence in global events, many countries and territories of color share similar feelings of resentment and hostility toward the United States.

I will include eight countries of color in greater detail at the bottom of this chapter which will explain in more detail why America and its citizens are held responsible for these initial hostilities and how our continued suppression of diverse ideologies has further exacerbated these tensions. It is also important to note that around 90% of the countries that seem to harbor hostilities toward America and Americans due to our historical treatment are countries of color.

Furthermore, we exploit even our territories and our allies that are countries of color, often without regard for the consequences of our actions.

I will include eight of those countries in greater detail in the comments of this post, explaining why America and its citizens are held responsible for these initial hostilities and how our continued suppression of diverse ideologies has further exacerbated these tensions. It is also important to note that around 90% of the countries that harbor hostilities toward America and Americans due to our historical treatment are countries of color.

Furthermore, we exploit even our territories and allies that are countries of color, often without regard for the consequences of our actions.

Here are eight of the countries of color we have exploited, some of which we continue to exploit, and these will be expanded upon in the comments: Puerto Rico, Venezuela, Cuba, Panama, Honduras, Mexico, Syria, and North Korea (Korea as a whole).

Resentment over U.S. interventions, economic sanctions, and support for opposition groups has significantly contributed to the longstanding tensions between the U.S. and these nations.

The relationship between the United States and Iran, in particular, is a complex tapestry woven from historical events, political decisions, and cultural misunderstandings, all of which significantly influence today's relations.

A central truth of this narrative is that American actions over several decades have not only shaped Iran's trajectory but also sown the seeds of resentment, anger, and hostility toward the U.S. The imperialistic and geopolitical maneuvers of the U.S. government have left lasting scars on Iranian society, making it crucial for Americans to acknowledge and confront the responsibility we bear in shaping this fraught relationship.

Acknowledging these histories and examining the ongoing implications of U.S. actions in all countries of color is crucial for fostering a more comprehensive understanding of international relations and repairing relationships adversely affected by American policies.

The origins of this complex relationship with Iran can often be traced back to critical events since the end of World War I, when the Middle East was divided into countries with borders.

The 1953 coup of Iran, when the CIA orchestrated the overthrow of Iran's democratically elected Prime Minister, Mohammad Mossadegh. This intervention aimed to secure Western control over Iranian oil resources and counter the perceived threat of communism during the Cold War. As a direct result, the Iranian people witnessed the crushing of their democratic aspirations and the undermining of their sovereignty. This coup set the stage for a monarch who ruled for decades as an authoritarian Shah Mohammad Reza Pahlavi.

Backed by the United States, the Shah ruled as a shadow puppet of the USA, with an iron fist, employing a brutal security apparatus known as SAVAK to suppress dissent.

During this period, the Iranian populace endured oppression, censorship, disappearances, and the ruthless enforcement of a regime that prioritized Western interests over the well-being of its citizens.

This painful chapter in Iranian history is what fostered deep-seated animosity toward the United States, a sentiment that continues to resonate in the Iranian consciousness today.

The 1953 coup, known as Operation Ajax, was a watershed moment in U.S.-Iran relations. The U.S. intelligence community viewed Mossadegh's nationalist policies, particularly the nationalization of the Anglo-Iranian Oil Company (now BP), as a direct threat to American and British oil interests.

Following the coup, the Shah instituted a regime characterized by widespread human rights abuses, which created long-lasting grievances among the Iranian people toward the United States of America.

The Shah's secret police, SAVAK, was notorious for its torture, killings, suppression, and the disappearance of Iran's citizens of political dissent.

Supported and trained by the CIA and Israeli intelligence, SAVAK played a crucial role in maintaining the Shah's regime, yet contributed significantly to public discontent toward Israel and the United States.

The Shah's alignment with the U.S. often alienated ordinary Iranians who felt their culture was being undermined in favor of Western values. Socioeconomic disparities increased, with much of Iran's wealth concentrated among a small elite, exacerbating widespread unrest.

The culmination of this resentment led to the 1979 Iranian Revolution, which resulted in the overthrow of the Shah and the establishment of the Islamic Republic under Ayatollah Khomeini. This marked a significant turning point in U.S.-Iran relations, as the new government adopted a vehemently anti-American stance, rightly blaming the U.S. for the country's previous hardships.

The animosity stemming from the coup and the subsequent years of U.S. support for the Shah has had enduring consequences. Events such as the U.S. Embassy hostage crisis in 1979 and ongoing tensions over

Iran's nuclear program have continued to exacerbate the adversarial relationship.

Acknowledging this history is crucial for understanding current dynamics in U.S.-Iran relations and the broader Middle East. A more nuanced perspective can help facilitate constructive dialogue and potentially mend the fractures of the past.

The lack of authentic democratic practices under the Shah's government exposed the contradictions in American foreign policy. The U.S. supported the Shah even as evidence of his systematic human rights and civil rights violations became increasingly apparent.

This collaboration meant that Iranian dissenters faced repression not only from local authorities but also from foreign influence. Such actions starkly contrast with the democratic values the U.S. professes to champion. This duplicity did not go unnoticed; it sparked revolutionary sentiments among Iranians who viewed the U.S. not as a promoter of democracy but as a key enabler of tyranny.

The complicity of the U.S. in these human rights violations and its indifference to the suffering of the Iranian people intensified feelings of betrayal, resentment, and hostility toward Americans, shaping the tumultuous relationship that persists to this day.

Under the Shah, various reports and accounts documented widespread human rights abuses, including torture, imprisonment of political dissidents, and censorship of the press. Organizations such as Amnesty International and Human Rights Watch have chronicled these abuses, noting that the U.S. turned a blind eye due to strategic and economic interests.

Cold War dynamics partly drove the U.S. support for the Shah, as American policymakers viewed Iran as a bulwark against Soviet expansion. This geopolitical strategy often overshadowed concerns about democracy and human rights, leading to a foreign policy prioritizing stability over ethical considerations.

The fact that the U.S. was complicit in the Shah's oppressive regime galvanized various factions in Iranian society, including leftists, Islamists, and nationalists, contributing to a coalition that ultimately led to the 1979 Iranian Revolution.

Anti-American sentiment was a unifying theme during this period, as many Iranians saw the U.S. as an imperialist power imposing its will on Iran.

The aftermath of the Iranian Revolution saw the establishment of a theocratic regime that maintained a hostile stance toward the United States. The U.S. Embassy hostage crisis in 1979 epitomized this animosity, leading to decades of adversarial relations characterized by sanctions, military standoffs, and mutual antagonism.

This history demonstrates the U.S.'s refusal to acknowledge any wrongdoing.

The events in Iran raise important questions about the ethical implications of U.S. foreign policy and the genuine promotion of democracy abroad. The tension between political realities and democratic ideals remains a sensitive topic in discussions about American intervention and foreign relations in the Middle East.

Understanding these complexities is vital for comprehending the current state of U.S.-Iran relations and the underlying tensions that continue to shape them.

By acknowledging the U.S. in the historical context and the repercussions of past actions, there is an opportunity for the U.S. to right its wrongs and foster a narrative through which both nations might find pathways to more constructive engagement in the future.

The consequences of American policy did not end with the fall of the Shah in 1979; instead, the U.S. decided to double down, and its actions evolved and magnified. The Iranian Revolution dramatically altered the political landscape, and the subsequent hostage crisis further strained an already tense relationship.

In response to the hostage situation, the U.S. imposed a series of severe economic sanctions aimed at isolating Iran. These sanctions were unilateral and drastic, effectively punishing the Iranian populace for the actions of their government.

As a result, ordinary Iranians faced dire hardships, starving to death and struggling with shortages of essential goods, medicines, and basic services. The elite in Iran felt none of these hardships, effectively punishing the right hand for what the left hand was doing.

The economic distress inflicted by these sanctions became a catalyst and served as fertile ground for the growing resentment and anti-American sentiment, as it reinforced the belief that the U.S. would sacrifice the welfare of the poor and disenfranchised Iranian people to meet its geopolitical objectives, which were only concerned with the Iranian elite.

The U.S. Embassy hostage crisis in 1979, in which 52 American diplomats and citizens were held hostage for 444 days, not only soured U.S.-Iran relations but also emboldened hardline elements within Iran, leading to an even more authoritarian political climate.

The sanctions imposed by the U.S. after the hostage crisis were comprehensive and targeted various sectors of the Iranian economy, including critical oil exports. Over the years, these sanctions have expanded to include measures that target financial transactions, trade, and access to key technologies.

While economic sanctions often aim to leverage change in government behavior, they invariably lead to unintentional humanitarian crises. Reports indicate that sanctions have adversely affected access to medical supplies and healthcare for ordinary Iranians, fostering further anti-American sentiments.

The long-term impacts of these sanctions have perpetuated economic instability in Iran. Inflation and unemployment rates have soared, with many Iranians facing poverty, starvation, and deprivation, which deepens their resentment toward the U.S. as they perceive it to be responsible for their suffering.

The sanctions policy has proven controversial, with various international bodies and humanitarian organizations arguing that such measures only hurt civilians more than they pressure the elite or the government. This dynamic has led to a complex relationship where calls for reform among Iranians are overshadowed by nationalistic sentiments opposing foreign interference, particularly from the U.S.

The ongoing sanctions and the U.S. withdrawal from the Joint Comprehensive Plan of Action (JCPOA) in 2018 have further complicated relations. Donald Trump's decision to reinstate sanctions has driven Iran to assertively pursue its nuclear program, fueling further tensions between the two nations.

These sanctions have laid an additional foundation for a humanitarian crisis, solidifying the perception of the U.S. as a harmful influence within Iranian society.

The sanctions severely damaged not only Iran's economy but also the lives of millions of non-political Iranian citizens, exemplifying how American foreign policy decisions can lead to devastating consequences for populations. When the U.S. employs economic sanctions as a diplomatic tool, it often overlooks their human impact, resulting in extensive suffering among innocent people.

Once again, the U.S. is willing to throw aside what it claims publicly and make decisions that reveal a broader pattern whereby human rights considerations are sacrificed for strategic ends, further entrenching mistrust and animosity in regions affected by American policies.

U.S. support for military interventions in the Middle East during the late 20ᵗʰ and early 21ˢᵗ centuries has further complicated the situation with Iran.

The U.S. backing of Saddam Hussein during the Iran-Iraq War (1980-1988) directly contradicted its stated goals of promoting stability and democracy in the region.

The U.S. freely provided Iraq with crucial military intelligence and financial support, even as Saddam's regime committed heinous atrocities against its people and neighboring nations.

By prioritizing a short-term alliance based on immediate strategic interests rather than investing in long-term peace-building initiatives, the U.S. caused lasting regional instability and conflict.

This pattern of duplicity fostered an environment of fear and mutual suspicion, leading Iran to feel compelled to seek its own security solutions, including the development of nuclear capabilities—a significant point of contention between Iran and the U.S. in recent decades.

Initially, the U.S. viewed Saddam Hussein as a counterbalance to the Islamic Revolution in Iran, supporting Iraq financially and logistically throughout the Iran-Iraq War. This support included providing intelligence and selling weapons, despite awareness of the humanitarian crises created by Saddam's regime.

During the Iran-Iraq War, Saddam Hussein's regime was responsible for numerous human rights violations, including the use of chemical weapons against Iranian troops and Kurdish civilians, resulting in the deaths of millions.

The U.S. government's knowledge of these actions did not deter its support, highlighting a complex and often contradictory foreign policy approach.

The lasting effects of U.S. interventions in Iraq extended beyond the Iran-Iraq War, leading to further instability in the region. The 2003 invasion of Iraq, following 9/11, exacerbated sectarian tensions, and the U.S. is responsible for the rise of various extremist groups in the Middle East, such as ISIS, al-Qaeda, and the Taliban, complicating the security landscape.

The perceived need for security has driven Iran to develop its nuclear program, which Tehran views as a deterrent against potential military threats. The U.S. response, including sanctions and military posturing, has created a cycle of provocation and distrust, significantly impacting diplomatic efforts.

The history of U.S. military interventions in the Middle East underscores the complexities of foreign policy driven by strategic imperatives. The contradictions in supporting authoritarian regimes while advocating for democracy and stability have contributed to enduring instability and conflict. This reality has not only shaped regional dynamics but has also spurred nations like Iran to pursue alternative security measures, complicating U.S.-Iran relations and raising questions about the efficacy of American involvement in the region.

The fallout from Trump's decision to withdraw the U.S. from the Joint Comprehensive Plan of Action (JCPOA) in 2018 further illustrates the pattern of American diplomacy that often overlooks broader implications. By unilaterally rescinding this agreement, which was designed to effectively curtail Iran's nuclear program in exchange for sanctions relief, the U.S. not only undermined diplomatic goodwill but also sent a clear signal to Iran and the international community that it could easily abandon its commitments.

This action triggered a renewed cycle of conflict and distrust, prompting Iran to reassert its sovereignty while beginning to explore its nuclear options.

Consequently, this decision further isolated Iran from the international community. It highlighted a retreat by the U.S. from constructive diplomacy, marking a shift from engagement to confrontation that entrenches divisions and alienates potential regional allies and beyond.

The consequences of such actions are profound, underscoring the complexities and possible pitfalls of American foreign policy rooted in short-term strategic calculations rather than long-term diplomatic vision.

The JCPOA, signed in 2015 between Iran and the P5+1 (the five permanent members of the UN Security Council plus Germany), aimed to limit Iran's nuclear capabilities in exchange for lifting economic sanctions. The agreement was seen as a landmark achievement in diplomacy.

Following the U.S. withdrawal, Iran began to gradually breach the limits set by the JCPOA, including expanding uranium enrichment levels and stockpiling enriched materials—actions that raised concerns among the international community regarding the potential for weapons development.

The withdrawal strained U.S. relations with European allies, who remained committed to the agreement and sought to salvage it. It illustrated a divergence in strategic priorities among traditional partners.

Trump and the U.S. are responsible for all of the actions that have taken place since the withdrawal, leading to increased military tensions in the region, including confrontations between U.S. and Iranian forces, as well as a series of attacks on shipping in the Gulf that were attributed to Iranian proxies. This environment has led to a renewed call for increased hostilities and fears of a wider conflict.

Subsequent attempts by the Biden administration to revive negotiations on a revised nuclear agreement have met with mixed responses from Iran, complicating efforts to restore the diplomatic framework established by the JCPOA.

The U.S. withdrawal from the JCPOA reflects a broader trend in American foreign policy that prioritizes immediate strategic gains over sustained diplomatic engagement.

The resultant instability raises questions about the viability of future diplomatic efforts and serves as a cautionary tale about the long-term consequences of unilateral actions on international relations initiated by the U.S.

Recognizing and addressing the historical grievances caused by U.S. actions is vital for improving U.S.-Iran relations and establishing a more stable and cooperative Middle Eastern landscape overall. Understanding the long-term consequences of interventionist policies and engaging in genuine dialogue rooted in mutual respect is essential for breaking the cycle of animosity and mistrust that has characterized U.S.-Iranian relations for decades.

To move forward, Americans must critically engage with their country's historical and ongoing actions in Iran and other nations of color by acknowledging how American actions have shaped the current state of relations.

The impacts of U.S. interventions, economic sanctions, and diplomatic failures have left an enduring imprint on Iranian society and continue to stoke animosity. Recognizing this responsibility demands a transformative shift in perspective that prioritizes diplomacy, respects national sovereignty, and honors the humanity of all individuals involved.

Historical U.S. interventions in Iran, particularly the 1953 coup, have fostered a narrative of external control that still resonates in Iranian society today.

Ongoing economic sanctions imposed by the U.S. have significantly affected the Iranian economy and civilian population, often leading to widespread hardship. Critics argue that these sanctions exacerbate anti-American sentiment and hinder diplomatic resolution.

The inability to constructively engage with Iran, especially following the Iran nuclear deal (the Joint Comprehensive Plan of Action) in 2015 and the subsequent U.S. withdrawal in 2018, has contributed to deteriorating relations. A lack of trust hampers progress toward mutual interests.

Engaging with nations of color requires cultural sensitivity and an understanding of historical contexts. This approach is vital for fostering relationships based on respect and equality rather than power dynamics.

Successful diplomacy must consider the lives and perspectives of ordinary citizens. Fostering people-to-people connections and understanding local political contexts can help mend relations at a grassroots level.

Acknowledging and addressing historical grievances is crucial for improving U.S.-Iran relations and ensuring a more collaborative Middle East. A commitment to understanding and respecting the complexities of these relationships will pave the way for more productive dialogue and cooperation in the future.

Only through this lens of accountability and understanding can the U.S. redefine its role on the global stage, fostering relationships grounded in respect, mutual understanding, and a genuine commitment to shared values rather than dominance or coercion.

Through such critical reflection, we can address the root causes of animosity and strive toward a more peaceful and cooperative future.

Acknowledging past mistakes and adopting a policy framework centered on empathy and constructive engagement can foster a more stable and prosperous relationship between the U.S. and Iran, ultimately benefiting both nations and the wider international community.

Historical U.S. foreign policy often leaned toward dominance, particularly during the Cold War. Shifting to a partnership model instead of a dominant and possessive stance would emphasize collaboration and respect for national sovereignty, which is essential for long-term stability.

Policies that prioritize empathy and understanding can help mitigate conflicts. By recognizing the unique historical, cultural, and political contexts that shape Iranian society, the U.S. can build trust and open lines of communication.

Identifying shared values, such as economic cooperation, regional stability, and the fight against extremism, can serve as a foundation for dialogue and collaboration between the U.S. and Iran.

Fostering constructive engagement requires consistent and open dialogues, highlighting the need for back-channel communications, cultural exchanges, and diplomatic initiatives.

A peaceful and cooperative U.S.-Iran relationship has implications beyond bilateral ties. Stability in Iran can contribute to broader regional stability, impacting global issues such as energy security, migration, and counterterrorism.

The U.S. must acknowledge historical grievances, make reparations, and shift towards an approach based on empathy and respect.

The U.S. can foster positive nation-to-nation relationships globally. Such a transformation would not only enhance ties with Iran but also contribute positively to the international community, paving the way for a more collaborative and peaceful world.

The following eight nations exemplify the complex and often damaging relationship the U.S. has fostered through its various forms of exploitation or intervention:

Puerto Rico: The relationship between Puerto Rico and the United States is fraught with historical, political, and economic tensions that contribute to resentment among many Puerto Ricans. Since becoming a U.S. territory in 1898, Puerto Rico has lost its sovereignty and operates under U.S. governance without full rights. Puerto Ricans are U.S. citizens but cannot vote in presidential elections and have no voting representation in Congress, leading to feelings of political marginalization. Furthermore, U.S. policies, such as the Jones Act, have adversely affected the island's economy, exacerbating issues like the recent debt crisis and contributing to a pervasive sense of economic exploitation and neglect. Culturally, many Puerto Ricans feel a loss of identity due to the imposition of American norms and values, alongside facing discrimination in mainland America. This complex dynamic fuels calls for either statehood or independence—a multifaceted grievance that illustrates the disconnect between Puerto Rico and the U.S. mainland.

Venezuela: The complex relationship between the United States and Venezuela is marked by long-standing resentment fueled by a series of interventions, economic sanctions, and perceived political meddling. Historically, the U.S. has intervened in Latin America under the pretext of promoting democracy and stability, but many Venezuelans view these actions as imperialistic. This includes U.S. support for various opposition groups during tumultuous times, notably during Hugo Chávez's presidency when the U.S. was perceived as backing a coup attempt in 2002. Such interventions fostered a narrative of the U.S. as a neocolonial power attempting to control Venezuela's political landscape, galvanizing nationalism and anti-American sentiment among both the populace and the government. Furthermore, economic sanctions targeting Venezuela's oil sector—the backbone of its economy—have exacerbated the nation's economic woes and contributed to a humanitarian crisis. Many Venezuelans blame these sanctions for widespread shortages of basic goods, food, and medicine, viewing them as punitive measures that deepen the suffering of ordinary citizens rather than encourage reform. This perception of U.S. interference has entrenched resentment and unified a national identity against what is seen as an external oppressor, deepening the rift between the two nations.

Cuba: Long-standing animosity between the U.S. and Cuba is rooted in the U.S. embargo and interventions in Cuban affairs. After Fidel Castro came to power in 1959, Cuba sought assistance from the U.S., but the latter's refusal to aid the island unless it aligned with American interests significantly contributed to Cuba's shift toward communism. The U.S. response included the embargo that economically isolated Cuba, escalating hostilities, and prompting Castro to turn to the Soviet Union for support. This realignment not only solidified Cuba's communist regime but also deepened anti-American sentiments within the country. The U.S. interventionist policies and economic sanctions pushed Cuba into the arms of a superpower willing to provide the aid and support that the U.S. denied, illustrating how U.S. actions can directly shape the political landscape of other nations. This historical context highlights the complexities of U.S. foreign policy and its unintended consequences on international relations.

Panama: Panama's animosity toward the United States has historical roots deeply embedded in its complex relationship with U.S. involvement in its sovereignty, particularly concerning the Panama Canal. The U.S. played a pivotal role in Panama's separation from Colombia in 1903, subsequently gaining control over the Canal Zone. This control was formalized through the Hay-Bunau-Varilla Treaty, which many Panamanians perceived as inequitable and forced upon them. For most of the 20th century, the U.S. exercised significant political and military influence in Panama, leading to resentment toward American interventionism. The Canal, a symbol of U.S. dominance, was critical to Panamanians, who felt that their land and resources were being exploited without fair compensation or respect for their sovereignty. This legacy fostered humiliation and anger exacerbated by U.S. military actions and political machinations, including support for the oppressive regime of Manuel Noriega. Noriega's eventual fall from grace led to the U.S. invasion of Panama in 1989, resulting in extensive casualties and damage, deepening distrust of American motives. Many Panamanians continue to harbor bitterness toward American policies, viewing them as exploitative and damaging to their national identity.

Honduras: Resentment and hostility toward the United States in Honduras can be traced back to a tumultuous history of U.S.

involvement in political affairs, particularly the backing of military coups that subverted democratic processes. One glaring example is the 2009 coup that ousted President Manuel Zelaya, who had initiated progressive reforms aimed at addressing social inequality and poverty. The U.S. response to the coup was perceived as tacit approval, as it did not take immediate action to restore Zelaya's leadership. This complicity entrenched distrust toward the U.S. among many Hondurans, who see American influence as undermining their sovereignty and democratic institutions. Additionally, economic exploitation linked to U.S. corporate interests has contributed to resentment, as American companies in agriculture and textiles have often employed exploitative labor practices with inadequate wages. This perception of the U.S. as a nation that exploits local resources fosters feelings of injustice, contributing to a cycle of resentment that affects diplomatic relations.

Mexico: Mexico's animosity toward the United States is rooted in colonial history, territorial disputes, and economic disparities. The Mexican-American War (1846-1848) dramatically reduced Mexico's territory, fostering a deep-seated resentment toward the U.S. Policies that maintain cycles of dependency and underdevelopment contribute to poverty and violence in Mexico, which are often oversimplified in American discourse focused on cartel violence. Many Mexicans view U.S. actions as imperialistic, undermining their sovereignty and exacerbating domestic challenges.

Syria: The United States' actions in Syria have significantly contributed to deep-seated distrust and hostility toward America among many Syrians. Historically, the U.S. has supported Israel in its conflicts with Syria, fostering animosity due to perceived imperialistic tendencies. During the Syrian Civil War, the U.S. intervened by backing various rebel groups, including those affiliated with extremist factions, which many saw as direct interference in Syria's sovereignty and governance. This military involvement was perceived as exacerbating the conflict rather than promoting stability, particularly as U.S. airstrikes targeted both ISIS and government forces, leading to civilian casualties and destruction of infrastructure. The consequences of U.S. sanctions and military actions have resulted in widespread suffering among the Syrian populace. The Caesar Act, aimed at crippling the Syrian regime, has further complicated the humanitarian crisis, inflicting economic pain on ordinary citizens rather than solely the governing elite. The lack of a comprehensive approach that represents the diverse voices of the Syrian population in peace negotiations has also bred resentment, solidifying a narrative that the U.S. prioritizes its strategic interests over the welfare of the Syrian people. As a result, many Syrians view the U.S. not as a promoter of democracy but as an imperialist entity that fuels suffering and instability.

Korea: America's need to dominate and control the political landscape after World War II significantly contributed to the animosity toward the United States in Korea. Following the end of the Japanese occupation, rather than supporting Korea's bid for independence, the U.S. and the Soviet Union chose to divide the nation along the 38th parallel. This move was not driven by an understanding of Korean aspirations for self-determination but rather by the superpowers' desire to establish military strongholds in the region. The division artificially imposed by foreign powers created deep divides within Korea and led to the establishment of two antagonistic regimes: a communist dictatorship in the North guided by the USSR and an authoritarian government in the South propped up by the U.S. Ultimately, this failure to honor the Korean people's desire for unity and autonomy sowed seeds of discontent and hostility toward the U.S. as a colonial participant in their ongoing struggle. In the years that followed, America's actions in Korea were largely dictated by the context of the Cold War, where containing communism became a critical objective. The U.S. chose to back Syngman Rhee, an anti-communist leader whose regime was marred by authoritarianism and corruption, further alienating the population. The U.S. arrogance and disregard for the Korean perspective resulted in increased instability, which contributed to the outbreak of the Korean War. Throughout this conflict, U.S. military intervention was less about supporting Korean independence and more focused on asserting control in the region, fueling the animosity that had already begun festering post-WWII. The desire to dictate the narrative of democracy, coupled with a lack of genuine engagement with the Korean populace, not only jeopardized the possibility of a cohesive Korean state but also led to profound, lasting repercussions that have shaped U.S.-Korean relations to this day.

At the heart of these issues lies a deeply ingrained attitude of American exceptionalism, which conveys the belief that the U.S. has both the right and obligation to intervene in the affairs of other nations. This mindset often disregards the historical contexts and complexities of foreign societies, leading to poorly conceived policies that exacerbate existing tensions. Nations like Iran and Cuba perceive American cultural and political imposition as a form of imperialism, fostering resentment and resistance.

Why We Should Pay Reparations to the Descendants of Enslaved People in the United States

The issue of restitution for the descendants of enslaved people in the United States has become a critical topic of discussion, igniting debates that encompass historical, economic, and social dimensions. Due to the complexities surrounding this issue, we must consider aspects such as eligibility, potential costs, forms of restitution, and the long-term implications for society.

Here is an overview of instances when the U.S. government has engaged in reparative actions:

Native Americans:
The Indian Claims Commission has paid billions of dollars to Native American tribes for land seizures, with total payments amounting to around $1.3 billion. Specific examples include payments to the Klamath Tribes of Oregon, the Sioux Nation of South Dakota, and the Chippewa Tribe of Wisconsin.

Japanese Americans:
The Civil Liberties Act of 1988 provided $1.2 billion in compensation and formal apologies to Japanese Americans interned during World War II.

Tuskegee Syphilis Experiment:
A settlement of $10 million was reached for the victims of the Tuskegee Syphilis Study.

Greenwood, Oklahoma:
In the aftermath of the 1921 Tulsa Race Massacre, the Oklahoma legislature provided reparations in the form of scholarships, economic development initiatives, a memorial, and medals to survivors.

Iran Hostages:
The U.S. government has paid reparations to American citizens who were held hostage during the Iran hostage crisis from 1979 to 1981.

Victims of the September 11 Attacks:
Financial assistance and compensation programs were established to support victims and their families following the September 11, 2001, terrorist attacks.

Slaveholders:
After the abolition of slavery, some slaveholders received compensation for the loss of their enslaved individuals, particularly in the District of Columbia, where a program was established to provide funds to slaveholders.

American Slaves:
No reparations we are even trying to cover up the history of slavery on the USA

Victims of Discriminatory Policies:
There have been instances of compensation for groups adversely affected by specific discriminatory policies, such as lawsuits against the federal

government concerning injustices related to the relocation and treatment of Native Americans.

For a more comprehensive list of reparations and discussions surrounding this topic, you can refer to: [UMass Reparations Guide](https://guides. library.umass.edu/reparations).

While these reparations have occurred, the issue of reparations for the descendants of enslaved Africans in the U.S. remains unresolved and is a topic of ongoing debate.

We compensated slaveholders but not the enslaved individuals themselves. Let that sink in. Why did we provide financial restitution to slaveholders for their immoral and unethical behavior while neglecting those who were kidnapped, tortured, held against their will, and forced to labor? This oversight is a profound injustice.

Historical context is vital to understanding the current discourse. Enslavement in the U.S. lasted for approximately 246 years, beginning in 1619 and continuing until the Emancipation Proclamation in 1863, with the official end of slavery occurring in 1865.

Juneteenth celebrates June 19, 1865, the day when the last enslaved people of African descent in Galveston, Texas, finally learned of their freedom from the system of slavery in the United States.

Freedom was proclaimed through the Emancipation Proclamation, which was signed by President Abraham Lincoln on January 1, 1863. However, Texas was the farthest of the Confederate states, and slaveholders there did not attempt to free the enslaved African Americans they held in bondage. This meant that President Lincoln's proclamation was unenforceable without military intervention, which eventually came nearly 2.5 years later.

The impact of slavery has left a profound and lasting legacy on the descendants of enslaved individuals, manifesting in systemic racism, economic disadvantages, and social inequities that persist today. This complex history creates a moral imperative for many to address the injustices that have unfolded over generations.

Due to 246 years of slavery and the ongoing legacy of racial discrimination, many in the Anglo population continue to see and treat Black people as inferior in various ways.

In support of restitution, proponents argue for a framework primarily focused on descendants of enslaved individuals. One proposed approach is to provide annual payments akin to what is currently given to Indigenous Americans through programs like the Bureau of Indian Affairs (BIA), which often provide per capita payments from tribal governments based on revenue generated from tribal enterprises. If we consider that Indigenous Americans receive annual payments that can vary widely depending on tribal membership, revenue sharing, and other factors, a similar structure could provide an ongoing source of income for descendants of enslaved people.

To put this in context, let's examine the dollar value from 1865. Following the end of slavery, the federal government considered compensatory measures for formerly enslaved people, but none were fully enacted. If we assume an annual payment would start from that point, amounts could be indexed for inflation. For example, if a free person were to $100 per year in 1865 as a reference point, this would translate to approximately $1,700 today when adjusted for inflation an estimate some might use for reparations discussions. By creating an annual payment model rather than a lump sum, proponents believe that this approach would provide long-term financial support while acknowledging the ongoing legacy of slavery.

The financial implications of reparations raise further complexities, particularly when comparing the historical value of proposed payments with contemporary standards. If one considers the potential structure involving annual payments, for instance, we might propose an amount of $1,700 per descendant of enslaved individuals. This would yield a total expenditure, amounting to $51 billion annually, that could serve as a starting baseline for discussions. A considerable expenditure, especially as estimates suggest that there are approximately 30 million descendants eligible.

$51 billion sounds like a significant amount to all of us, but it is a small percentage compared to the estimated $8 trillion the wealthy tax cuts will cost us.

Expanding on the potential costs and indexing the payments to historical value further complicates the total reimbursement figures. When calculating a timeline that extends from 1865 to the present day, annual increments would accumulate dramatically, leading to considerably high totals, even as they adjust for inflation. Many advocates for such structures argue that they would allow descendants to build wealth gradually and mitigate the immediate financial burden that a lump sum might create on the federal budget.

One potential method for determining the funding for these ongoing payments could involve tax adjustments, similar to how many states fund programs for Indigenous individuals or how federal budgets are allocated across various social programs. Such measures could help achieve dynamic funding based on national income levels, allowing payments to reflect not only inflation but also the growing economic needs of historically marginalized communities.

In addition to direct payments, alternative forms of restitution could include investments targeting education, healthcare, housing, and community development initiatives. For example, scholarships and grants aimed at African American students could significantly improve educational outcomes and increase access to higher education, thereby fostering long-term change. Establishing a mechanism for ongoing assessments of systemic racial inequality would be crucial for adjusting restitution measures as socioeconomic conditions evolve.

The political landscape significantly influences the reparations conversation. Recent actions and statements from figures such as President Donald Trump and the MAGA Republicans underscore a concerning trend in which the "dark side" of American history is either downplayed or dismissed altogether.

This refusal to fully acknowledge past injustices inhibits the nation's ability to reckon with its history and hinders opportunities for meaningful dialogue about reparations. Many believe that to properly address historical wrongs, we must candidly admit when we have erred. While some argue that slavery ended 160 years ago, the systemic mistreatment of the Black community has remained largely unchanged. The persistent inequities experienced by Black Americans indicate that the effects of slavery are woven into the very fabric of society today.

Critics from the white community often claim that they bear no responsibility for past injustices because they were not alive during the time of slavery. However, such a stance overlooks the ongoing impact of that history, which continues to affect contemporary racial dynamics.

Many argue that as a collective society, we cannot distance ourselves from the legacies of our ancestors. Just as every nation must grapple with its failings, so too must we confront the realities of our past. Acknowledgment, reconciliation, and reparative actions should not be viewed as burdensome obligations; rather, they are essential steps toward achieving justice. All individuals, regardless of their background, seek acknowledgment and restitution when wronged, and it is fundamentally unjust to expect marginalized communities to plead for redress.

Opposition to the idea of restitution, often articulated by those with a perception of superiority, is similarly compelling and multifaceted. One central argument centers on practical challenges, particularly the difficulties involved in accurately identifying eligible descendants. Current genealogical methods may not suffice to comprehensively trace family histories for all potential recipients. This verification process is not only intricate but could also incur significant administrative costs.

Social and political feasibility further complicates the narrative surrounding reparations. Many U.S. policymakers and constituents view the concept of reparations as politically unviable, with public opinion showing deep divisions on the matter. Enacting such measures could lead to backlash or further polarization, complicating ongoing efforts for racial justice. Similar arguments were used regarding LGBTQ+ marriages.

Critics also advocate for alternative approaches focusing on systemic reforms rather than direct payments. They suggest that investing in policies that promote socioeconomic growth—such as universal basic income initiatives, housing vouchers, job training programs, and improved access to education—may be more effective in addressing the racial disparities that have emerged over centuries. Emphasizing systemic change rather than providing specific payments could lead to sustainable progress without the perceived punitive nature of reparations.

As discussions around restitution continue, questions regarding the involvement of future generations remain prominent. Determining how to include descendants in any restitution framework raises ethical concerns. Would payments continue indefinitely for future generations, and how would eligibility be determined? Critics argue that this could create a system in which individuals are rewarded or penalized based on ancestry, leading to further division rather than unity and progress.

The discourse surrounding restitution for the descendants of enslaved people in the United States is complex. Proponents of reparations see these measures as necessary to redress historical wrongs and foster true equality, often advocating for ongoing payments based on the model established for Indigenous Americans, which recognizes that real justice takes time and sustained effort. Conversely, critics emphasize the practical challenges and potential societal ramifications of enacting such measures.

By considering historical motivations such as systemic racism, economic disparities, and social injustices as well as discussions of indexed value adjusted for inflation and sustained annual payments rather than one-time lump sums, we can engage in meaningful dialogue about reparations. This conversation also highlights the importance of acknowledgment and reconciliation. Ultimately, achieving a long-term impact requires a multifaceted approach that involves continuous dialogue among historians, policymakers, community leaders, and the descendants of enslaved Africans. Together, we must strive to identify the most equitable and effective paths forward in addressing the enduring legacy of slavery and working toward a more just society. An unflinching acknowledgment of our past is crucial as we move forward, ensuring that history is not forgotten and that no one has to beg for justice.

Public opinion on reparations for dependents of the enslaved and racial injustice in the United States is deeply divided, reflecting a complex landscape of historical, ethical, and political considerations. Surveys reveal significant disparities in support for reparations among different demographic groups and political affiliations.

General support for reparations shows that while Black Americans support reparations in some form, only about 18% of White Americans express similar support. This dichotomy underscores the racial gap in perceptions of the necessity and fairness of reparations.

Among political party affiliations, Democratic voters generally exhibit a more favorable view toward reparations compared to their Republican counterparts. A survey from Data for Progress found that 55% of Democrats supported some form of reparations, reflecting a notable expectation among this group to address historical injustice.

A majority of Republicans express skepticism or outright opposition to reparations. A Gallup poll indicated that around 75% of Republicans were against the idea of reparations for slavery, viewing it as an unfair method of addressing injustice.

Support for reparations tends to vary significantly with race and age. Younger generations, particularly those in the millennial and Gen Z cohorts, tend to show more support for reparations than older generations, suggesting evolving perceptions of equity and justice within younger demographics. Among Black Americans, support for reparations is significantly higher among younger respondents compared to older generations. Economic factors also play a role; many Americans express a preference for investments in systemic reforms such as education, job training, and housing over direct payments. Polls reveal that substantial numbers of White Americans are more comfortable with policies that promote socioeconomic improvement rather than reparations framed as payments for historical injustices.

The opposition to reparations is particularly pronounced among members of the MAGA (Make America Great Again) faction within the Republican Party. Several factors contribute to this opposition. Many MAGA Republicans embrace a philosophy rooted in individualism and meritocracy, believing that reparations contradict these ideals. They assert that resources should be allocated based on individual needs rather than historical grievances tied to ancestral injustices.

This opposition is further fueled by racial narratives; the MAGA base often frames discussions on race and history through a "colorblind" ideology, which posits that recognizing race-based injustices perpetuates division. Consequently, they may view reparations as an unnecessary complication in the pursuit of a unified national identity. Additionally, economic concerns play a significant role, with opponents often arguing against the feasibility and fairness of funding reparations. They question where the funds would come from and advocate for policies that assist all impoverished individuals, regardless of race. This economic argument aligns with broader conservative views on taxation and government spending.

Many MAGA Republicans also fear that supporting reparations could alienate their voter base. Given that surveys indicate widespread opposition to reparations among conservative voters, MAGA representatives might perceive support for reparations as political suicide in maintaining favor with their constituents.

While support for reparations is stronger among Democrats, a notable contingent within the party remains skeptical or opposed. Some moderate and centrist Democrats caution against reparations for fear that it could detract from broader policy initiatives aimed at racial equity. They argue that focusing on direct payments might overshadow essential conversations on systemic reform and reconciliation.

Disagreements within the Democratic Party about the best path to achieving racial justice also contribute to this opposition. Some members advocate for policies that promote equity, focusing on marginalized communities more broadly rather than solely targeting descendants of enslaved individuals. Ethical considerations also play a role; many Democrats are concerned about the implications of defining eligibility based on ancestry, fearing it could reinforce division rather than promote healing among communities. They may look for solutions that address current inequalities without the complexities attached to reparations.

The discussion surrounding reparations in the United States is emblematic of broader societal tensions around race, history, and justice. Public attitudes are influenced by deep-seated beliefs, demographic differences, political affiliations, and differing views on the role government should play in addressing historical injustices. The ongoing discourse highlights the necessity for constructive conversations that balance acknowledgment of past wrongs with pragmatic approaches to achieving racial equality today.

I don't care that anyone believes it should not be about race. White Americans have shaped our society and how it works with race since the first person set foot in North America.

What is your opinion regarding reparations to the descendants of the enslaved?

The Historical and Ongoing Marginalization of Non-Anglo Immigrants in the U.S.

The history of the United States is deeply intertwined with the treatment of immigrants, particularly those who are not male and of Anglo descent. This systemic persecution has been present since the nation's inception and continues to manifest through various government policies and societal attitudes. Despite different political administrations over the years, a troubling pattern emerges that reveals an enduring commitment to controlling and dehumanizing these marginalized communities.

From the very founding of America, immigrants of color, including people forced here who served in slavery, the Indigenous peoples, and those fleeing violence and persecution, have been subjected to mistreatment and discrimination. This treatment has often been influenced by prevailing views among Anglo citizens, leading to a culture of exclusion and hostility. The evolution of U.S. immigration policies reflects a historical trajectory that often places the lives and rights of non-Anglo immigrants as secondary to national security and political interests.

A key element in understanding this pattern is the intersection of national security, undocumented immigration, and the treatment of people of color. Presidential decisions over the decades reveal a consistent trend wherein policies are shaped by fear and suspicion toward marginalized communities rather than a commitment to human rights and dignity. Notable shifts in our modern history in this regard can be traced from Gerald Ford's administration to Donald Trump today, each reflecting a unique yet disturbingly similar approach to immigration and national security.

President Gerald Ford's tenure coincided with significant geopolitical changes following the Vietnam War. The U.S. faced an influx of Vietnamese refugees, and while Ford demonstrated some measures of compassion, the stories of those fleeing oppression highlighted a complex interplay of empathy and systemic barriers. I know that when I grew up a number of Vietnamese refugees bought and owned shrimp and family shiny boats. Their livelihood was vandalized and some boats were burned overnight.

Throughout American history, the foundational principle encapsulated in the iconic phrase "We the People" suggests a democratic ethos that emphasizes equality, justice, and opportunity for all, regardless of race, gender, or background. However, the reality has often fallen short of this ideal, particularly regarding the treatment and opportunities afforded to marginalized groups, including people of color, women, and immigrants. From the outset, the rights and freedoms declared in the Constitution and the Declaration of Independence were not universally applied. Historical documents such as the Constitution initially protected the interests of a predominantly white, male, land-owning class, intentionally excluding enslaved individuals, women, and Indigenous people. This exclusion laid the groundwork for systemic inequalities that have persisted throughout American history.

The institution of slavery entrenched severe racial hierarchies, establishing a paradigm that prioritized the rights of white Americans over all others. Even after the Civil War and the abolition of slavery, systemic racism remained deeply ingrained in laws and social structures through Jim Crow laws and other discriminatory practices. Throughout the 20th century and into the 21st, policies like redlining, voter suppression, and unequal access to education and employment opportunities further marginalized communities of color. These systemic barriers have created enduring disparities in wealth, health, and social mobility.

The concept of the American Dream, a vision where hard work leads to prosperity and opportunities for all, has often been out of reach for many populations, particularly for immigrants who are not Anglo or are perceived as "other." Immigrants of color frequently face additional obstacles compared to their Anglo counterparts. Policies over the decades have oscillated between periods of openness and periods of hostility, often reflecting broader societal fears and prejudices. Undocumented immigrants, for example, endure the heavy burden of systemic discrimination, living under threat of deportation while being denied many legal protections available to citizens. Ongoing racial profiling and discriminatory practices in law enforcement and immigration policy have disproportionately affected immigrants of color. The depiction of these individuals as potential threats contributes to a climate of suspicion and fear, overshadowing their contributions to society as workers, community members, and family members.

Political discourse in the U.S. has historically reflected and reinforced these unequal structures. The rhetoric surrounding national identity, immigration, and security often marginalizes non-Anglo individuals. From the Chinese Exclusion Act of 1882 to more contemporary measures that perpetuate a narrative of "us versus them," policy decisions have often been driven by fear rather than a genuine commitment to equality and inclusion. In recent years, the rise of populism and nationalism has further exacerbated divisions. Politicians have found electoral success by appealing to sentiments that prioritize the interests of a particular demographic at the expense of others, deepening existing inequalities and tensions.

To realize the promise of "We the People," the United States must critically examine its values and practices, ensuring that all individuals, regardless of their race, nationality, or immigration status, are treated with dignity and respect.

Developing fair immigration policies that recognize the contributions of immigrants, protect their rights, and prioritize humane treatment would be essential for fostering a more equitable society. Ensuring equal access to opportunities in education, employment, and healthcare for all, actively working against systemic barriers, and addressing historical injustices that have contributed to current disparities is crucial. Implementing policies that eliminate racially biased practices and enhance accountability within law enforcement can help build trust within marginalized communities, fostering a sense of safety and belonging. Encouraging active participation from a diversity of communities in the political process ensures that the voices of marginalized groups are heard and considered in decision-making.

The promise of equality envisioned at the nation's founding remains an ongoing struggle, necessitating constant vigilance, advocacy, and reform. For the U.S. to truly embody its foundational values, it must confront its historical injustices, dismantle discriminatory practices, and commit to an inclusive vision that ensures that every individual—whether a citizen or an immigrant, regardless of race or gender—has equal opportunity to thrive. Only then can the country move closer to achieving its ideal of being "for the people" and "created equal."

Understanding the Disenfranchised Voter's Choice and Why Some Democrats Supported Trump

As Democrats, we continually seek to understand why a significant percentage of disenfranchised voters chose to support Trump.

We touted, "This is the most important election in our lifetime. We are voting to save our democracy!"

Everyone understood what that meant to them individually, but did anyone think to ask a disenfranchised individual what it meant for them?

I didn't ask, but the information was volunteered to me. Once I was told how they felt, I could see how someone might say, "I have tried this my whole life and I wasn't included, but I haven't tried that, so I'm going to try it."

Could it be that the root of this issue lies in our failure to consider the deeper historical context, alongside today's systemic oppression and its impact on their belief in a democratic republic?

We must ask ourselves: What has our conception of freedom truly offered these individuals? We must engage in an honest reflection about the circumstances that led to their disaffection with our party and take proactive steps to address these concerns.

The interplay between the promotion of freedom and the enactment of repression against marginalized communities deserves rigorous exploration, particularly when examining both historical and contemporary political dynamics.

The paradox of a democratic republic is steeped in a historical backdrop of suppression within democratic frameworks. Democracies, especially in the United States, were founded on principles of freedom and equality; however, these ideals have often been applied selectively.

The treatment of Black individuals, Indigenous populations, LGBTQ+ communities, people of color, and undocumented immigrants showcases a long-standing history of systemic oppression that exists alongside the country's professed democratic values.

One glaring example of this foundational hypocrisy is the systematic repression of Black Americans through slavery, segregation, and ongoing systemic racism, which occurred within a democratic structure that claimed liberty for all. This relationship epitomizes the contradiction inherent in a system that promotes freedom while simultaneously undermining it for specific groups.

Another example can be seen in the criminalization of homosexuality through anti-sodomy laws and the marginalization of LGBTQ+ identities, which were implemented in a society that celebrates personal freedoms. The violent backlash against LGBTQ+ communities, especially following the Stonewall Uprising, further illustrates how societal acceptance can be selectively enforced.

Moreover, undocumented immigrants frequently face severe repercussions, including deportation and violence, despite the nation's reliance on their labor and its professed democratic ideals. Policies targeting these individuals reveal deeply entrenched xenophobia and racism within our governance.

The current political landscape, particularly initiatives such as Project 2025, illustrates troubling shifts toward authoritarianism. Proposed by conservative groups in the United States, this initiative aims to fundamentally reshape federal governance and policy when Donald

Trump, a Republican, regains office in January. Specifically, he appears focused on deporting all immigrants, rolling back progressive reforms, and restoring certain policies that could adversely affect marginalized communities.

The underlying notion of loyalty to a specific political figure, Donald Trump, over constitutional principles represents a disturbing trend; individuals may be categorized not only by party loyalty but also by their identity traits.

As the political landscape becomes increasingly polarized, those who diverge from the prevailing ideology may face repercussions, including public shaming, loss of employment, and even violence. In such an environment, individuals may feel compelled to compartmentalize aspects of their identity, hiding parts of who they are to avoid backlash. As the LGBTQ+ community often says, they are "back in the closet."

This instinct mirrors historical experiences where marginalized communities developed strategies for survival, often living discreetly to evade scrutiny or violence.

As significant political shifts occur, the expression of dissent or nonconformity may become subdued, leading to self-censorship.

People may become increasingly cautious about disclosing their beliefs or identities in public spheres, contributing to an atmosphere of mistrust and anxiety.

In response to escalating repression under initiatives like Project 2025, organized resistance will become necessary.

Liberal and progressive forces must unite to confront authoritarian trends, emphasizing collective advocacy for democratic principles, human rights, and equitable treatment.

Anticipating the consequences of repression is crucial, as the ongoing threat of violence not only impacts immediate victims but also creates a cycle of trauma that affects future generations.

The normalization of fear can stifle societal growth and diminish community spirit and resilience.

The potential regression of rights and freedoms could set a dangerous precedent, unraveling decades of progress and reinforcing systemic inequities.

Vigilance is essential to counteract this trend and reclaim rights for all marginalized groups. The tension between the democratic ideals of freedom and the reality of oppression presents a compelling narrative of systemic injustice.

As political landscapes evolve, particularly under initiatives that may seek to undermine the principles of equality and justice, understanding historical lessons becomes critical.

The call for accountability, advocacy for intersectionality, and recognition of shared fears across identities remains vital.

Mobilizing toward a just and equitable society requires solidarity among those historically faced with repression, as well as those navigating newfound vulnerabilities in an increasingly hostile environment.

In doing so, communities can create a unified front to resist authoritarian tendencies and reaffirm the principles of liberty, justice, and protection for all individuals, regardless of identity.

This requires acknowledging that the fight for freedom and rights is interconnected across marginalized identities. Only through a concerted effort rooted in shared understanding and mutual support can we effectively confront these impending challenges and work toward a society that embodies the values of true democracy for everyone.

The Importance of Engaging in Difficult Discussions: A Call for Reflection

In recent weeks, I've received a plethora of comments on my social media posts regarding the reluctance many feel to engage with supporters of the MAGA movement.

The two primary reasons cited are a belief that these individuals won't listen and a fear that any discussion will devolve into pointless arguments. If you've commented on my post, I encourage you to reflect on whether there's a parallel between your reasons for disengagement and the responses you provided.

We lost, and it's time to pull up our big girl or big boy pants, dust ourselves off, and get back to work. The longer we remain idle, the more detrimental policies and actions the opposing side will push through, tearing down hard-won progress. Rebuilding what has been lost will ultimately be much harder than repairing what already exists.

Constructive engagement is crucial in our increasingly polarized environment. If the Democratic Party aims to reclaim lost ground, a significant reevaluation of strategies is paramount. We can't accomplish anything outside of our party until we stop lashing out and attacking each other. It's essential to recognize that we only fail in the 2024 election if we give up. Failing is quitting, which leads to forever losing, while learning from our experiences can make us better for the next round.

Communities of color, Indigenous Americans, and the older LGBTQ+ community have long understood the importance of engaging in challenging discussions. They take on these discussions not for immediate gain but to promote education and gradually dismantle oppressive structures. Each succeeding generation that engages in these battles contributes to a greater impact, and slowly but surely, we inch closer to achieving social justice.

However, we must recognize that true equality may take generations, even if the law suggests that we've already arrived.

Interestingly, there are parallels between current Democratic behaviors and the more combative tactics observed within segments of the MAGA base after the 2020 election. While violence and law-breaking are not present, we have assumed the approach of refusing accountability and casting blame which can create similar dynamics of anger and division. A prevailing sense of superiority can lead to a lack of empathy for the broader electorate. If you choose not to participate, that's fine; it's your decision. But please stop trying to talk others into quitting. Be a cheerleader if you can't be a participant.

The reluctance to engage in discussions reflects larger challenges that political movements face following setbacks. Comparing us to them highlights how similar dynamics of anger and division can manifest across the political spectrum.

Learning from losses, adapting, and fostering meaningful conversations even when they are uncomfortable must become our focus. Acknowledging these dynamics and committing to constructive dialogue is essential for progress in the political arena and achieving true social justice.

Let's take these battles on together, knowing that our efforts today will lay the foundation for a more equitable tomorrow. Together, let's resolve to not just learn from failure but to actively work towards improvement, moving forward with renewed purpose and unity.

Always avoid physical violence. My mom always told us, "If you end up having to fight don't back down. You may end up getting your ass kicked but you do what you have to do to make sure they suffer even with their victory."

The Paradox Of Inclusivity, Unraveling Hidden Biases And Prejudices In Liberal Movements

The suggestion is that personal connections to diverse groups often disguise deeper biases. Genuine inclusivity goes beyond surface-level relationships and requires confronting unexamined prejudices and understanding systemic inequalities.

The liberal movement has long championed the ideals of inclusivity, advocating for the rights and dignity of diverse groups based on race, religion, sexual orientation, economic status, and educational background.

However, beneath this surface commitment to inclusivity exists a complex web of biases, prejudices, and hidden intolerances that often go unacknowledged within the very movements that espouse these values.

This paradox highlights the disparities between proclaimed beliefs and actual behaviors, presenting significant challenges for those within the liberal fold.

Understanding these tensions requires exploring the intricate relationships among identity, experience, psychology, and social interactions, all of which shape our perceptions of inclusivity.

The heart of the paradox lies in the distinction between acceptance and true inclusivity.

Many individuals believe that having friends from diverse backgrounds or marrying someone of a different nationality automatically makes them open-minded or tolerant.

However, this perceived enlightenment often masks deeper biases and emotional responses that remain unexamined.

Knowing a single individual from a marginalized group does not provide a comprehensive understanding of their experiences, struggles, or cultural nuances.

For example, while one may be quick to identify as accepting after forming a bond with a member of the LGBTQ+ community, it is crucial to recognize that such relationships don't necessarily translate into a broader acceptance of LGBTQ+ individuals as a whole.

The limits of personal experience often lead individuals to conflate their narrow experiences with universal understanding.

As someone with personal connections to marginalized communities, one can still fall short of grasping the full breadth of their challenges and realities.

Take the example of an adopted sister with Choctaw heritage; genuine affection and admiration do not equate to an authentic understanding of the systemic issues faced by Indigenous peoples.

The complexities of identity and experience cannot be reduced to anecdotal understandings based on limited interactions.

To claim acceptance of a group in its entirety, individuals must engage with the broader historical and societal contexts that shape each community's unique narratives.

The concept of tolerance itself is often misinterpreted in liberal movements.

While liberals may pride themselves on being more tolerant than other demographics, this tolerance is sometimes superficial and conditional.

Tolerance, as a psychological phenomenon, may manifest as mere passive acceptance rather than active engagement with difference.

For instance, an individual may tolerate the existence of a diverse group of people but harbor unexamined prejudices that remain hidden beneath a veneer of civility.

This discrepancy can lead to problematic attitudes and behaviors that undermine the very principles of inclusivity.

Many may support LGBTQ+ rights publicly but engage in harmful rhetoric or actions privately when discussing issues that affect that community.

The disconnect between public affirmation and private attitudes is both a psychological defense mechanism and a reflection of societal pressures.

Psychologically, a phenomenon known as cognitive dissonance arises, wherein individuals hold contradictory belief systems that create internal tension.

To alleviate this discomfort, many may suppress or ignore their biases rather than confront and work through them.

Much of the hidden prejudice retained within liberal spaces can be traced back to social conditioning.

People are raised within cultural, social, and familial frameworks that instill biases from childhood.

Even within apparent liberal environments, individuals may inherit a worldview that subtly encourages judgment or exclusion of those who differ from them in significant ways.

For example, socioeconomic differences can lead to divisions among liberal allies; those from privileged backgrounds may struggle to empathize with the lived realities of those entrenched in poverty.

This gap in understanding often manifests as paternalism rather than genuine solidarity, wherein those in power may attempt to "help" marginalized individuals without truly listening to their needs or seeking their input.

To address the paradox of inclusivity within liberal movements, several steps can be taken to promote a deeper understanding of the issues at hand and foster genuine relationships that encompass all identities and experiences.

Encouraging open conversations about biases and prejudices enables individuals to confront uncomfortable truths.

Creating safe spaces where people can share their experiences can help build understanding and empathy, allowing individuals to learn from one another constructively.

Individuals must commit to ongoing self-examination of their beliefs and behaviors, recognizing and addressing subconscious biases essential for creating a truly inclusive environment.

Providing comprehensive education on the histories, cultures, and experiences of diverse communities can foster deeper empathy and understanding.

Investing in historical education ensures that individuals grasp the systemic issues impacting marginalized groups and begin to recognize the subtleties inherent in each unique culture.

In this context, the inclusion of critical race theory (CRT) in educational curricula offers significant benefits.

CRT asserts that race is a social construct that shapes our experiences, and it frames systemic racism as an ingrained aspect of U.S. law and policy, affecting various facets of life, including education, employment, and housing.

Teaching CRT from the earliest educational stages through to doctoral programs allows students to understand the historical roots of racial dynamics and how they play out in contemporary society.

By examining the intersections of race with other identities, students will better understand how personal experiences relate to societal structures.

This theoretical framework encourages critical thinking and promotes the importance of examining power dynamics within our institutions.

Moreover, integrating CRT into educational settings encourages a dialogue about privilege, allowing individuals to recognize how their social positions shape their perspectives and actions.

It compels students to engage in discussions that go beyond the mere existence of diversity, delving into the underlying systemic issues that influence inclusion and equity.

This proactive approach ensures that discussions around race and identity are not relegated to a single course or moment in an academic journey but instead become ingrained in the overall educational experience.

Advocating for marginalized groups necessitates action and allyship beyond mere acceptance.

This means standing in solidarity with communities when they face discrimination, fostering advocacy efforts that support systemic change, and engaging in dialogues that challenge dominant narratives.

The paradox of inclusivity within liberal movements serves as both a challenge and an opportunity for growth.

By recognizing and addressing the biases, prejudices, and hidden intolerances within ourselves, we can work toward authentic inclusivity that embraces all individuals, regardless of race, religion, sexual orientation, economic status, or education level.

Understanding that acceptance is not synonymous with true inclusivity fosters the groundwork for deeper connections and commitments to the values of solidarity and justice.

In examining our relationships and attitudes candidly, we can begin to dismantle the barriers that prevent genuine understanding and collective action.

Ultimately, leading the way toward a more inclusive and enlightened liberal movement requires not just open hearts but also open minds, as we endeavor to embrace the rich tapestry of human experience.

Unveiling the Consequences of American Interventionism: Arrogance, Greed, and Exploitation

In our quest for power and influence, the United States has often approached foreign intervention with an attitude steeped in arrogance and driven by greed.

This pursuit has led to a troubling legacy of manipulation, exploitation, and disregard for the well-being of the nations we engaged with.

As we delve into this complex history, we must confront the uncomfortable truth about the consequences of our actions on vulnerable societies.

A Legacy of Manipulation and Exploitation

The United States' belief in Manifest Destiny not only justified the westward expansion but also led to the systematic displacement and suffering of Native American populations.

The government's insatiable thirst for land resulted in broken treaties, violent confrontations, and the cultural erasure of indigenous peoples, all pursued with little regard for their humanity.

The Mexican-American War exemplified American expansionism cloaked in claims of liberation.

Motivated by greed for fertile land and resources, the U.S. pursued a brutal conflict that resulted in the loss of significant Mexican territory.

This land acquisition was pursued with little thought for the people who lived there or the sovereignty of Mexico.

Interventions in nations like Cuba, Nicaragua, and Guatemala were designed not to foster democracy but to protect American economic interests.

The CIA-backed overthrow of Guatemalan President Jacobo Árbenz in 1954 is a striking example of U.S. arrogance, where geopolitical strategizing prioritized corporate profits over the democratic aspirations of the Guatemalan people.

Such actions often left these countries in chaos, facing political instability and economic decline long after the U.S. had retreated.

The Cold War: A Time of Arrogance Wrapped in Ideology

Throughout the Cold War, the U.S. intervened in Latin American countries under the guise of combating communism.

These interventions often resulted in the installation of dictatorships aligned with U.S. interests, leading to widespread human rights abuses.

For instance, in Chile, the U.S. supported a coup that ousted democratically elected President Salvador Allende, replacing him with Augusto Pinochet, whose regime was marked by brutality and repression.

The U.S. was indifferent to the suffering imposed, more focused on its ideological warfare than on the lives of the citizens caught in the crossfire.

U.S. involvement in Vietnam was driven by a combination of fear of communism and an unwillingness to engage in diplomatic resolutions.

The war devastated Vietnam, costing millions of lives and leaving the country in ruins.

This intervention reflected a profound arrogance, believing that American ideals could be imposed through military force without regard for the cultural context or the actual desires of the Vietnamese people.

The Modern Era: Continued Indifference

In the 21st century, the U.S. continued its pattern of intervention in the Middle East, most notably in Iraq and Afghanistan.

The invasion of Iraq in 2003 was justified by fabricated claims about weapons of mass destruction and the pursuit of democracy.

However, the aftermath was a destabilized region and the rise of extremist groups, with little concern for the welfare of the Iraqi people.

This arrogance in foreign policy reflected a troubling belief that U.S. interests could override local needs and aspirations.

Time and again, after exerting significant influence, the U.S. has withdrawn from regions, leaving chaos in its wake.

The abrupt withdrawal from Afghanistan in 2021, following 20 years of presence, is a poignant reminder of this pattern.

The aftermath saw a rapid resurgence of the Taliban and a humanitarian crisis, illustrating the reckless disregard for the stability of a nation that had relied on U.S. support.

The Cost of American Arrogance: A Call for Reflection

The history of U.S. foreign intervention is stained by arrogance and greed, embodying a pattern of manipulation, exploitation, and abandonment.

In our pursuit of power, we have often disregarded the rights and welfare of the very populations we claimed to help.

This pattern has left behind scars that endure long after our departure, highlighting the urgent need for a more ethical approach to international relations one that seeks to uplift rather than exploit, to listen rather than impose.

As we reflect on this legacy of interventionism, it is crucial to acknowledge the consequences of our actions and to advocate for policies that prioritize genuine collaboration, respect, and the well-being of nations around the globe.

Only through such a shift can we hope to foster a more equitable world.

A Comprehensive Overview of U.S. Immigration History: From Colonial Times to the Present Day

The history of immigration in the United States is characterized by cycles of openness and restriction, driven by economic needs, social dynamics, and political pressures. Over the centuries, laws and policies have evolved amidst ongoing debates about how best to balance national interests with the principles of a nation built by immigrants.

During the colonial period, British policies primarily dictated immigration practices. Citizenship was selectively granted, often to sustain economic growth while limiting political rights to non-citizens. The colonies were populated by various groups, including indentured servants and, more tragically, African slaves forced into bondage.

The institution of slavery dramatically reshaped demographic patterns in North America. From the early 1600s onward, over 388,000 Africans were forcibly brought to the colonies, vastly outnumbering any other group arriving against their will. The unique cruelty of slavery, with its complete denial of freedom and human rights, creates a stark contrast with other forms of migration.

With the achievement of independence, the new American government had to establish its approach to defining citizenship. The concepts of jus soli(right of the soil) and jus sanguinis(right of blood) were balanced by the notion of allegiance, reflecting the revolutionary spirit of founding a nation on loyalty rather than lineage.

The Naturalization Act of 1790 was the first significant legislative effort, granting citizenship to "free white persons" while excluding many others, notably slaves, Native Americans, and non-whites, from naturalization pathways. This created an ideal of citizenship that was racially and ethnically exclusive from the outset.

Throughout the 19th century, immigration continued to fluctuate. Economic downturns and political upheavals abroad, such as the Irish Potato Famine and European revolutions, increased the flow of immigrants to the United States. This influx prompted anxiety among native-born citizens, manifesting in the form of the Nativist movement, which sought to extend naturalization periods and limit voting rights for immigrants.

Legislation such as the Chinese Exclusion Act of 1882, which temporarily halted the immigration of Chinese laborers, reflected growing xenophobia and racial discrimination. This period also saw the federalization of immigration policy, gradually transferring control from states to the federal government.

Court rulings in the late 19th century, like the significant 1889 decision in Chae Chan Ping v. United States, granted Congress plenary power over immigration, cementing the federal government's dominion over these policies. This period of judicial endorsement allowed sweeping immigration restrictions, focusing chiefly on quotas and exclusions that primarily affected Asian immigrants.

The early 20th century witnessed conflicting pressures brought about by industrialization and world wars. While the 1920s saw restrictive quotas based on national origin and racial bias, the post-World War II era marked a turning point. The civil rights movement, combined with geopolitical pressures during the Cold War, led to notable reforms.

The Immigration and Nationality Act of 1965 abolished the national origins quota system, reflecting broader social changes and opening doors to immigrants from Latin America, Asia, and Africa. This ushered in a new era of diversity but also new challenges related to undocumented immigration and border security.

Into the 21ˢᵗ century, the United States continues to grapple with comprehensive immigration reform amidst debates about security, economics, and human rights. Complex visa systems, asylum policies, and border enforcement are subjects of extensive discussion. The challenge remains: how to reconcile a legacy of immigration with contemporary needs and threats, ensuring that the system remains fair yet secure.

As of 2019, approximately 86 million individuals had immigrated to the United States since 1783. The persistent challenge of crafting an immigration policy that aligns with American values of freedom and opportunity, while addressing modern realities, underscores the enduring complexity and importance of this issue.

Understanding the intricate history of U.S. immigration—shaped by factors ranging from colonial expansion and the tragic legacy of slavery to the rise of industrial capitalism and modern political challenges— demonstrates the depth of its impact on the nation's identity. Today, as always, immigration remains integral to the American story, demanding attention to past lessons in forging future policies.

Manifest Destiny and Territorial Acquisition

The ideology of Manifest Destiny was a powerful driver of U.S. policy in the 19ᵗʰ century. This belief that the U.S. was destined to expand across the continent was rooted in a sense of American cultural and racial superiority. It provided a moral justification for the annexation of lands and the displacement and eradication of indigenous peoples.

The people, from the south of today's United States, populated almost all of the Southwest of what we now know as the US. The Mexican-American War (1846-1848) was a direct manifestation of this ideology. The war culminated in the Treaty of Guadalupe Hidalgo, which forced Mexico to cede approximately 55% of its pre-war territory to the U.S., including present-day California, Nevada, Utah, Arizona, and parts of Colorado, Wyoming, New Mexico, and Texas. The financial compensation of $15 million was minimal compared to the vast resources and strategic advantages the U.S. gained. This annexation had profound implications for the indigenous and Mexican populations living in these regions, who suddenly found themselves under U.S. jurisdiction, facing new laws, cultural pressures, and often discriminatory practices.

The U.S. also attempted to purchase additional Mexican territory after the war, such as in the Gadsden Purchase (1853), emphasizing its relentless pursuit of territorial expansion. The combination of military action and economic inducements highlights the aggressive nature of U.S. expansionism during this era.

Throughout U.S. history, immigration policies have favored certain groups over others, reflecting broader societal attitudes and prejudices. In the late 19th and early 20th centuries, policies were designed to encourage immigration from northern and western Europe, regions seen as culturally compatible with the U.S.

However, immigrants from non-European regions, particularly Latin America, Asia, and Africa, faced restrictive measures. For instance, the Chinese Exclusion Act of 1882 was one of the first major laws restricting immigration based on ethnicity, setting a precedent for future policies that discriminated against non-European immigrants.

In the 20th and 21st centuries, immigration debates have increasingly centered around the U.S.-Mexico border. Policies such as the Bracero Program during World War II indicated a willingness to allow Mexican laborers into the country when economically beneficial, yet subsequent periods saw heightened restrictions and border enforcement. This reflects a dynamic where economic considerations occasionally overrode racial biases, yet these were not sustained beyond periods of immediate economic need.

Before European contact, indigenous peoples in North America had diverse societies, ranging from nomadic tribes to advanced civilizations with agricultural networks, cities, and trade systems. European colonization severely disrupted these societies, leading to massive population declines caused by disease, warfare, and displacement.

The Spanish colonization of Mexico, while also brutal, involved more integration between Europeans and indigenous peoples. Intermarriage and cultural blending led to a mestizo identity that is a fundamental part of modern Mexican culture. This contrasts sharply with the United States' approach, which frequently involved the marginalization and forced relocation of Native American peoples onto reservations, often in undesirable or remote areas.

Today, the U.S.-Mexico border is a focal point of immigration policy and debate, complicated by historical context and ongoing racial dynamics. Many immigrants crossing the border seek to escape violence, economic hardship, or political instability, driven by factors often linked, directly or indirectly, to U.S. policies in Latin America.

The treatment of immigrants at the border has been widely criticized, with reports highlighting overcrowded detention centers, family separations, and inadequate access to basic services. These issues are often exacerbated by underlying racial biases, where immigrants from Latin America are treated differently from those from European countries. For example, in moments of crisis, U.S. immigration policies have sometimes shown preferential treatment to refugees from European nations, reflecting deeply ingrained racial and cultural prejudices.

To address these complex issues, it is critical to acknowledge the interconnected histories of the U.S., Mexico, and indigenous peoples, understanding the legacies of displacement and cultural erasure. Promoting equitable immigration policies requires dismantling racially biased frameworks and ensuring that all individuals, irrespective of their heritage or skin color, are treated with dignity and respect.

Moreover, meaningful reform must address both immediate humanitarian concerns at the border and broader systemic issues that drive migration. This includes support for economic development, political stability, and human rights in Latin American countries. Engaging in international cooperation, alongside domestic policy changes, is essential for fostering a more just and equitable approach to immigration that honors shared histories and upholds human dignity.

By reflecting on these profound historical narratives and inequalities, we can work towards policies that not only address immediate concerns but also promote long-term justice and reconciliation.

A Case for Open Borders Across the Americas: Embracing Our Shared Heritage

In the modern-day pursuit of freedom and opportunity, the concept of open borders within the Americas is emerging as not only a practical solution to economic and societal challenges but also as a profound acknowledgment of our shared historical and cultural heritage. Imagine an America where people from all over the continent, North, Central, and South, move and interact freely, fostering richer communities and a deeper sense of unity. This vision, rooted deeply in historical continuity, economic pragmatism, and ethical considerations, calls for a reevaluation of contemporary borders.

Long before European colonization defined the geopolitical landscape of the Americas, the indigenous peoples of the continent were interconnected through complex networks of trade, kinship, and cultural exchange. This pre-colonial mobility allowed for fluid movement across vast territories, a tradition abruptly altered by colonial borders but never fully extinguished. These historical networks remind us of a world where the peoples of the Americas were one, long before the territorial claims of distant empires drew lines upon maps.

The colonial era saw the mingling of indigenous, European, and African cultures, creating a shared legacy that continues to resonate today. This mixing of heritages laid the foundation for regions in the United States that were once part of New Spain and later Mexico, California, Texas, New Mexico, and Arizona, to become cultural beacons of this continental blend. These states' names themselves are a testament to their deep cultural ties with Latin America, suggesting that the notion of separate, impermeable borders stands in contrast to centuries of interconnected histories.

From an economic perspective, the benefits of open borders within the Americas are profound. Greater freedom of movement can unlock tremendous economic potential through inter-American trade and collaboration. Allowing people to move freely would enable a more dynamic allocation of labor and skills, spurring innovation and economic growth across the continent. Such mobility is not merely an ideal; it is a practical step toward economic synergy.

The U.S. economy, in particular, has long benefited from the labor of immigrants, especially from neighboring countries. Migrant workers play critical roles in various industries, from agriculture to technology, often addressing labor shortages and helping maintain economic stability. Furthermore, remittances sent by immigrants to their home countries in Latin America and the Caribbean are vital economic lifelines that reduce poverty and promote development. Open borders could strengthen these economic ties, creating a more stable and prosperous region, where the pressures driving migration are significantly alleviated.

At the heart of the call for open borders lies a profound ethical obligation to recognize and uphold the rights and dignity of all individuals. The current immigration system subjects many to dangerous journeys, detention, and separation from loved ones conditions that starkly oppose the ideals of human rights. Embracing open borders for people of the Americas is a step towards respecting and affirming their inherent dignity, treating the movement of people as a natural and legitimate act.

Addressing historical inequalities also forms a crucial part of this ethical discourse. Socio-economic challenges driving migration often stem from past policies and interventions that have destabilized regions, leading to cycles of poverty and displacement. The U.S., acknowledging its role in this shared history, bears a responsibility to pursue equitable solutions that foster opportunity for all peoples of the Americas.

An open-border policy invites cultural reciprocity, enriching societies through the exchange of ideas, customs, and traditions. It echoes the multicultural fabric of the Americas, celebrating the diversity that defines our continent.

Reimagining U.S. borders to be open to individuals from anywhere across the Americas is not merely a dream. It is a practical and ethical imperative that acknowledges our intertwined destinies. Such a policy would honor the longstanding tradition of interconnectedness, address economic needs, and rectify historical injustices, laying the groundwork for a more equitable and harmonious future.

We can create a society rooted in the principles of freedom, opportunity, and justice an America that acknowledges its shared heritage and looks towards a united future. In doing so, we transform borders from barriers into bridges, strengthening our communities and honoring the impeccable continuity of the Americas, a land meant to be open to all its people.

Why the Great Democracy Experiment Is Failing And How To Fix It!

The Enduring Legacy of Donald Trump's Presidency

Trump's goal has been to be remembered as a significant figure in the history of the United States, regardless of whether that legacy is viewed in a positive or negative light. Much like a child seeking attention, he seems to prioritize visibility and recognition over the nature of his popularity.

The impact of Donald Trump's presidency on American society and its international standing has been profound and complex. Throughout his tenure, several policy decisions have introduced substantial challenges at both domestic and global levels. Notably, the withdrawal from significant international agreements and changes in domestic policies affecting essential services have marked a shift towards prioritizing national interests over global cooperation and welfare. These actions have led to uncertainty and potentially increased human suffering.

Addressing the aftermath of these policies and rebuilding relationships will require sustained efforts from future generations. Emphasizing collaboration, inclusivity, and sustainability is essential to progress toward a more stable and equitable future. By actively re-engaging with the global community, reinforcing domestic cohesion, and restoring essential services, the U.S. can work towards repairing its reputation and fostering a more harmonious international and domestic landscape.

The policies affecting healthcare, food security, and humanitarian aid have had profound effects on human life, including the potential loss of tens of millions of lives.

Healthcare: The Trump administration's efforts to roll back Medicaid coverage impacted approximately 17 million people. Without access to necessary healthcare, there is a risk of preventable illnesses going untreated, potentially leading to increased morbidity and mortality. Studies have shown that a lack of healthcare can significantly reduce life expectancy and raise mortality rates, particularly among vulnerable populations. Research suggests that losing healthcare can lead to millions of premature deaths, especially among low-income individuals who lack alternative forms of coverage.

Food Assistance (TANF and SNAP): Reductions in Temporary Assistance for Needy Families (TANF) and the Supplemental Nutrition Assistance Program (SNAP) affected 11 million people, limiting their ability to secure basic nutrition. Food insecurity is linked to numerous health problems, including malnutrition, compromised immune function, and increased risk of chronic diseases. Estimates indicate that food insecurity can elevate mortality rates, particularly among children and the elderly. Access to adequate nutrition is crucial for children's development and academic performance.

Education and Free Lunch Programs: Ending free lunch programs for poor students can exacerbate educational disparities and affect millions of children. Proper nutrition is vital for cognitive development and learning. A lack of adequate meals can lead to poorer academic performance, which has long-term implications for economic mobility and health outcomes. Studies indicate that food insecurity can negatively impact students' concentration, behavior, and academic achievements, potentially leading to lifelong consequences.

Foreign Humanitarian Aid: Ending foreign humanitarian aid will have global repercussions, affecting millions in need of basic services like food, medical care, and shelter. Such reductions can exacerbate conditions in regions already suffering from poverty, conflict, and natural disasters. Humanitarian aid is often a lifeline for vulnerable populations, and its absence can lead to worsened health outcomes, increased mortality, and prolonged crises. International organizations have highlighted the critical role aid plays in saving lives and stabilizing regions.

While Hitler was in power, between 60-80 million people lost their lives, 50 million of whom were civilians. We have no war, but civilian loss of life worldwide while Trump is president will number in the tens of millions. The loss of life will surpass the concentration camps. Most of the loss of life will be in third-world nations since we ended humanitarian aid.

Healing political polarization and repairing international relations, as well as addressing social and economic inequalities, could require three generations (60 years) or more of sustained efforts. To fully address the impacts, especially concerning climate change, it may take ten or more generations (200 years or longer) given the scale of environmental setbacks.

The presidency of Donald Trump is characterized by significant policy changes across various sectors. As we examine these changes, it's important to understand both their immediate effects and their potential long-term impacts. This article delves into eight critical areas influenced by Trump's administration and explores the complexities involved in addressing these impacts over time.

Environmental Policy: The Trump administration withdrew the United States from the Paris Agreement and rolled back over 100 environmental regulations. Notably, it reduced restrictions on carbon emissions from industrial sources and eased protections for endangered species. The impacts include increased greenhouse gas emissions, contributing to global warming, while reduced protections can lead to biodiversity loss and disrupted ecosystems. Reversing such environmental damage could take 30 to 50 years, depending on the success of international cooperative efforts and advances in clean energy technologies.

Increased Greenhouse Gas Emissions: The withdrawal is likely to lead to a continuation of policies that allow for higher carbon emissions, exacerbating climate change.

Global Temperature Rise: Without U.S. participation in the Paris Agreement, efforts to limit global warming may falter, resulting in more severe climate impacts.

Biodiversity Loss: Eased regulations can lead to habitat destruction and more species at risk, disrupting ecosystems and threatening food security.

Climate Change Feedback Loops: Higher emissions contribute to feedback effects like ice melt, which can further accelerate global warming.

Economic Costs: Increased climate-related disasters can strain infrastructure and lead to significant economic losses.

Public Health Risks: Reduced air quality and pollution can lead to health crises, increasing healthcare costs, and impacting communities.

International Relations and Leadership: The U.S. losing credibility as a leader in climate negotiations can hinder global cooperation on environmental issues.

Future generations may face difficulties in reinstating credibility and negotiating meaningful climate agreements.

Trump appointed over 200 federal judges, including three Supreme Court justices who shifted the judiciary to a more conservative stance. These lifetime appointments influence decisions on a wide range of issues, including reproductive rights, healthcare, and immigration. Decisions reflecting conservative legal interpretations can persist for decades, affecting legislation and civil liberties. Judicial philosophy shifts are slow, lasting 30 to 40 years unless changes in political control lead to a rebalancing of the judiciary.

Trump's presidency exacerbated existing political and social divisions, amplifying partisan tensions and impacting public discourse. This polarization is evident in the increased partisanship in Congress and heightened social conflicts. Polarization leads to legislative gridlock, reduced bipartisan cooperation, and increased social unrest. Healing such divisions could take 20 to 40 years, requiring efforts in education reform, political engagement, and grassroots movements to foster dialogue and understanding.

The "America First" policy altered traditional U.S. alliances as the administration renegotiated key trade agreements and challenged NATO's role, among others. This shift affected global diplomatic dynamics and trade relationships. Strained relationships with allies can impact global trade systems and international security. Restoring international trust might take 10 to 20 years, contingent on consistent foreign policy and diplomatic outreach from subsequent administrations.

Trump's immigration policies, including the termination of DACA and family separations, had profound impacts on immigrants and their families, affecting millions of lives. Increased fear and instability among immigrant communities, potential labor shortages, and social tensions due to these measures. Addressing these impacts involves legal reforms and social integration initiatives over a span of 20 to 30 years.

Economic strategies such as tax cuts, protectionist tariffs, and deregulation aimed to stimulate growth but also increased the federal deficit and intensified income inequality. While tax cuts provided short-term economic boosts, they contributed to long-term budget deficits and exacerbated wealth disparities. Implementing corrective measures could take 10 to 20 years, involving strategic tax reforms and targeted economic policies to address inequality.

Efforts to dismantle the Affordable Care Act led to uncertainties in healthcare markets and access challenges for millions of Americans. Increased premiums, reduced coverage options, and heightened instability in the insurance market. Significant healthcare reform could require a decade of legislative effort and policy innovation to ensure stable and affordable coverage for all.

Policies favoring school choice and reduced federal oversight impacted public education funding and expanded the educational achievement gap. Disparities in education quality and access, particularly affecting low-income and marginalized communities. Comprehensive education reform could take 15 to 20 years to implement, demanding increased investment in public education and shifts in policy at the federal and state levels.

Undoing or mitigating the impacts of the Trump administration's policies involves addressing multiple complex and interrelated issues. The timelines for recovery are estimated and depend heavily on future political leadership, societal engagement, and economic conditions. As the U.S. navigates these challenges, informed dialogue and active participation are crucial in shaping a sustainable future.

The long-term effects anticipated from the political polarization exacerbated during Trump's administration are significant and multifaceted, impacting various aspects of American society and governance. Here are some key potential outcomes:

Increased polarization can lead to persistent legislative stalemates, where bipartisan cooperation becomes rare. This gridlock can hinder the passage of essential legislation on critical issues such as healthcare, infrastructure, and climate change, ultimately stalling progress on policies that address pressing societal needs.

Heightened polarization may contribute to a decline in respect for democratic norms and institutions. As partisan loyalty takes precedence over civic duty, there may be increased acceptance of anti-democratic behaviors, such as voter suppression or challenges to election results, undermining the integrity of the electoral process.

Political polarization can exacerbate social divisions, leading to the entrenchment of communities along partisan lines. This fragmentation can diminish social cohesion and trust among individuals from different political backgrounds, making constructive dialogue and compromise more challenging.

The rise in politically charged rhetoric and divisive narratives can lead to heightened tensions and potentially increase the risk of political violence. Instances of extremism and politically motivated attacks may become more common as individuals feel compelled to act on their beliefs.

Many individuals may become disillusioned with the political process and disengage from civic participation, feeling that their voices are not represented. This alienation can lead to lower voter turnout and reduced involvement in community and political organizations, further entrenching polarization.

Polarized environments can lead to ineffective governance, where elected officials focus more on party loyalty than on collaboration and problem-solving. This can result in a lack of effective responses to national crises, such as public health emergencies or economic downturns.

The current state of polarization may shape the political attitudes of younger generations, who may grow up in an environment marked by division and conflict. This could lead to a cycle of polarization that persists as new voters carry their experiences and beliefs into adulthood.

As political polarization affects the U.S. ability to present a unified front on international issues, it may weaken the nation's global standing. Allies may become uncertain of U.S. commitments, impacting international agreements and cooperation on global challenges such as climate change and security.

The enduring effects of polarization may lead to a realignment of political parties and ideologies. As factions within parties become more pronounced, new political movements or parties may emerge, further complicating the political landscape and potentially leading to instability.

The media landscape may become increasingly polarized, with outlets catering to specific ideological perspectives. This can create echo chambers where individuals are exposed only to information that reinforces their beliefs, further entrenching polarization and reducing the likelihood of encountering diverse viewpoints.

Addressing these long-term effects will require concerted efforts from political leaders, civil society, and citizens to promote dialogue, understanding, and cooperation across partisan lines. Fostering a culture of engagement and respect for democratic processes will be crucial in mitigating the impacts of polarization on the future of American democracy.

The Opulence of Leadership: Examining Donald Trump's Presidential Approach

In the history of American presidencies, personal style and leadership approach have varied significantly.

Some presidents have preferred a subdued manner, aligning closely with the democratic-republic ideals upon which the United States was founded, a stark contrast to the opulence commonly associated with any monarchy.

Donald Trump's presidency, however, marks a departure from these norms, inviting discussion on the nature and symbolism of leadership in a democratic-republic society.

American presidents have occupied a unique position. They are heads of state in a democratic republic that prides itself on its foundational rejection of hereditary rule and monarchy.

The White House, while grand, symbolizes a temporary seat of power, not a royal palace for kings or queens. Its elegance lies in its symbolism of an office serving the people, where leaders reside temporarily to execute their duties before passing the mantle to their successors.

Donald Trump has embraced opulence, a characteristic more closely associated with monarchical rule than democratic leadership. This preference for grandeur and spectacle was evident in both policy and demeanor, setting his presidency apart from those of his predecessors.

From gold cherubs to lavish decor and building a grand ballroom, these elements not only contrast with historical norms but also invite criticism for what is viewed as an extravagant use of taxpayer money.

It's easy to argue that all these trappings will need to be removed when Trump leaves office, further increasing expenses and waste.

Beyond aesthetics, Trump's policies are also drawing scrutiny. Everyone can point to decisions that, in their view, prioritize extravagant spending over essential public services.

Trump's choices will have tangible consequences, such as 17 million people losing Medicaid and millions facing food insecurity. These two outcomes fuel concerns that Trump and his administration's priorities are skewed, prompting echoes of the infamous phrase, "Let them eat cake," often attributed, though perhaps inaccurately, to Marie Antoinette.

One arena where Trump's approach has drawn additional scrutiny is his admiration for certain Middle Eastern leaders. This admiration often focused on the power exerted by kings and princes in these regions, figures who wield authority often unchecked by democratic norms.

It's easy to point out that these leaders can suppress dissent and opposition without accountability.

This starkly contrasts with democratic-republic principles, where leaders are expected to be accountable to their constituents, ensuring that power is balanced and checked.

The discourse surrounding Trump's admiration for such leaders underscores a broader conversation about governance, power, and accountability. It prompts reflection on why democratic leaders might find allure in autocratic styles of leadership where opulence and exertion of power go unchallenged. This tension between democratic ideals and autocratic allure raises important questions about the kind of leadership that best serves the principles of freedom, justice, and equality.

The contrast between opulence and elegance in leadership reflects deeper tensions in how power is perceived and exercised. While elegance in leadership emphasizes humility and service, opulence can signify a preference for power without accountability.

As America continues to navigate its democratic-republic journey, these discussions remain critical in understanding the path forward and ensuring that leadership always aligns with the foundational ideals of the democratic-republic.

Balancing spectacle with substance, and ensuring policies serve the public rather than personal grandeur, are central to this ongoing dialogue.

The Role of Patience and Prudence in a Democratic Judicial System

In a democracy, the judiciary serves as a cornerstone of justice, upholding the principles of fairness, equality, and due process. When individuals assume the roles of judge, jury, and executioner, whether metaphorically in positions of influence or literally within the legal system, it underscores the importance of a balanced approach to justice. An effective judicial system is not driven by haste or bias, but by a careful, deliberate examination of the facts at hand.

One key lesson often emphasized in democratic societies is the importance of waiting for all evidence to surface before making a judgment. The integrity of a democratic judicial system relies heavily on the patience and thoroughness of its legal professionals. They must diligently gather evidence and conduct comprehensive interviews with all parties involved. This process ensures that decisions are informed and judgments are rendered with the fullest insight into a situation.

The danger of acting on the testimony of a single, potentially manipulative source cannot be overstated. History and numerous legal precedents remind us of the risks of hasty conclusions. Individuals versed in manipulation may present a convincing yet ultimately deceptive narrative. As such, the courts must exercise extreme caution, distinguishing between truth and manipulation through critical analysis and cross-examination.

It is incumbent upon the judiciary to learn from past experiences. If patterns emerge where certain types of individuals consistently mislead or manipulate the system, the court must adapt and account for these tactics. This adaptation does not imply prejudice against individuals but highlights the need for heightened scrutiny and a robust mechanism to protect the integrity of the legal process.

Ignoring these lessons can have grave consequences. Should the courts fail to address manipulative tactics appropriately, the administration of justice could suffer. Outstanding cases may recur, each potentially more severe than the last, undermining public trust in the judicial system. Thus, the judiciary must remain vigilant, continually refining its processes and strategies to address deceit while maintaining a commitment to fairness and justice.

Democracy requires the judicial system to serve not just as a mechanism of punishment, but as a bastion of fairness and a model of patience. Those in positions of judicial power must exercise their authority with wisdom and restraint, ensuring that justice is not only done but seen to be done by all members of society. By doing so, the judiciary safeguards the principles of democracy and reinforces the social contract that binds the community together.

Democracy in Action: How Sanctions Reflect Global Unity Against Aggression

In today's interconnected world, democracy extends beyond borders, shaping global responses to crises. A striking example of this is the way democratic nations have responded to Russia's invasion of Ukraine, showcasing a powerful, non-military method that aligns with democratic ideals: economic sanctions.

While the United States and European nations have chosen to avoid direct military conflict, they have rapidly mobilized to impose a diverse array of financial sanctions intended to severely impact Russia's economy. This strategy demonstrates the influence and speed with which democratic alliances can act. By restricting Russia's access to crucial foreign currencies like the dollar and euro, freezing assets of Russian banks, and cutting off access to the SWIFT financial messaging system, these democracies are applying heavy pressure on an aggressor without resorting to warfare.

Countries like Japan and even neutral Switzerland have joined the sanctions, signaling a rare and powerful global coalition. This unity illuminates the collective strength democracies hold when they coordinate efforts against violations of international law and peace.

Russia, in response, has tried to mitigate the economic damage by hiking interest rates and leveraging foreign reserves—reserves that are largely inaccessible due to sanctions. The Russian government's aggressive economic responses highlight the significant pressure sanctions impose, further proving their effectiveness as a tool of diplomatic and economic warfare.

For the Russian populace, however, these sanctions translate into economic hardship, illustrating a tragic byproduct of global diplomacy where ordinary citizens bear the brunt of their government's actions. This underlines a critical point about the nuances of democracy; it seeks to balance action against wrongdoers while minimizing harm to innocents—a challenge in any international conflict.

The sanctions have potential ripple effects. With Russia and Ukraine being major players in commodities such as oil, gas, and agriculture, these actions have already led to rising global prices, thus affecting economies worldwide. Democracies must navigate these economic shifts while maintaining internal support for sanctions, a testament to the complex interplay between domestic and foreign policy in democratic governance.

Corporations have also taken a stand, with firms like BP withdrawing investments from Russia. This corporate action not only reflects ethical stances but also emphasizes democracy's multifaceted nature, where public sentiment and corporate responsibility intertwine with governmental policies.

The sanctions serve as a testament to democracy's potential as a peacekeeping and justice-seeking entity. They represent a form of democratic consensus, a collective statement against aggression, underlining the values of dialogue, crisis management, and non-violent resolution at the international level. This seminal moment could redefine the dynamics of international conflict resolution, showcasing how democracies can unite to defend global peace and justice without direct conflict.

Amidst the complexities and hardships, these sanctions remind the world of the enduring power of democratic unity and the shared responsibility to uphold international law and order, proving that democracy extends far beyond domestic governance, it is a global force for good.

Why Politics Attracts Narcissists and Corrupt Individuals

In the grand theater of politics, where individuals often emerge as heroes or villains, the power to shape nations' destinies becomes both an alluring and perilous play. Beneath the surface of democratic ideals lies a persistent question: why do so many politicians appear corrupt or narcissistic?

So by delving into the structural, psychological, and cultural factors that make politics a magnet for such personalities, and exploring whether they are more prevalent in any political party.

Politics, by its very nature, is synonymous with power, a magnetic field for those who crave influence and control. Individuals with narcissistic tendencies often pursue political careers to fulfill their needs for admiration and authority.

According to Dr. John Gartner, a psychologist known for his study on political personalities, politics offers a stage for visibility and acclaim, highly appealing to narcissists.

Narcissism is characterized by grandiosity, a desire for excessive admiration, and a lack of empathy, traits that thrive in high-stakes environments where attention is currency.

For many, the electoral process becomes less about public service and more about self-serving ambitions.

The structure of political systems can contribute to corruption, with loopholes and a lack of accountability enabling unethical behavior. Practices such as lobbying, campaign financing, and political patronage are often criticized for fostering environments where money and personal connections can outweigh the public interest.

Historically, financial motivations have been attributed more to parties traditionally associated with business interests, such as the Republican Party in the United States. Conversely, the Democratic Party is often seen as more socially driven, focusing on policies that prioritize social welfare and equity.

However, this distinction can be overly simplistic, as both parties are susceptible to financial influences when they engage in social policymaking.

The role of the media cannot be underestimated in amplifying the perception of corruption and narcissism in politics. Headlines dominated by scandals and controversies often overshadow narratives of public service and positive change. This focus on sensationalism feeds into the public's confirmation bias, reinforcing perceptions of widespread political decay.

Social media platforms have given rise to a new type of political engagement driven by quick consumption of information and emotional reactions. The social media environment boosts the profiles of individuals adept at using these tools to manipulate public perception and craft personal brands, regardless of their political efficacy.

When examining whether these traits are more prevalent in certain political parties, the tribal nature of politics comes into play. Research shows that political biases can lead individuals to perceive opposing parties in a more negative light, including assumptions about the prevalence of corruption or narcissism.

Dr. Jennifer L. Raymond, a political psychologist, notes that our brains are wired to support our in-group beliefs and to criticize the out-group, often leading to skewed perceptions based on political affiliation.

To transform politics into an arena where public service prevails over personal ambition, systemic changes are essential. Enhancing transparency in campaign financing, enforcing strict conflict of interest laws, and empowering independent watchdogs can curb the influence of corrupt individuals.

Educational reforms that encourage civic engagement and critical thinking from an early age can help future generations recognize and reject narcissistic leadership. Promoting a political culture that values humility, empathy, and accountability can shift the focus back to public service.

Implementing psychological assessments and screenings for political candidates raises ethical and practical considerations but could be instrumental in identifying potentially harmful personality traits. Establishing ethical guidelines and non-discriminatory criteria can help ensure candidates possess the emotional intelligence and leadership qualities necessary for effective governance.

Analyzing the prevalence of narcissism and corruption across different political systems and cultures offers valuable insights into systemic vulnerabilities and effective reforms. By examining successful models in various countries, policymakers can adapt and implement reforms tailored to their national contexts, fostering a more accountable political environment.

Case studies of politicians known for their narcissistic traits and those who exhibit altruistic integrity provide lessons in leadership. By examining historical and contemporary figures, we can identify behaviors and policies that lead to effective governance or exacerbate corruption and self-interest.

It is generally safe to say that corrupt politicians can cost taxpayers billions of dollars each year. Trump for example is suspected of most of the following: Corruption can manifest in various forms, such as embezzlement of public funds (Trump requires all visitors to the president stay on his property and overcharged the taxpayers he also overcharged the taxpayers for the secret service staying on his propoerty), bribery (accepting a $400,000,000 jet that will cost taxpayers a Billion dollars for it to be retrofitted and he intends to keep it when he leaves office), fraud Trump opening private club with a membership requirements to meet with trump one on one so he will do their bidding. Also requiring buying Trump crypto coin to bribe him to push agendas), and misallocation of resources (sending the military into American cities to do Trump's bidding, all of which lead to substantial financial losses for our country's taxpayers.

These practices not only waste taxpayer money but can also undermine public trust in government, lead to inefficient public services, and stymie economic growth. Quantifying the exact cost will be challenging, as it varies by incident and depends on the scope and scale of Trump's corruption. However, the impact is widely acknowledged to be substantial.

Addressing the complexities that draw narcissistic and corrupt individuals to politics requires a multifaceted approach focusing on public perception, education, psychological assessment, and global best practices. By fostering a culture that values transparency, accountability, and ethical leadership, we can create a political environment that genuinely aligns with democratic ideals. Through informed citizen engagement and systemic reforms, the goal of ensuring public service triumphs over personal ambition becomes more attainable.

Addressing Domestic Violence: A Democratic Imperative for Lasting Change

In the quest for a truly democratic society, addressing domestic violence is a vital undertaking that demands a comprehensive and multifaceted approach. Such efforts focus on protection, accountability, and cultural transformation, ensuring that every individual can live without fear of harm.

At the heart of a democratic response is the need to overhaul existing laws. Current penalties must be revised to reflect the true severity of domestic violence, moving beyond minimal fines to enforce significant consequences. This could include mandatory counseling and the possibility of incarceration for repeat offenders. By implementing such legal reforms, a democratic society sends a clear message: the protection of victims and the pursuit of justice are paramount.

Supporting victims is equally essential. Democracies should prioritize funding for shelters, hotlines, and counseling services, giving survivors the resources they need to find refuge and rebuild their lives. Crucially, the financial burden of abuse must not fall on victims; they require assistance to regain their independence and well-being without economic strain.

Education plays a pivotal role in shifting societal attitudes. Investing in public education programs that promote respect, equality, and non-violent conflict resolution can help change cultural norms. By engaging schools, communities, and media outlets, democracies can create environments where violence is not tolerated, fostering a culture of empathy and understanding.

Judicial reform is critical to this effort. Training judges, police, and legal professionals is necessary to ensure domestic violence cases are handled with sensitivity and urgency. Special units within police forces and courts can focus on these cases, offering expertise and prioritizing victim safety and justice.

Empowering women is fundamental to achieving meaningful change. Democracies must work towards increasing women's representation in politics and leadership roles, fostering economic independence, and dismantling patriarchal norms that often underpin domestic violence. By promoting equal opportunities and amplifying women's voices, society moves closer to lasting, positive change.

Community involvement is another crucial element. By encouraging community engagement in addressing domestic violence, it becomes a collective issue, not just a private one. Democratic societies should promote programs that support victims and rehabilitate offenders, helping to create a culture where violence is universally condemned.

Ultimately, tackling domestic violence within a democracy involves leveraging legal, educational, and social reforms to build a society where every individual is protected, valued, and free from harm. This holistic approach aims not only to address immediate concerns but also to drive long-term cultural change, reinforcing the democratic ideals of equality, justice, and human dignity for all.

The Ethical Landscape of Reproductive Rights: Bodily Autonomy and the Reality of Choice

The classification of a fetus as distinct from a human life until birth is a topic that intertwines biological, ethical, and legal dimensions. From a biological perspective, particularly in the early stages of gestation, a fetus does not exhibit the characteristics typically associated with fully developed human beings, such as consciousness, the ability to survive outside the womb, or a complete nervous system.

Viability is usually recognized at around 24 weeks of gestation, when a fetus may survive outside the womb, but even then, the chances, approximately 40%, often require extensive medical intervention, including considerable time on life support.

This scenario brings forth critical questions, such as who is responsible for the medical bills accruing from the care required for a premature infant. The costs of neonatal care can be substantial, in the millions, leading to complex discussions involving insurance coverage, parental financial responsibility, and the broader responsibilities of healthcare systems.

Infants born prematurely are at an increased risk of facing various severe physical, mental, and emotional challenges. Physical health issues might include complications like respiratory distress syndrome, chronic lung disease, and developmental delays, while mental and emotional impacts could range from difficulties in bonding with caregivers to long-term conditions such as anxiety or attention deficits. These potential outcomes necessitate a multidisciplinary approach to long-term care that addresses not just the immediate medical needs but also the lifetime developmental needs of these vulnerable infants.

Philosophically, the discourse revolves around personhood, moral consideration, and bodily autonomy. A central tenet is that a fetus exists within the body of a pregnant individual, the mother is a fully developed person with unique rights, emotions, and a distinct life narrative.

This perspective underscores the right of individuals to have control over their own lives. Autonomy is fundamental to adulthood; adults can make decisions about their bodies, careers, and relationships. Pregnant individuals should similarly retain this authority over their bodies and decisions regarding reproduction.

For full disclosure, I must acknowledge that abortion has never been a conversation I have had with someone who was struggling with the decision. However, I recognize that it is ultimately a woman's body, and the choice should be hers. While I might privately hope she would consider changing her mind, I respect her decision completely. I have spent considerable time volunteering as an escort for women to get past protestors to enter the clinic. I believe men have no right to dictate or influence this deeply personal choice, as we cannot fully understand or empathize with what a pregnant woman or any woman experiences. Men need to mature mentally and emotionally and recognize that women are fully capable of making their own decisions.

Contrary to persistent myths, the idea that women frequently use abortion as a form of birth control is misleading. Research indicates that the majority of individuals seeking abortions report already having children and cite reasons such as medical necessity, financial instability, lack of support, or not feeling prepared for another child.

Although those who support forced births often oppose birth control, many also oppose comprehensive sex education. Access to effective contraceptive methods is crucial for reducing unintended pregnancies. The ongoing lack of comprehensive sex education and access to contraception perpetuates higher rates of unplanned pregnancies, highlighting the need for informed choices rather than restrictive policies.

Another myth is that abortions lead to significant mental health issues. While it is crucial to acknowledge that the decision to terminate a pregnancy can be emotionally complex, studies indicate that the majority of individuals do not experience long-term psychological harm. The negative mental health outcomes often cited are typically the result of societal stigmatization rather than the procedure itself.

One more myth worth addressing is the belief that abortion is inherently unsafe. Safe, legal abortions performed by qualified medical professionals are exceedingly safe. The World Health Organization has noted that unsafe abortions, which account for an estimated 25 million globally, lead to significant maternal morbidity and mortality. Access to safe abortion services is associated with decreased maternal mortality rates, underscoring the importance of legal and safe options.

When individuals are compelled to continue unwanted pregnancies, the risks extend not only to the pregnant mother but also to the children born into difficult circumstances.

Research shows that children from families facing economic challenges or instability are more likely to experience health issues and socioeconomic struggles.

In the U.S., the estimated cost of raising a child in the lower middle-income bracket from birth to age 18 is approximately $233,611, highlighting the need for robust support systems to ensure healthy development.

Personal accounts from those who have endured forced pregnancies often illustrate the profound emotional and financial struggles involved in raising a child in such environments.

Data shows that approximately 30% of non-custodial fathers are considered "deadbeat dads," failing to provide financial support for their children. This statistic complicates the conversation about responsibility, revealing the societal structures that may leave single parents without adequate support.

Studies suggest that a significant number of "deadbeat dads" align with conservative views, often advocating forced birth policies while placing the burden of parenting responsibilities solely on women. The potential inconsistencies in these positions highlight the ethical dilemmas surrounding forced pregnancies and the responsibilities that accompany them.

These forced pregnancies create an environment where the rights of the pregnant individual are subordinated to the interests attributed to the fetus.

This represents a troubling dichotomy: a system that prioritizes the potential life of the fetus while neglecting the immediate rights and needs of the individual carrying it.

This inconsistency raises critical ethical concerns, if the rights of the fetus are prioritized, what mechanisms are in place to care for the subsequent life it leads?

Evidence shows that in societies with heavily regulated reproductive health, maternal and infant health outcomes can deteriorate rather than improve, contradicting the initial justification of protecting life.

It's vital to consider the broader implications of reproductive health policies. When individuals have the autonomy to make informed choices about their reproductive health, they are more likely to achieve educational and career success. This not only benefits them and their children but also contributes positively to society.

Studies consistently show that when individuals can choose if and when to have children, it leads to better outcomes for families and communities, including improved educational attainment and economic stability.

Access to safe and legal abortions contributes to overall public health. Countries with supportive reproductive health policies typically see lower rates of abortion overall, as individuals have the resources and education needed to prevent unintended pregnancies. By investing in comprehensive reproductive health services, societies can mitigate the need for abortions and promote healthier outcomes.

The emphasis on choice is not solely about the act of abortion; it speaks to a broader context of reproductive rights, safety, and health.

Supporting the pro-choice movement recognizes the complexities of human life and the realities faced by pregnant individuals. It affirms the necessity to empower individuals to make their own reproductive choices and acknowledges the systemic support essential for ensuring those choices are viable.

Advocates for pro-choice policies emphasize that true respect for life entails ensuring that every human being both potential and realized has the opportunity to thrive. This approach transcends a binary debate on abortion; it embodies the fundamental principle of honoring the rights, dignity, and agency of those navigating the multifaceted landscape of reproductive health.

An Evolutionary Perspective on Abortion and In Vitro Fertilization

The story of Amber Nicole Thurman tragically underscores the stark consequences of restrictive reproductive policies following the overturning of Roe v. Wade.

A 28-year-old Black mother with aspirations of becoming a nurse, Amber faced insurmountable barriers to accessing abortion services in her home state.

Planned and determined, she made arrangements to terminate her pregnancy in North Carolina but ultimately missed her appointment due to unforeseen traffic.

Regrettably, she became the first documented woman to die as a result of abortion bans since the Dobbs decision, suffering a preventable death in a Georgia hospital where doctors refrained from performing a necessary procedure due to legal constraints.

Amber's harrowing story illuminates the urgent need for societal recognition of reproductive autonomy and its impact on maternal and child health.

Forced unwanted pregnancies not only jeopardize the well-being of mothers but also place future generations at risk.

As the U.S. faces dwindling population growth amid increasing restrictions on reproductive rights, it is crucial to empower women with the ability to make informed choices about their bodies.

To cultivate healthier families and thriving communities, preserving access to comprehensive reproductive health services is paramount, ensuring that no woman faces Amber's tragic fate again.

Let's examine reproductive choices through the lens of evolution.

To clarify, I am not suggesting that women are comparable to animals or mere instruments for reproduction.

Instead, my goal is to present an alternative perspective.

While my focus is primarily on human evolution, I recognize the difficulty in articulating this viewpoint from a religious standpoint that believes in creationism over evolution.

Reproductive decision-making is fundamentally intertwined with biological and evolutionary significance.

As society confronts the complex issues surrounding early termination and assisted reproductive technologies, such as in vitro fertilization (IVF), it is essential to explore these topics from an evolutionary standpoint.

Understanding the implications of natural and aided reproductive choices can illuminate the importance of autonomy in motherhood and highlight the diverse pathways of family creation.

This understanding fosters a more empathetic view of pro-choice and pro-IVF positions.

The principles of natural selection drive evolution, wherein the survival and reproduction of individuals influence the genetic transmission to succeeding generations.

For mothers, maternal fitness, defined as a mother's ability to invest resources effectively in her offspring, plays a crucial role in evolutionary success.

The decision to continue or terminate a pregnancy can be a pivotal factor in a woman's overall reproductive success.

My hypothesis posits that this ability to make informed choices reflects enhanced cognitive capacities, suggesting that human beings have transcended traditional evolutionary processes in reproductive contexts.

In nature, animals exhibit instinctive behaviors that ensure the survival of their lineages.

Unplanned natural pregnancy termination and miscarriages are primarily caused by chromosomal abnormalities, where the genetic material fails to support viable development.

Other contributing factors that can cause unplanned natural terminations include hormonal imbalances, infections, anatomical issues, and various health conditions affecting the mother.

Intentional termination of pregnancy, can happen naturally in nature, but is induced through medical interventions, including medication and surgical procedures for women

This distinction is crucial, as miscarriages represent a natural outcome dictated by biological circumstances, whereas induced terminations reflect a conscious decision-making that individuals undertake based on various factors.

The ability to induce pregnancy termination is not an evolutionary adaptation in itself but rather a result of evolutionary advancements in cognitive ability, which gave us medical science and a deepening understanding of reproductive health.

As society has progressed, women have gained increased autonomy over their reproductive choices, allowing them to make informed decisions rather than relying solely on the unpredictable outcomes of nature.

This empowerment reflects a significant shift in how reproduction is perceived, moving towards a model where individuals control their bodies and reproductive outcomes.

This evolution of choice may ultimately shape future generations, influencing how society approaches reproductive health and family planning.

It raises important considerations about the intersection of technology, medicine, and individual agency in the ongoing narrative of human evolution and reproductive rights.

Both mechanisms demonstrate how biological and medical factors interact with reproductive health, shaping the complexities of human reproduction.

These biological factors can significantly influence reproductive success and overall maternal health.

Wild mammals can "self-terminate" pregnancies through natural processes for a myriad of reasons.

The ability and occurrence of pregnancy termination in wild mammals are predominantly driven by natural processes influenced by environmental conditions, health status, social dynamics, scarce resources, and species-specific reproductive strategies.

Similarly, for human mothers, decisions about pregnancy must consider a range of factors, including physical and emotional well-being, socioeconomic stability, and the ability to care for existing children or the ones she is carrying.

These decisions are not made lightly; they reflect an innate drive for survival that aligns with evolutionary principles.

By allowing women the choice regarding their reproductive rights, society respects this fundamental aspect of maternal instinct that has been honed through millions of years of evolution.

Throughout history, regulating female reproductive rights has often been tied to societal values and religious beliefs

Societies that have empowered women with autonomy in their reproductive choices tend to thrive, benefiting from the health and vitality of their populations.

Empowering women to make informed decisions about pregnancy and motherhood can improve maternal and infant health outcomes and positively contribute to community resilience.

As human culture evolves, so do the technologies and methods that assist reproduction.

IVF epitomizes advancements in reproductive technology, granting women autonomy by providing alternatives to natural conception.

This technology enables women facing infertility or health issues to achieve their reproductive goals, representing a modern adaptation of the evolutionary principle of ensuring the survival of one's genes.

Forcing women into unwanted pregnancies can have detrimental effects, not only on maternal health but also on the outcomes for the child and the family unit.

Historically, societies that restricted women's autonomy, such as in various periods of human history, experienced significant population declines or even collapse.

In the United States, attempts to control women's autonomy can be traced back to as early as 1847, and today, the country faces an almost 0% growth rate.

The ability to choose is paramount, as each woman's situation is unique.

Contextual factors such as age, health, relationship stability, and financial security heavily influence personal decisions regarding reproduction.

Acknowledging these complexities aligns with a compassionate worldview that honors the evolutionary principles of survival and adaptability.

Supporting pro-choice policies is not merely about the right to choose; it is about ensuring that children are brought into environments where they are nurtured and can thrive.

This acknowledges that while some pregnancies may be desired, various factors can significantly impact a woman's decision to continue with a pregnancy.

Medical complications that endanger the health of the mother or fetus are critical considerations.

Issues of consent, such as rape or coercion, can heavily influence this decision.

Emotional and psychological readiness to become a parent is essential.

Socio-economic factors, including financial instability and lack of support, also play a role.

Cultural and societal pressures regarding unplanned pregnancies can further impact a woman's choice.

So many reasons can affect women and sway them to make this decision that I cannot list them all in a post.

Creating a societal framework that understands these complexities and facilitates access to comprehensive reproductive health services is crucial.

By advocating for pro-choice policies, we reinforce the notion that every child deserves to be in a situation where they are cared for, valued, and can reach their full potential.

By fostering a culture emphasizing reproductive autonomy, society can promote healthier families and communities, ultimately driving progress.

Furthermore, the acceptance of reproductive technologies such as in vitro fertilization (IVF) reflects the changing landscape of family formation.

As societal norms continue to evolve, embracing these advancements allows for a greater diversity of family structures, reinforcing that there is no singular pathway to parenthood.

This openness respects individual choices and acknowledges the necessity for collective adaptability in the face of new reproduction and family life challenges.

Viewing abortion and IVF through an evolutionary lens highlights the significance of maternal autonomy and reproductive choices as essential components of human survival and community success.

By recognizing that women's reproductive rights are deeply rooted in the intrinsic drive for maternal fitness and societal well-being, we can cultivate greater empathy for differing perspectives on these critical issues.

Allowing women to make informed choices about their bodies and families aligns with our collective evolutionary journey, supporting the development of healthier generations and thriving societies.

As we progress, embracing both pro-choice and pro-IVF perspectives can foster a more inclusive and compassionate society, ultimately enriching our shared human experience.

Understanding the Disenfranchised Voter's Choice and Why Some Democrats Supported Trump

As Democrats, we continually seek to understand why a significant percentage of disenfranchised voters chose to support Trump.

We touted, "This is the most important election in our lifetime. We are voting to save our democracy!"

Everyone understood what that meant to them individually, but did anyone think to ask a disenfranchised individual what it meant for them?

I didn't ask, but the information was volunteered to me. Once I was told how they felt, I could see how someone might say, "I have tried this my whole life and I wasn't included, but I haven't tried that, so I'm going to try it."

Could it be that the root of this issue lies in our failure to consider the deeper historical context, alongside today's systemic oppression and its impact on their belief in a democratic republic?

We must ask ourselves: What has our conception of freedom truly offered these individuals? We must engage in an honest reflection about the circumstances that led to their disaffection with our party and take proactive steps to address these concerns.

The interplay between the promotion of freedom and the enactment of repression against marginalized communities deserves rigorous exploration, particularly when examining both historical and contemporary political dynamics.

The paradox of a democratic republic is steeped in a historical backdrop of suppression within disemocratic frameworks. Democracies, especially in the United States, were founded on principles of freedom and equality; however, these ideals have often been applied selectively.

The treatment of Black individuals, Indigenous populations, LGBTQ+ communities, people of color, and undocumented immigrants showcases a long-standing history of systemic oppression that exists alongside the country's professed democratic values.

One glaring example of this foundational hypocrisy is the systematic repression of Black Americans through slavery, segregation, and ongoing systemic racism, which occurred within a democratic structure that claimed liberty for all. This relationship epitomizes the contradiction inherent in a system that promotes freedom while simultaneously undermining it for specific groups.

Another example can be seen in the criminalization of homosexuality through anti-sodomy laws and the marginalization of LGBTQ+ identities, which were implemented in a society that celebrates personal freedoms. The violent backlash against LGBTQ+ communities, especially following the Stonewall Uprising, further illustrates how societal acceptance can be selectively enforced.

Moreover, undocumented immigrants frequently face severe repercussions, including deportation and violence, despite the nation's reliance on their labor and its professed democratic ideals. Policies targeting these individuals reveal deeply entrenched xenophobia and racism within our governance.

The current political landscape, particularly initiatives such as Project 2025, illustrates troubling shifts toward authoritarianism. Proposed by conservative groups in the United States, this initiative aims to fundamentally reshape federal governance and policy when Donald Trump, a Republican, regains office in January. Specifically, he appears focused on deporting all immigrants, rolling back progressive reforms, and restoring certain policies that could adversely affect marginalized communities.

The underlying notion of loyalty to a specific political figure, Donald Trump, over constitutional principles represents a disturbing trend;

individuals may be categorized not only by party loyalty but also by their identity traits.

As the political landscape becomes increasingly polarized, those who diverge from the prevailing ideology may face repercussions, including public shaming, loss of employment, and even violence. In such an environment, individuals may feel compelled to compartmentalize aspects of their identity, hiding parts of who they are to avoid backlash. As the LGBTQ+ community often says, they are "back in the closet."

This instinct mirrors historical experiences where marginalized communities developed strategies for survival, often living discreetly to evade scrutiny or violence.

As significant political shifts occur, the expression of dissent or nonconformity may become subdued, leading to self-censorship.

People may become increasingly cautious about disclosing their beliefs or identities in public spheres, contributing to an atmosphere of mistrust and anxiety.

In response to escalating repression under initiatives like Project 2025, organized resistance will become necessary.

Liberal and progressive forces must unite to confront authoritarian trends, emphasizing collective advocacy for democratic principles, human rights, and equitable treatment.

Anticipating the consequences of repression is crucial, as the ongoing threat of violence not only impacts immediate victims but also creates a cycle of trauma that affects future generations.

The normalization of fear can stifle societal growth and diminish community spirit and resilience.

The potential regression of rights and freedoms could set a dangerous precedent, unraveling decades of progress and reinforcing systemic inequities.

Vigilance is essential to counteract this trend and reclaim rights for all marginalized groups. The tension between the democratic ideals of freedom and the reality of oppression presents a compelling narrative of systemic injustice.

As political landscapes evolve, particularly under initiatives that may seek to undermine the principles of equality and justice, understanding historical lessons becomes critical.

The call for accountability, advocacy for intersectionality, and recognition of shared fears across identities remains vital.

Mobilizing toward a just and equitable society requires solidarity among those historically faced with repression, as well as those navigating newfound vulnerabilities in an increasingly hostile environment.

In doing so, communities can create a unified front to resist authoritarian tendencies and reaffirm the principles of liberty, justice, and protection for all individuals, regardless of identity.

This requires acknowledging that the fight for freedom and rights is interconnected across marginalized identities. Only through a concerted effort rooted in shared understanding and mutual support can we effectively confront these impending challenges and work toward a society that embodies the values of true democracy for everyone.

LAW ENFORCEMENT HAD NO OBLIGATION TO DO ANYTHING TO PROTECT THE KIDS IN UVALDE, ACCORDING TO THE US SUPREME COURT

In 2005 the Supreme Court ruled that the police did not have a constitutional duty to protect a person from harm.

Marjory Stoneman Douglas High School in Parkland, Florida, students filed suit, naming six defendants, including the Broward school district and the Broward Sheriff's Office, as well as school deputy Scot Peterson and campus monitor Andrew Medina.

On Monday, though, a federal judge ruled that the government agencies "had no constitutional duty to protect students who were not in custody."

This latest decision adds to a growing body of case law establishing that government agencies including police agencies have no duty to protect citizens in general

The US Supreme Court has made it clear that law enforcement agencies are not required to protect the citizens who are forced to pay the police for their "services."

Neither the Constitution nor state law imposes a general duty upon police officers or other government officials to protect individual persons from harm — even when they know the injury will occur. Police can watch someone attack you, refuse to intervene, and not violate the Constitution.

The Supreme Court has repeatedly held that the government has only a duty to protect persons who are "in custody."

Courts have rejected the argument that students are in the custody of school officials while they are on campus. Custody is narrowly confined to situations where people lose their freedom to move freely and seek assistance on their own — such as prisons, jails, or mental institutions.

Considering these facts does not necessarily lead us to the conclusion that law enforcement agencies are somehow on the hook for every violent act committed by private citizens.

This reality does belie the often-made claim; however, that police agencies deserve the tax money and obedience of local citizens because the agencies "keep us safe."

Nevertheless, we are told there is an agreement here — a "social contract" — between government agencies and the taxpayers and citizens.

And, by the very nature of being a contract, we are meant to believe this is a two-way street. The taxpayers are required to submit to a government monopoly on force and to pay these agencies' taxes.

In return, these government agents will provide services. In the case of police agencies, these services are summed up by the phrase "to protect and serve" — a motto that numerous police agencies have in recent decades adopted.

But what happens when those police agencies don't protect and serve? What happens when one party in this alleged social contract doesn't keep up its end of the bargain?

The answer is very little.

The taxpayers will still have to pay their taxes and submit to police agencies as lawful authority. If the agencies or individual agents are forced to pay due to lawsuits, it's the taxpayers who will pay for that too.

The senior leadership positions may change, but the enormous agency budgets will remain, the government agents themselves will continue to collect generous salaries and pensions, and no government will surrender its monopoly on the use of force.

Red and Blue States and the Integrity of Democracy

In the United States, the integrity of democratic processes is increasingly compromised by gerrymandering, voter suppression, and voter intimidation, practices that collectively undermine fair representation. While both red and blue states engage in gerrymandering, it is often more pronounced in red states, where voter intimidation also prevails. Redistricting, restrictive ID laws, and polling place closures systematically limit ballot access for minorities and low-income individuals. The visible presence of law enforcement at polls, misleading signage, and threats of legal consequences further discourage participation among vulnerable communities.

When Democrats controlled Congress, they could have enforced existing laws to secure their dominance in the executive branch for decades. Gerrymandering and voter suppression are widespread concerns across both political spectrums. While blue states also use gerrymandering, it tends to be less overt than in red states.

The Republican Party argues that easing voting access risks electoral security, while Democrats contend that such restrictions disenfranchise voters, particularly in locations with long wait times.

The Democratic Party is willing to compromise on certain seats in some districts to implement laws that promote broader voter participation, such as increasing polling places, offering transportation, expanding mail-in voting options, and supplying resources for voters waiting to cast their ballots.

Enhancing voter access could involve automatic voter registration, extended hours, same-day and online registration, voter education, early voting opportunities, reducing ID requirements, providing assistance hotlines, allowing individuals with felonies to vote, affirming that prisoners are still citizens and should have the right to vote, and partnering with grassroots organizations.
While these strategies could improve voter access, numerous other approaches could also enhance engagement.

The struggle for voting access reveals a fundamental divide: Democrats seek to expand access, while Republicans frame these initiatives as threats. This tension arises from the potential Democratic voter base significantly outnumbering that of the Republican Party. In states like Georgia, Republicans have curtailed voter assistance initiatives, such as distributing water and snacks at polling places.

With the 2026 elections approaching, and Donald Trump's fear of losing a majority both parties might redraw congressional districts ahead of the 2030 census, influenced by the country's unrest and unsatisfactory performance of the present Administration. This process could strengthen either party's majority.

Analysis shows several red states could turn blue with increased participation among registered Democrats if suppressive laws and intimidation are eliminated.

Georgia: The state has experienced demographic changes and increased community turnout. While it went Democratic in 2020, it reverted to Republican in 2024. Ongoing restrictive laws raise concerns about voter access.

Texas: A diverse population challenges Republican dominance, but gerrymandering limits Democratic influence in urban areas.

North Carolina: New voter ID laws and gerrymandered districts have diminished Democratic representation.

Arizona: Transitioning to a competitive battleground, it faces voter suppression challenges that complicate access.

Florida: Voter suppression measures disproportionately affect Democratic-leaning communities, complicating competitive districts.

Voter intimidation practices also hinder participation in communities of color in states like Mississippi, Alabama, and Louisiana, despite their Democratic majority.

As demographics shift, states may become more competitive if barriers like voter intimidation are addressed:

Mississippi: Low turnout due to intimidation tactics.

Alabama: Potential for increased mobilization supported by grassroots efforts.

Louisiana: Needs to overcome intimidation measures and improve voter education.

Arkansas, Tennessee, West Virginia, Indiana, South Carolina, and Kentucky:

Each has urban areas with potential for Democratic support if turnout improves and districts are redrawn:

In blue states, challenges might emerge that could enable Republican gains if gerrymandering is corrected:

California: Growth of conservative voices in rural areas may require redistricting.

New York: Dense urban packing could dilute Republican influence.

Illinois, Maryland, Massachusetts: Redistricting could enhance Republican representation.

The electoral dynamics in both red and blue states illustrate how gerrymandering and voter suppression detract from fair representation for all parties. Without these practices, the Electoral College would better reflect public sentiment, which may justify calls for terminating the Electoral College altogether.

A proposed solution to gerrymandering includes establishing an independent, bipartisan commission to redraw district lines equitably after the 2030 Census.
This commission should be sequestered with no outside contact and should represent major political parties and independent voices until unbiased redistricting is completed, using census data that reflects changing demographics.

As the 2030 Census approaches, states may face shifts in political competition as populations grow and diversify.

Republicans advocating for fair access and Democrats addressing their own gerrymandering practices can enhance electoral competitiveness and credibility.

Implementing independent redistricting commissions could promote balanced representation, fostering inclusivity and public trust in electoral processes.

Achieving fairness, equality, and inclusivity remains essential for American democracy.

The Return of the Democratic Republic

Democracy is not a castle we inherit; it is a bridge we repair while crossing. In our time, the structure most in need of reinforcement is the span between public power and private wealth. The bridge lists because of the weight of money, its volume, its velocity, and its invisible channels, have warped how we set public priorities and how we consent to be governed. This should lay out, in full, a plan to straighten and strengthen that bridge: we have to end the domination of money in politics, limit the purchase of influence, impose a civic premium on extreme wealth until the damage it has caused is repaired, and make the democratic republic truly inclusive, capable of moving people along the spectrum from bigotry to civil acceptance without abandoning liberty.

The work has to begin with holding those responsible and a clear-eyed acknowledgment of who and what they are willing to sacrifice to pad their wallets. This includes the president and everyone who invested in his gift. When a small class can spend without limit to shape elections, purchase access to rulemakers, and arbitrage the tax code, the many are asked to be subservient.

You do not save a democratic republic by pleading for better behavior from those most advantaged by the loopholes. You save it by closing the loopholes, auditing the incentives, and setting rules that honor citizenship over checkbooks. You make it worth saving by ensuring every person, regardless of race, faith, gender, origin, or identity, can see themselves in the laws and the life of the nation.

What follows is an in-depth blueprint, and an argument, for how the citizens of the USA can remove elite financial influence from American self-government while cultivating a civic culture that rejects dehumanization and embraces equal dignity. Central to this blueprint is a 40 percent tax floor on annual income and profits above three million dollars, with no exemptions and no deductions, it has to last until trust and balance are measurably restored.

Sadly, we have to tax the elite to force them to do the right thing. It is sadder that they and our executive branch have decided our democracy is for sale.

It is hard to say aloud that a free society must protect the freedom to speak, even offensively, while refusing to normalize the abuse, exclusion, or violence that drives people from the public square. Both truths must be held at once if the democratic republic is to endure.

The United States has cycled through eras of concentrated wealth before, from the Gilded Age to the leveraged 1980s. What makes the current era distinct is not merely the scale of fortunes but the engineered permeability between private money and public power.

Elections are saturated with private spending. Following the Supreme Court's 2010 decision in Citizens United and subsequent cases, independent expenditures by corporations and wealthy individuals face few limits so long as they are nominally uncoordinated with campaigns. Dark money vehicles obscure donors. The loudest voices are amplified further by the architecture of digital advertising and microtargeting, which allows immense resources to drown out ordinary speech.

Policy is shaped in the anterooms of government. Lobbyists fundraise for the officials they meet, draft bill language, and hire the very staff who once regulated them. The revolving door between public service and private advocacy undermines impartiality, while access, not argument, too often determines outcomes.

The tax code tilts the table. Preferential rates on certain income, the deferral of gains, shifting profits across borders, and bespoke deductions have reduced effective tax rates at the top even as public investment lags. The result is a government asked to govern with fewer resources, while private fortunes grow increasingly capable of steering it.

Put plainly, we have privatized the on-ramps to public power. To reverse this, we need simple, enforceable rules that return politics to the people. The reforms below are structural, not symbolic. They must be joined to a second recognition: a democracy awash in money and closed to difference will repeatedly re-elect the conditions of its own decline.

A pivot away from money-dominant politics requires legal change and institutional redesign. It begins with overturning or neutralizing the framework that treats unlimited spending as sacrosanct speech while permitting secrecy and coordination in all but name.

A constitutional amendment is one path, clarifying that the First Amendment allows reasonable limits on political spending to prevent corruption and its appearance. A comprehensive federal statute is another, aimed at requiring real-time disclosure of all political spending, conditioning corporate political expenditures on informed shareholder consent, and setting enforceable anti-coordination rules that reflect modern campaign practices.

Disclosure must be real-time and reliable. Public reporting within hours or days, beneficial ownership transparency that pierces shell entities, and criminal penalties for willful evasion create a deterrent effect. Anti-coordination rules must be bright-line and technology-aware. Shared vendors, shared creative assets, and data pipelines between candidates and supposedly independent groups should trigger presumptions of coordination, with meaningful sanctions and an independent, well-funded enforcement body empowered to act quickly.

Power should be shifted deliberately toward small donors. Two proven tools are small-donor matching and democracy vouchers. Matching multiplies modest contributions, while vouchers give every eligible voter a set of public credits to allocate to candidates who meet qualifying thresholds. In both models, candidates who accept public funds abide by spending caps that focus campaigns on persuasion, not auctioneering. The practical effect has been demonstrated in places like Seattle and Maine, where candidates spend more time with constituents, donor pools diversify, and attention follows the many instead of the wealthy few.

Lobbying at its best educates officials; at its worst, it is a market for outcomes disguised as persuasion. The goal is not to ban advocacy but to prohibit influence-for-sale and make public business public.

The first repair is to sever the money line between lobbyists and officials. Fundraising by registered lobbyists for sitting officials should be barred, as should the use of leadership political committees as conduits for concentrated money. Cooling-off periods need to be lengthened and enforced. Members of Congress and senior executive officials should be prevented for years, not months, from lobbying the bodies they served. Shadow lobbying, in which influence is sold under the label of strategic consulting, should be explicitly covered.

Open the doors and show the drafts. Public, searchable calendars of meetings and calls between officials and paid advocates, posted within days, restore visibility. Mandatory publication of lobbyist-drafted bill language and formal submissions to agencies enables citizens, journalists, and watchdogs to see who is writing the rules and to compare competing inputs.

Enforcement must be independent and capable. Fragmented ethics offices should be consolidated into a single authority with subpoena power, civil penalty authority, criminal referral capacity, and protected budgets. Whistleblowers should be shielded against retaliation. Outcomes of enforcement actions should be reported publicly and promptly. Many peer democracies already meet these baselines; the United States can match them without chilling legitimate speech.

Wealth is not villainy. But when market success mutates into political impunity, a democratic counterweight is required. A non-negotiable 40 percent federal tax rate on annual income and realized profits above three million dollars is that counterweight.

The scope must be clear. The floor applies to individuals' total annual income and realized capital gains above three million dollars, as well as pass-through business profits distributed to owners above that threshold. Income at or below the threshold continues under existing brackets. The rule admits no exemptions or deductions at the covered level. Clarity here removes the maze of carve-outs that invite industrial-scale avoidance and political horse-trading.

Guardrails must be designed to prevent avoidance. A general anti-avoidance rule allows the government to disregard transactions that lack a substantial economic purpose beyond tax reduction. Third-party reporting and withholding obligations for brokers, private equity administrators, law firms, and family offices ensure high-value transactions are visible. Beneficial ownership transparency, with full look-through to natural persons across domestic and foreign entities, enables enforcement agencies to follow money rather than paper shells.

Deferral strategies must be narrowed. For easily valued, tradable assets held by ultra-high-income taxpayers, mark-to-market methods can reduce the incentive to park gains indefinitely. Deemed realization at death for very large estates, carefully designed not to harm family businesses or farms below the threshold, complements this. Exit taxes and robust international information-sharing reduce the payoff from expatriation or arbitrage. Alignment with global minimum tax standards reinforces these protections.

Sunset provisions must tie the floor to measurable repair. The floor is a tool, not a creed. The tax rate will have the ability to change when evidence shows money dominance has receded and public investment has recovered.

Political finance milestones would include reductions in independent expenditures as a share of total election spending and broader donor participation across income brackets. Integrity milestones would track verified decreases and the cessation of lobbyist fundraising, compliance with cooling-off periods, and reductions in policy capture indicators.

Social investment milestones would measure sustained increases in education, infrastructure, and research funding alongside improvements in public trust and mobility. A nonpartisan commission should publish five-year scorecards and Congress can vote on reauthorization or refinement based on those results.

A democratic republic repaired but inhospitable to difference is a structure rebuilt without a floor. True inclusivity is not a mood or slogan; it is the daily architecture of law, culture, and contact that moves people along the spectrum from bigotry to civil acceptance while guarding freedom. The task is to hold two commitments at once: defend robust free expression, and draw firm civic lines against dehumanization, exclusion from public goods, and violence.

The legal floor of inclusion is equal protection and equal access. Anti-discrimination laws in housing, employment, education, healthcare, credit, and public accommodations must be enforced predictably and promptly. The standard is simple: no person is denied an opportunity or their safety because of who they are. This requires accessible reporting systems, credible investigations, due process for all parties, and meaningful remedies. It also requires the government itself to be exemplary: accessible voting sites, language access where needed, and neutral, non-harassing public services.

The cultural pathway from prejudice to acceptance is rarely moved by edict; it is moved by proximity and practice.

Programs that increase sustained, cooperative contact across lines of difference such as service corps that mix participants by region and background, integrated school projects and magnet programs, shared civic deliberations on local budgets and zoning, mentorship networks that cross race and class so we can change attitudes because they change relationships.

Community-led dialogue, grounded in restorative practices, gives people a place to speak candidly, hear harms named, and agree on forward commitments. These are not performative sessions; they are agreements to help us live together with dignity.

Speech policy must be principled. A free society tolerates offensive ideas; it does not tolerate targeted harassment, threats, or intimidation that drive others from the public square.

The line is conduct, not viewpoint. Universities, workplaces, and online platforms can align around this by publishing narrow, viewpoint-neutral rules against doxxing, stalking, and incitement, while protecting debate, even vehement debate, about policy, identity, and belief.

Transparency about moderation rules and consistent enforcement builds trust that inclusion is not a pretext for censorship.

Education is the long lever. A civics curriculum that teaches the architecture of the Constitution alongside the history of groups once excluded from it prepares students to argue without denying each other's place. Media and digital literacy inoculate against manipulation and dehumanization by teaching people how propaganda and algorithmic amplification work. History taught honestly, including the hard chapters, is not a confession; it is a toolkit for not repeating errors.

Workplaces and public institutions can foster belonging without abandoning fairness. Selection and promotion should be merit-based and transparent, with outreach designed to widen pools, not lower bars. Training that centers on practical norms, how to disagree, how to report misconduct, and how to build mixed teams that perform always beats exercises that sort people into moral camps. The measure of success is whether people from different backgrounds want to stay and thrive, not whether they attend a seminar.

Safety is nonnegotiable. Hate crimes must be tracked and prosecuted. Communities at risk should have trusted liaisons to law enforcement and access to preventive resources. The same state that protects expression must protect people from violence and coercion, regardless of the ideology behind it.

Inclusivity must be tangible in the distribution of opportunity. A credible democracy delivers basics that let people participate as equals. Broadband for every household, clinics that accept every patient, schools funded equitably across neighborhoods, fair housing that breaks cycles of segregation, and courts that move quickly and treat like cases alike are not luxuries. They are the daily proofs that belonging is real.

Inclusivity is not unanimity. It is a disciplined way of living with difference: Argue hard, humanize always, and leave no one outside the law's protection. When citizens see that they cannot be erased and that they cannot erase others, the center holds.

Critiques deserve answers. Limiting the size and opacity of political spending is not censoring ideas; it is preventing corruption and its appearance, which courts have long recognized as a compelling interest. Public financing expands speech by enabling more voices to be heard. A 40 percent floor does not crush innovation when it applies only above three million dollars in yearly income or realized gains. Strong incentives remain to create and invest, and history shows that healthy public investment in science and education fuels private breakthroughs.

Concerns about capital flight can be mitigated. Coordinated international standards, exit taxes, and information-sharing blunt flight. Many high-net-worth individuals prize the rule of law, infrastructure quality, and market depth public goods sustained by fair taxation. The temporary and evidence-based nature of the floor is another stabilizer. Philanthropy remains valuable, but it is not a substitute for democratically determined priorities. Under a no-deductions floor, donations are treated like any other top-level spending choice, ensuring that core public obligations are not outsourced to private discretion. Small businesses are largely unaffected, since only distributed profits that push individuals above the threshold are covered, and reinvested earnings continue under ordinary rules with simplified compliance for smaller firms.

Free speech and inclusivity can coexist. The rule of thumb is that ideas compete, and people are protected. A society confident enough to let offensive ideas be aired, and strong enough to protect targeted people from harassment and violence, grows more cohesive over time. That is not a contradiction; it is constitutional maturity.

Ambition must be paired with execution. The near term should focus on transparency and public financing legislation, enforceable anti-coordination rules, and the creation of an empowered independent enforcement agency. Lobbying and ethics reforms, fundraising bans for lobbyists, longer cooling-off periods, public meeting logs, and a consolidated anti-corruption authority, can pass concurrently. The Internal Revenue Service should be resourced to modern standards, including a high-wealth unit capable of using beneficial ownership databases and mandated third-party reporting from key financial intermediaries.

In parallel, inclusivity must be operationalized. Justice Departments at the federal and state levels should publish clear hate-crime reporting pipelines and response times. Education agencies should update civics, history, and media literacy standards to teach both constitutional architecture and the narratives of those historically excluded.

National and state service programs can expand with deliberate demographic mixing and incentives for local problem-solving. Public institutions, from libraries to city councils, should adopt transparent, viewpoint-neutral speech and conduct policies that protect debate while prohibiting harassment and threats.

In the mid-term, the 40 percent floor can be implemented with clear definitions of covered income and robust anti-avoidance measures. International information-sharing agreements should go live alongside domestic enforcement upgrades. A constitutional amendment clarifying authority to regulate election spending can proceed in parallel with statutory reforms. Election process improvements, such as independent redistricting and ranked-choice pilots, can reduce the incentives for polarization fueled by concentrated money. Inclusivity efforts should be evaluated by participation rates, safety indicators, and trust surveys, with adjustments made publicly.

In the long term, the tax floor should be evaluated against public scorecards. If milestones have been met, the floor should be reduced or retired; if not, it should be refined and reauthorized.

Public financing should be normalized nationwide. Transparency should become routine, and ethics enforcement should remain independent, visible, and well-funded. As new technologies emerge, from generative political content to crypto-based funding channels, rules should be updated continuously to preserve the spirit of the reforms.

Inclusivity should be embedded as a habit. Cross-community service as a rite of passage, honest history as a shared language, legal protection as a lived constant.

Repair is lived, not proclaimed. Campaigns powered by millions of small donations transform the daily work of candidates from dialing for dollars to listening to people. Legislative text drafted in public, with visible author attributions and version histories, allows citizens to see where ideas come from and who is pushing them. A tax system that is short, legible, and robust at the top supports budgets with room to invest in the future because the present is not mortgaged to loopholes. A civic culture where people of differing identities argue vigorously and still trust one another's right to belong is visible in schools that integrate excellence and equity, public forums that are heated but not hateful, and neighborhoods where safety is shared.

None of this is speculative. Versions of each element already function in American cities and states and in peer democracies. The task is to connect these successes, scale them, and defend them.

It is unsettling to assert that we must tax the elite to make them do the right thing. Civic virtue should be voluntary. But systems that reward exploitation will be exploited. A democratic republic cannot rest on the hope that those with the most power will restrain themselves. It must structure incentives so that private advantage aligns with public duty.

It is also unsettling to insist that a free people tolerate speech they dislike. Yet a republic cannot keep its promise if every hard idea is banished and every hard person is banished with it. The moral center is firm but capacious, protects people, debates ideas, and keeps the circle of belonging wide enough that no one mistakes defeat in argument for exile from the community.

The 40 percent floor is not a shackle on prosperity. It is a stopgap against the shackling of democracy. The inclusion project is not a demand for uniformity. It is a discipline of pluralism. Together, they buy time and space to re-level the field so that when the floor sunsets and the culture steadies, we inherit fair rules and a common life worth keeping.

A compact of governance rather than grievance. Citizenship is equal even when wealth is not. Elections must be contests of ideas and organization rather than bank accounts.

Public office is a trust rather than a springboard to private gain. Those who benefit most from our shared system owe most to sustain it until the system is rebalanced, and then no more than fairness requires. And belonging is not a favor bestowed by the majority; it is the starting condition of every person under the law.

We will not be subjects of money.
We will be the authors of the law.
We will live with differences without denying each other's place.

If we mean that, if we end the money veto, sever influence-for-sale, adopt a temporary civic premium at the very top until repair is real, and weave inclusion into the daily fabric of law and life, then the old promise breathes anew. The United States does not need to be saved from its people. It needs to be returned to them.